CW01390254

secret mothers' business

Joanne Fedler is a full-time mother and writer, former law lecturer and advocate for women's rights. She is the author of six books and the co-founder of Moonstone Media. She grew up in Johannesburg and now lives with her husband and two children in Sydney.

secret mothers' business

one night, eight women, no kids, no holding back

Joanne Fedler

ALLEN&UNWIN

First published in 2006

Allen & Unwin
83 Alexander Street
Crows Nest NSW 2065
Australia
Phone: (61 2) 8425 0100
Fax: (61 2) 9906 2218
Email: info@allenandunwin.com
Web: www.allenandunwin.com

National Library of Australia
Cataloguing-in-Publication entry:

Fedler, Joanne.
    Secret mothers' business: one night, eight women, no kids, no holding back.

    ISBN 1 74114 715 8.

    1. Motherhood. 2. Mothers. 3. Female friendship. 4.
    Women - Family relationships. I. Title.

306.8743

Set in 10.75/15 pt Adobe Caslon Pro by Bookhouse, Sydney
Printed in Australia by McPherson's Printing Group

10 9 8 7 6 5 4 3 2 1

This book is dedicated to all mothers everywhere.
Whenever you feel like a bad mother,
and utterly alone—you're not.
You're not.

contents

author's note

In June 2003, I was working on an article about Andrea Yates, an American woman who drowned her five children in the bath. During the course of my research, the horror that had compelled me to start writing shifted, making way for a reluctant empathy. I was ashamed of my compassion, uncertain as to how my outrage could sit together with this unlikely companion.

While I was battling with my response, Kathleen Folbigg exploded, through the media, into the Australian psyche—another mother who had killed her own children, four of them over a period of ten years. Nauseated, I was drawn into the tabloid gossip about the diaries she had kept, in which she wrote about how self-annihilating motherhood felt to her. I was startled by her confessions. Partly because they so closely resembled those I had penned during some gruelling times when my children were little.

My article, which appeared in the *Good Weekend* magazine of the *Sydney Morning Herald*, ended with the sentence, 'Perhaps if

hell exists, Folbigg will burn for what she has done. But thankfully, I am not the one who will be judging her'.

To tell you the truth, I was nervous about how people would respond. I anticipated condemnation. But apart from the odd outraged letter from more elderly readers, I was met with a quiet concession from other mothers that none of us would welcome a jury's scrutiny of our own mothering. Mothers everywhere identified with the point of my article—that though the actions of mothers who kill their children are unimaginable, their desperation and loneliness are not unique—which could so easily have been misunderstood.

Some months later, I got together with a group of my female friends for a sleepover. Over a sumptuous feast—and too many daiquiris—we began revealing the stories of our lives as mothers, wives, working women and the individuals we were before we became parents. There were revelations and confessions, lots of laughter, wine, foot massages and excruciatingly bad DVDs.

At the urging of my friend and agent Jane Ogilvie, I was spurred to write a book about that island of time, a sacred space of sharing. *Secret Mothers' Business* emerged from that gathering and maps the events and emotions of a single evening in which eight women spend a night together, alone, husband- and child-free.

All the conversations between these covers are based on true conversations with real women. I know, because I am one of them. The narrator is me. I have not altered any of the facts of my own life, other than the names of my husband and children and a few details to protect people I love (although in real life I'm less of a bitch, honestly!). All the other women are 'fictionalised'—I have merged characteristics of several friends into one character and invented scenarios that are not necessarily true to the lives of the particular women who were there that night. This is to protect the identities of the women involved. It is also to safeguard my precious friendships with these women, and to honour the trust that allowed these conversations to happen.

I wrote this book because I have faith in the power of truth-telling and I believe in the endurance of women's friendships. I did it because motherhood is undervalued, over-romanticised and a hell of a ride, and if you're in it, you know exactly what I mean.

Finally, I wrote this book to honour my children, my greatest teachers about my worst imperfections. I did it because I love them, and I have undertaken to be ruthlessly honest with them about life so that they can make informed choices in their lives.

No narrative can be enjoyed on an empty stomach, and so this one is dotted with a constellation of courses, to invoke the creativity and sensual delight that women derive from a beautiful plate of food, lovingly prepared. Like me, I'll bet you too have shared tearful and uproarious conversations with women friends around kitchen tables, between mouthfuls of homemade cooking and that blessed glass of wine . . .

All of the stories presented in the following pages are true—they either happened to me or someone, somewhere, told them to me. But all writing is an alloy of truth-telling, imagination and exaggeration. If this book makes you uncomfortable, it was just a story. If there is relief or comfort to be found, well then, enjoy.

Joanne Fedler

what you need to know about us

The narrator (a.k.a Me)

Age: 37 (same age as Marianne Faithfull's Lucy Jordan when it dawned on her that riding through Paris in a sports car with the warm wind in her hair was just never gonna happen . . . sigh).

Marital Status: Recently married Frank, father of my children, after eight years together.

Kids: Jamie (7½) and Aaron (4).

Occupation: Writer (once law teacher and women's rights activist).

Issues: Will our kids forgive us for robbing them of grandparents and cousins who we left in South Africa four years ago? After Bali, is Australia 'safe'? Aaron recently identified as a 'bully' by his preschool teacher; Atkins or Weight Watchers? Oh, and sun damage to the cleavage.

Fantasies: To write like Amy Tan or Toni Morrison and become a world-famous novelist; to own my own home in Sydney in the next decade; failing these, anything involving Robbie Williams without a shirt on.

Don't Mention: Writers under thirty with bestsellers. Estate agents and landlords. Cancer of anything.

Hidden Alliances: I know it sounds very 'high school-ish', but Hel's my best friend. Among all these Aussies, I sometimes feel culturally marginalised.

Three Self-descriptive Adjectives: Mother, writer, immigrant.

Helen (a.k.a Hel)

Age: 43

Marital Status: Happily married to David, who owns 'Burly', manufacturers of workmen's overalls (in khaki, navy and grey and, next year, beige).

Kids: Nathan (6), Sarah (5) and Cameron (3). Pregnant with number four.

Occupation: Full-time mother.

Issues: Sarah recently asked what a 'blow job' is; told her 'it's what you have done to your hair after a cut'—it was the best I could do at such short notice; whether to go to Byron Bay for end-of-year holiday or to save money to go to Bali next year; the light beige or terracotta tiles for around the pool? Nathan's weight.

Fantasies: For David to come home before eight p.m. just one night a week; to wheedle Jo's salad dressing recipe out of her; and maybe, in a previous life, some lesbian sex (but that's *really* not for publication).

Don't Mention: The mother-in-law's cooking. The cost of new school shoes. Days when the gym crèche is full.

Hidden Alliances: Jo and I live to eat and someday we'll go on an eating tour of Italy. But I get on with everyone.

Three Self-descriptive Adjectives: Mother, wife, housekeeper (and there's nothing wrong with that).

Tamara (a.k.a Tam)

Age: 41

Marital Status: Married to Kevin, a plastic surgeon, who specialises in breast augmentation (and no, isn't it obvious I haven't had mine done?).

Kids: Two boys, Kieran (6) and Michael (7).

Occupation: Trained as a remedial teacher, currently an office administrator.

Issues: Is Kieran (a gifted child) being properly extended at school and stimulated to maximise his potential? Is Michael's bed-wetting related to feelings of inferiority to his younger brother, because he is not 'gifted'? (But I'd never discuss that in front of him.)

Fantasies: For both kids to excel at sports, music, academics and social skills; to have a family holiday sometime—Kevin's a workaholic; to wean myself off the Prozac—but I'm not in any rush.

Don't Mention: Gluten. Preservatives. Food additives.

Hidden Alliances: I don't have any—I do see Dooly more than the others because Michael and Luke are good mates.

Three Self-descriptive Adjectives: Mother, health fanatic, reader.

Liz

Age: 42

Marital Status: Comfortably married to Carl.

Kids: Chloe (6) and Brandon (3).

Occupation: Self-made businesswoman with own advertising agency, 'Craze'.

Issues: Have just discovered a white pubic hair (what a drag!); overdue for a mammogram (Mum died of breast cancer at the age of 41); work too hard to find time to potter in the garden (the only place of tranquillity in this mad world).

Fantasies: For Craze to become listed; for kids to grow into secure, independent, well-adjusted individuals; for Lily (Korean nanny) to never leave (couldn't manage without her).

Don't Mention: Kids' parties. Mum's death. Financial year-end.

Hidden Alliances: Was at school with Fi—we've seen each other through the dark times.

Three Self-descriptive Adjectives: Businesswoman, visionary, expert delegator.

Ereka

Age: 40

Marital Status: Married to Jake, undisputed soul mate and the best SNAG (Sensitive New Age Guy) of the lot.

Kids: Olivia (6) has slight brain-damage and Kylie (4½) still on the breast.

Occupation: Self-employed artist (more of a salvation than an occupation, but did sell two paintings in the past year. Admittedly it was to an aunt but, hey, she paid cash and I bought myself a Gucci handbag and matching shoes with the money—someday I might even get a chance to wear them).

Issues: The 25 kilos I've put on since Olivia's birth; why not a single one of these up-and-coming young designers has thought to launch a range of sexy clothes for fat people; how to reconcile with Jake's family since Olivia's birth; people feeling sorry for me; how to wean Kylie.

Fantasies: Liposuction; an ordinary life; to start all over again (I can dream, can't I?).

Don't Mention: Girls in bikinis (they just depress me). The fat content in Peking duck—some things are just worth it. Photos of myself ten years ago (I was thin and gorgeous).

Hidden Alliances: I don't have any—sometimes I exclude myself. It's just too hard feeling like a misfit.

Three Self-descriptive Adjectives: Fat, artist, mother.

Courtney-Jane (a.k.a CJ)

Age: 42

Marital Status: Divorced from Tom (a.k.a TFB, a.k.a That Fucking Bastard).

Kids: Scarlett (4)—a real whinger, Jorja (6)—quiet, a loner and Liam (8)—the light of my life.

Occupation: Family lawyer.

Issues: Men who divorce their kids when they divorce their wives; how all women suffer—financially, socially (and let's not forget sexually) after divorce; a libido, all dressed up with nowhere to go; crippling migraine headaches; nicotine withdrawal (gave up smoking 84 days and 13 hours ago); teacher thinks Liam may have ADHD, but I don't have the energy to investigate it.

Fantasies: A man who finds a 42 year old with three kids 'sexy'. That's about it, really.

Don't Mention: Cigarettes. Unpaid maintenance due from TFB. Sex. Cigarettes.

Hidden Alliances: Liz and I are the two full-time professionals, but she's got no clue how hard it is for single mothers. Can't stand Jo's left-wing politics. As the only divorcee, I guess I'm the misfit here.

Three Self-descriptive Adjectives: Single, sex-starved, ex-smoker.

Fiona (a.k.a Fi)

Age: 42

Marital Status: Married to Ben (62).

Kids: Gabriel (5) and Kirsty (17) stepdaughter from Ben's first marriage.

Occupation: Recently qualified as a massage therapist; run my own business, 'earthtouch' (small 'e') from home.

Issues: Too much plastic on the planet; why people who can afford it, don't sponsor a child through World Vision—people don't realise we're all in it together on this earth; trying to be a bit more relaxed about the inevitable mess and dirt of living with other people.

Fantasies: To meet the Dalai Lama; a three-month silent retreat at a Buddhist monastery in Nepal at some point in my life; to leave a delicate ecological footprint on the earth—use less electricity, consume less, become more environmentally in-tune; to find a cleaner who can match the way I clean.

Don't Mention: The war in Iraq. John Howard and George Bush. Hidden dirt.

Hidden Alliances: I've known Liz since I was thirteen—she's always been bossy, but she's got a heart of gold. She's the one who encouraged me to open my own business.

Three Self-descriptive Adjectives: Healer, protector of the planet, cleanliness um . . . oh all right, fanatic.

Louise (a.k.a Dooly—nicknamed after Dr Doolittle because of all our pets)

Age: 39

Marital Status: Married to Max (manic depressive).

Kids: Tyler (4) and Luke (7).

Occupation: Qualified social worker, currently working with aged people four mornings a week.

Issues: Ongoing anxiety about money—outstanding bills; the cost of Max's medication; interest rate increases—may have to stop some after-school activities, for now; that incident last year, obviously.

Fantasies: I don't really have any . . . Maybe just to pay off the mortgage; for life to feel easier day-to-day; I actually wouldn't mind losing ten kilos, but it's the last thing on my mind.

Don't Mention: Helen's pregnancy. Animals overdue for vaccinations (just can't afford it right now). That poor budgie.

Hidden Alliances: Tam's Michael and my Luke play soccer together and are good friends so I see Tam more than the others.

Three Self-descriptive Adjectives: Caregiver, chocaholic, can't think of another one.

the menu

Strawberry daiquiris

Canapés of bocconcini, fresh basil leaves,
    sundried tomatoes and capers

Smoked salmon dip with mascarpone cheese

Sushi (homemade)

Salad of beetroot, avocado, rocket, roasted pumpkin, pine nuts,
    Spanish onion and shaved parmesan cheese with homemade dressing

Thai prawn curry (with coriander)

Vegetarian lasagna (made by Lily)

Butternut and ricotta pancakes

Artichokes with balsamic dressing

Frozen berries with melted white chocolate

Zabaglione

Butterscotch schnapps

Fresh figs, four cheeses and glazed ginger

Enough chocolate to make you sick

a handful of ordinary women

'What the fuck do you think you're doing?' Helen asks me as I chop a bouquet of coriander with my latest acquisition—a gorgeous scalpel-sharp Victorinox vegetable knife made in Switzerland that slices like a dream. I have a weakness for knives. It's one of the things you need to know about me if you are ever going to be counted as one of my inner circle. My friends will tell you that I am a great cook, a slack cow at returning phone calls and I once posed nude for a photographer. They will also divulge in bemused tones that recent obsessions of mine include Robbie Williams, anything written by Amy Tan and making sure all my girlfriends go for regular pap smears. I had a brush with cancer several months ago and now I'm on a mission. Cervical cancer is so easy to detect and treat. And we all have lots to live for: we all have little kids.

Helen already has three and now her period is late—very late. At the ripe old age of forty-three, when your uterus is practically a fossil, that's either menopause kicking in a little early, or (yet another) pregnancy. Either way, it's tricky to figure out how

to greet her news. With exaggerated joy? (Even Robbie Williams in wet undies couldn't tempt me back into pregnancy's last gruelling stretch and those first punishing months of a newborn.) Genuine jealousy? (Who wouldn't give up caffeine and fried foods in perpetuity for that blessed chance to embrace her own freshly birthed baby in her arms again?) Mild irritation? (Isn't sex education like riding a bicycle or does my friend need a refresher course?) Relief? (I've been on Frank's case about a vasectomy since I missed my period in January—three cheers for the morning-after pill . . . ahem . . . guess it can happen to anyone.) Maybe just honest ambivalence will do for now.

'I'm putting coriander in the Thai curry,' I say, mincing the bunch of leaves with merciless dexterity. It responds flirtatiously with its nutty aroma so that my mouth aches for its flavour. I swear if coriander were a perfume, I'd wear it.

'I hate coriander,' she says, shaking her mop of black curls which could do with a wash. Who's got the time these days for the luxury of self-hygiene?

'Yes, and you need to see someone about that,' I quip. 'Problems like that, if left to fester, only get worse . . .'

'Have pity on me—I'm pregnant,' she whines. 'The taste makes me want to throw up even when I'm not knocked up.' This she says as she dips a spoon into the bubbling coconut milk and slurps it up with the gusto I adore in her.

The thing you need to know about Helen is that despite her unpardonable hostility towards coriander, she is also a great cook. Together she and I share an almost spiritual love of food. She has been known to arrive at my door, tatty and sweaty, three kids shrieking in the car, to drop off a small container of delicious leftovers. 'Taste this,' is all she says before clambering back into her station wagon. And there she leaves me, at my door with my face in a plastic bowl relishing the sheer ecstasy of three spoonfuls of Indonesian lamb curry or chicken liver pate she has just whipped up. Words between us are usually about two topics: food and the kids. How to get the pan juices of the roast chicken free of fat; what foods or household cleaning agents might be causing Cameron's eczema; does chicken stock enhance the flavour of dhal better than salt; should Aaron be tested for ADHD, or does he just need a bloody good hiding; that townhouse on the water in Salamander Bay for the July holidays or the apartment in Batemans Bay?

Helen is sane and sensible and deliciously irreverent, without an ounce of pretentiousness to her short, stocky frame. Happiness— that old fashioned quality—is tacked to her like an invisible cloak. Just about any fetid mood of mine, whether induced by PMS, homesickness or my son's latest atrocity, can be dispelled within minutes of being in her boisterous presence. I tell her all my secrets and as long as I preface them with 'Do not repeat this to *anyone*', I can probably rest easy that she's managed to keep them to herself; though, knowing Helen, if something slips out she'll usually confess her lapse before it comes back to me. I do need to tell her that forgiveness is *not* implicit in owning up. Keeping secrets and honesty are two distinct talents, though she's inseparably blended them in her head like a pate of cream cheese and red capsicum.

At school, Helen would have been the girl you'd have voted for as house captain. She takes charge. She starts new trends. And she's a cheerleader all the way. She is fully to blame for my oyster conversion. Last July on our annual week-away-from-husbands-but-with-all-the-kids, she plied me with Bloody Mary shots, each concealing the viscous yolk of what I had initially sneered at as 'gobs of snot'. Maybe the incremental Vodka lent a hand, but by the end of that evening I'd ditched the Bloody Mary and was slurping back those snot balls like they were manna from heaven. Since then, the mere sight of black pepper, a lemon and Tabasco sauce jointly or singly causes me to salivate like a Pavlovian hound. Helen doesn't do Tabasco sauce, but it is one of her lesser faults which I am willing to overlook. Not so the coriander.

'I'll put a bit of the curry in a separate pot for you, but the main pot gets coriander,' I say in my strictest voice. I make no apology for the fact that I am inflexible when it comes to coriander. In fact, in mean-spirited moments I question the authenticity of her love for food. It just doesn't add up, this repugnance she has for this heavenly herb which elevates a culinary experience to a whole new plane. 'It's like ditching the oral sex from sex,' I always tell her. 'I'd rather read a book.' And then she starts to laugh, and believe me, once you've heard Helen laugh, you'll spend your time looking for ways to bring it on again. It is infectious and ridiculous, and just the sound of her unbridled guffaws makes me laugh so hard in turn I sometimes wet my undies.

'What if I want seconds?' she asks, dipping a spoon in the curry again and sucking it clean.

'I'll put enough aside for seconds,' I say. 'Now make yourself useful and put out some candles. The others will be here soon.'

'You're a bossy cow,' she says, pinching my arm. 'And don't scrimp on the prawns,' she mutters, heading for the cupboard in her worn-down Ugg boots, and getting out the tealights to scatter around the lounge room. I'm big on ambience—it hides the worst and brings out the best. And tonight, we all deserve a little help from the shadows.

•

These dinner parties or girls' nights out are Helen's creation. More so than any other early-forty-something maternally burdened person I know, Helen makes and keeps her fun appointments with fastidious regularity. She carries within her broad and delicious smile, a teenage energy and a passion for celebration that magnetically draws everyone to her. Helen, like me, carries more weight than is strictly speaking necessary but, in keeping with her philosophy about fussing children, she just pays no attention to it. While I am cursing my flabby arms and pondering the pinchable size of my fat belly, she hides all her wobblies, as she calls them, under oversized t-shirts and baggy shorts. She couldn't care less how she looks. I, on the other hand, do care and therefore suffer.

A few months ago she organised my hen's party, the day before I married Frank, my partner of eight years and my children's father. She overrode all the squawks of anxiety from the others and hired a boat for the day, which in her enormous floppy white sun hat and stretched blue bathing costume, she skippered. She wanted me to hold onto the wheel and steer as we sailed beneath the Sydney Harbour Bridge. So I did. She wanted us to moor the boat in a quiet alcove and eat wonderful food. So we did. She wanted to shave all my pubic hair for my wedding night. So she did. Unfortunately while she was concentrating on this unenviable task—with the others inspecting and yelling out intermittently, 'You missed a spot!'—the tide went out and we spent the next six hours stranded. With the help of the coastguard and the returning tide, it only took us another two hours to get off the sandbank. Despite the owner of the boat, several husbands, a husband-to-be and the water police frantically trying to locate us, the sun went down without a single arrest or divorce. And I made it to my wedding in one piece, if you exclude pubic hair.

Since then, Helen has insisted on regular reunions. Given the daring events of the Founding Day, which for some of us qualified as *the best fun and most trouble we'd ever been in*, no one dares miss these. The time away from our husbands and kids is so precious, few of us are late. Tonight is a special night. It is a sleepover. A genuine bona fide bring-your-PJs-and-toothbrush sleepover. I haven't had one of those since I was about fifteen and, admittedly, I'm a little nervous. We're in Helen's parents' magnificent home on Darling Point (they're in Italy for a month) and despite the sweeping views I am quietly anxious about sleeping arrangements (there are only five official beds in the house, with a few couches for the rest). I am not the best sleeper—seven years of disturbed nights with kids will do that to you. These days all it takes is a small fart from Frank's side of the bed to wake me from my REM sleep, to make me sit bolt upright in bed and say, 'What? Who?' And that's it. I can't go back to sleep. And ask my kids: I'm a witch when I'm tired.

When I emailed all the girls about the sleepover, I got a flurry of breathless and giggly emails in response. Tam emailed back first that she'd love to come but doubted she'd be able to sleep over. CJ, of course, had to bribe her sister to stay the night, not having a husband to pick up the slack. Dooly might also have had to rally some paid help or call up a favour—Max can barely cope with himself let alone with the kids. But apart from a few logistical difficulties we've all made a plan to be here.

We are a handful of ordinary women, a collection of gutsy, passionate, adorable, intelligent mothers. Some of us are also deeply neurotic. At least two of us are on Prozac, that I know of (but Helen's sworn me to secrecy, Dooly sort of told her 'it's not official, so don't say you heard it from me'). Something happens when we congregate in this manner, free from our children and significant others. Our voices change. They become more high pitched. We sit unselfconsciously with our legs apart and tease each other about the state of our undies. Our jokes—if you can call them that—are so awful you can't tell whether our laughter, led by Helen's, is

induced by the pathetic punchline or the equally crap delivery. We snigger about penis size (if only men knew just how much size counts). And though we'd love to drink like we're twenty-three, none of us can afford a gratuitous hangover. So instead we dance, but no one would ever want to witness this cacophony of quaking and shuddering body parts. And we eat as if gluttony alone could make us all young and sexy again.

Do not underestimate the importance of food in these get-togethers. Helen is an insatiable list maker and gets a rush of anticipatory excitement from planning the food. Who will bring and make what. Only those of us who are real foodies are entrusted with actually making anything. That's Helen and I. The rest have to pitch in with the booze and the chocolate.

Each of us has her secret vice. Helen has spent an unconscionable amount of money on a huge tub of strawberry daiquiris and has brought with her a collection of music I've never even heard of—the soundtrack to the movie *Mermaids* of all things ('Just wait till you hear the fourth track,' she says). When Ereka arrives, she will have five marijuana cigarettes in her purse which will emerge at hourly intervals during the evening. Liz will come with a bottle of red wine that could technically be classified as an antique. Tamara will surely bring some gluten-free delight as well as her mobile but which, after much heckling, she will agree to switch off. If she doesn't it will ring half a dozen times before dessert—despite being able to reconstruct a nipple from a sliver of labia majora, Kevin still cannot put two kids to sleep without her help. Dooly will not come without chocolate—I suspect a mud cake or a chocolate mousse. Even knowing this about her will still not prepare me for her arriving with a bucket of chocolates, literally five litres of those little Favourites. Fiona no doubt will bring her aromatherapy kit to mix us up our own perfect oil combination based on whether we want to be relaxed, refreshed, calmed, soothed or stimulated. Of course, CJ will yell that she desperately needs the latter and will nudge us all into giving each other foot massages. And she will bring Harvey with her. He goes everywhere with her, and at some point in the evening, she will whip him out and place him on the plate of someone who has momentarily left the room to do a wee. He will be a source of much hysterical laughter and possibly induce an early departure by Tam.

•

Tam is the first to arrive. I suppose she thinks being on time, or even early, makes up for being a wet blanket later on (though being a fastidious Virgo myself I do appreciate the tidy virtue of punctuality). She is wearing pink tracksuit pants and a matching pink and white tracksuit top. Someone—not me—should tell her that peachy pink is really not her colour, not with all those freckles and that pale skin. She is slim and attractive in a plain sort of way. She doesn't believe in makeup but spends a small fortune—with which you could do greater justice in an Italian deli—on having her hair coloured chestnut brown, which you've got to admit, is a cop-out when there's fire-red, blueberry and butterscotch blonde to choose from. But that's Tam. She's made a virtue of unremarkable mousiness when it comes to her appearance.

She rabbits on, and so requires a lot of patient listening. And it's mostly about her two boys. We've all got kids, and this time away from them is meant to be just that—a break from it all. You need to be in the mood for Tam. She is not entirely relaxing company, but in a big group like this she'll mellow. Or we'll just get her drunk. One daiquiri should do it.

She strides in with a green recyclable grocery bag. 'How great is this?' she says with an enthusiasm that wouldn't withstand the mildest of cross-examinations. 'Long overdue, this get-together,' she chirps. 'Though I can't stay too late. I have to be up early tomorrow. Kieran's got a chess tournament—they've put him in the under-tens. Some of the mothers of the kids his age complained that their kids were losing confidence with him always beating them after only three moves, so they've moved him up.'

Helen and I both raise our eyebrows. 'Impressive,' Helen says. 'He's a little savant, that Kieran of yours.'

Tam smiles. 'I just want him to be happy,' she says, emphasising this word as if it's just recently been added to the English language and she's trying out how it sounds. 'Tall poppies don't make happy kids.' I want to tell her there's no magic in it—let the poor child breathe and he'll be happy. She takes out some odourless hand and cuticle cream, and squeezes out a glob onto the back of her left hand before gesturing to Helen and I to take some. We both decline.

'Oh, I don't know about that,' I say. 'Strikes me Einstein and Goethe were happy enough.'

'Yes, but did they have friends?' Tam looks at us with large eyes as she removes her wedding ring and rubs the cream into her neat, short-nailed jewellery-less hands.

'Geniuses don't need friends. They've got too much going on inside their heads,' Helen says, taking cutlery out of the top drawer.

'Genii,' I correct her, 'you genius.'

'Oh yeah,' she sneers. 'Not all of us can be clever. Some of us have to be satisfied with just being beautiful,' and she winks at Tam. Tam actually laughs a little patter of a chuckle, returning her wedding ring to her fourth finger.

'How many of us are there?' Helen asks me.

'Eight, including you,' I say. She hands me a fistful of knives and forks.

Out of her bag Tam retrieves three dips, one with eggplant (aah that queen of vegetables), one with olives and tomatoes, and some tzatziki. They are all laden with garlic. In moments of indulgent reflection, I have occasionally mused whether the full sensual bounties of life would not be exponentially diminished in the absence of that gorgeous little bulb, nestling in bunches, feathered in white cocoons. Garlic. There really are three basic ingredients to any good cooking. Helen and I fight over only two of them. We agree on garlic. For me chili and lemon form the Holy Trinity. For Helen it's ginger and basil. It's the source of a simmering tension in our friendship.

Tam has also brought with her a box of frozen berries and a slab of white chocolate. 'This is for a white chocolate sauce to pour over the frozen berries,' she says. She has brought this as an offering to us because she, of course, won't have any of it—too much fat. Too much sugar. Too much of a good time, if you ask me.

Tam embodies the questionable beneficence of maternal selflessness, exaggerating personal fulfilment from the sidelines. It's nauseating. I'm not one of those mothers who believes in living through her children. Seven years in the harsh sun of endless giving as a mother has baked me brittle. If Tam's brain just stopped processing everything for five minutes, the fun would kill her.

'Oh my gawd . . .' Helen gasps at the thought of that combination of icy little pebbles melting, but only on the outside, from the hot sweet chocolatey sauce.

'Chocolate makes pimples worse,' I say to Helen, alluding to the spot on her chin which is poised for eruption.

'Oh really?' she says. 'Thanks so much for drawing attention to it. And I suppose this top makes me look fat . . .' and then to Tam, 'I'm happy to make the sauce,' just as the doorbell goes again. 'Will you get that?' she asks me.

'Happily,' I reply. I leave Tam and Helen in the kitchen to discuss the dessert and to let Helen field the hundred questions about whether the evening's food contains gluten or any possible traces of gluten.

Gluten. The resident evil. Given a few drinks in her, I am sure you could get Tam to assert it's to blame for everything from global warming to racial intolerance. I wish I had her certainty, so I could identify 'The One' ingredient in life that makes things go awry and that, once eliminated, restores harmony and balance. Tam's conviction used to unnerve me. I'd always walk away from our conversations utterly insecure about the way I mother my kids. It's not like she maliciously plants these tapeworms of doubt in my belly, she just can't help herself. Helen and I have worked out that Tam needs a world of cause and effect where explanations bob like unseen but life-saving morsels beneath the surface, there for the hooking if you're willing to put in the hours. And put in the hours she does, by endlessly reading and researching, until she reels in a remedy.

Tam has effectively fashioned a career out of her kids. Though she's qualified as a remedial teacher (and was a bloody good one by all accounts) she works in a miserable little job as an office administrator for a small accounting software firm in the city. She's the first to admit that her work is tedious and that she's functioning at minimal brain capacity, but she loves the hours—she can make school drop-off and pick-up without any stress. And the job doesn't demand her time or energy outside the office. Which is just as well, because most of that is consumed at the naturopath, the kinesiologist, and all the other alternative doctors she keeps in business with appointments for her kids' ailments, everything from a bad dream to full blown pneumonia. The rest of us judiciously follow the immunisation schedule they hand out at postnatal clinics and zap our kids with antibiotics when the doctor says so. Not Tam. It's fascinating how a lack of trust plays itself out—Tam won't take anyone's word for anything, even if his name has sixteen letters after it. She investigates every issue motherhood raises and makes up her own mind. You've got to respect that about her. I, on the other hand, am wearily grateful when someone in a white coat tells me 'the right thing to do'. I just want to get it done. Getting it right is for people who don't have a life.

On days when motherhood feels too hard, I take heart in the fact that I'm a rookie. I was thrown into this job without training, seminars or a single test. I'm an unlicensed mother. When you consider the scrutiny to which prospective adoptive parents are subject—everything from their personal hygiene habits to their opinions on corporal punishment are potentially fatal to the administrative go-ahead—those of us who blithely trundle from heavy petting to full cervical dilation in labour get off lightly. I'm not advocating pre-kid screening, though it's hard to deny that some of us are way too screwed up to be procreating. Some of us can barely keep our own lives together, let alone take on the liability of others.

Tam, however, has arguably earned her licence in parenting specialising in correct nutrition, immunisation, education and socialisation. She's always got her nose in a book, a library or the internet, scouring for the latest research, and has succeeded in weaving a veritable technicoloured dreamcoat out of the mantle of motherhood. Without any encouragement, she will launch into a monologue about the latest theories on discipline, sensitivity, emotional wellbeing, brain development, ADHD, childhood obesity and effective use of boundaries.

I always listen, bristling with irritation when she gets that slightly superior tone in her voice, which if broken down into its semantic components would reveal that she thinks we are a bunch of remedial parenting-retards. She is softly critical of the way most of us bring up our kids—absentmindedly, on-the-run, reactively. In my lesser-evolved moments, I think: 'Hey, I may feed my kids McDonald's and I may raise my voice, but whose kid is wetting the bed? Huh? Not mine.'

Apparently, it is quite common for boys of seven to still pee in their beds at night. So the research says. But Helen's considered assessment is that Michael is a 'regressive mummy's boy, who still wants to be in nappies'. With the amount of attention his bed-wetting gets him, he'd be crazy to give it up in a hurry. Tam has schlepped this poor kid to music therapy, kinesiology, sacro-cranial therapy, and even talked him into acupuncture 'by explaining the benefits and of course allaying his fears and promising a reward'. If he didn't have a reason to piss in his pants before, he's bound to have one now.

Tam's two boys Kieran and Michael are, on the surface, positively Anne Geddes. My kids shriek and fuss, hers quietly listen. Mine call each other (and me sometimes) arse-wipe and poo-poo face, hers say, 'Thank you for dinner', and 'May I leave the table?' Mine turn their noses up at anything that resembles plant-life on their dinner plates, hers gobble up their broccoli and may even ask for seconds. To Kieran and Michael a 'treat' is carob-covered rice-cakes. Organic strawberries with yoghurt. Celery sticks with hummus. While I have to threaten TV deprivation for the rest of their lives to get mine to do their swimming lessons without spitting water at the teacher, hers have a busy schedule of cricket, soccer, judo and taekwando—all voluntarily attended.

They are the dullest kids I know—when Tam's around that is. I once had them over when Tam had a parent-teacher interview. They raided my lolly stash and Kieran broke Aaron's butterfly net with a look of such satisfied glee that I didn't know how to tell Tam. I'd put money on the fact that they'll both be adrenalin junkies at sixteen when testosterone outmuscles the noose of Tam's zealous scrutiny—that's if Tam doesn't discover some research that shows an extra spoon of sunflower seeds in their morning muesli can actually stall the advance of teenage rebelliousness.

Tam speaks to her boys in a calm and measured voice and treats them with vigilant equality, as if they were both gifted. Though it is only Kieran, the youngest one, who has been deemed by whatever body decrees such things as 'highly gifted' (after Tam took him off gluten). Since then, God help us, Tam has pinned her every waking moment to the corkboard of 'maximising his potential'. He is not allowed to be bored in class. Any irritable conduct is a red flag that he must be understimulated.

Tam corners his teacher, poor Ms Kramer, after school each day. (She is all of twenty years old and her Dip.Ed. certificate is probably still at the framers.) Tam demands a run-down on how his day was, getting ruffled with consternation if he was 'quiet', 'a bit hyperactive', or 'withdrawn'. She arrives at home time armed with a stack of photocopied articles on gifted children for Ms Kramer to read, which Ms K. probably dumps in the bin on her way out of the school grounds. But she keeps smiling, her compassion to mothers who still need to be the driving force in their children's lives evident despite her youth.

Helen and I quietly cringe, but Tam is quite resilient to our judgment of her. When it comes to her boys, she has a core of gritty courage in the face of our stifled derision. CJ once said behind her back, 'Good on her for taking a stand and being so committed to her kids.' But that was followed with, 'But she really should lighten up and let Kieran be a bit ordinary for once. I can't imagine that would do him any harm.'

'In fact, he may actually acquire a bit of personality,' I had said. But look, don't hold my assessments up as gospel. I'm no seer on childrearing. I'm still fresh off the starting block, undertrained, unprepared. To me, motherhood often assumes the proportions of an endless highway stretching beyond the visible horizon, with no street signs about how far I've come, or how long I've still got to go. I can't even be certain I've got enough fuel to make it, largely because I've got no idea where I'm going. I'm just going. I suppose I'll know when I've arrived. I've come to believe that despite the best intentions and the most dedicated effort, we're all pretty much on that same road to inflicting deep psychological damage on our kids. As soon as we just accept that reality, the relief is like Valium. Not that I'd know what Valium feels like.

If any of us manages to escape that one-way ticket to parental failure, it will be Tam. And, to be fair, she deserves to succeed. She's the Little Red Hen among us, asking, 'Who wants to come with me to a lecture by the Department of Sport and Recreation on active kids?' 'Not I,' says I. 'Not I,' says Helen. 'Then I shall go by myself.' And off she toddles with her notebook. And she always returns armed to the hilt with theories: television causes ADD. Vaccinations cause autism. Sugar causes hyperactivity. And gluten is to blame for everything from depression to schizophrenia. But apparently, not for bed-wetting.

Helen and I used to joke privately that Tam's Kevin, one of the top plastic surgeons in Sydney, is the most fuckable of all of our husbands. He's got that lean and hungry look, oozes the arrogance of men who cut and paste women's features like they're messy phrases in a Word document. He talks about himself in the third person as 'The Doctor', capital letters and all—I mean, can you take a guy like that seriously? I guess the fact that you've got to book six months in advance to get onto his operating lists for breast

implants and facelifts feeds his delusion that he's God's gift to women. He once came on to me. Admittedly he was drunk, and I was being harmlessly flirtatious. But I nearly choked on my vodka when he leaned over and whispered in my ear, 'The Doctor would examine your breasts for free.' I told Helen about it. And we both agreed that he's just a creep. Infidelity is not my thing. I may have fantasised about other men occasionally—that's normal, isn't it?— but I'd never actually act on it. Now we don't joke about Kevin any more. Not since Tam had that (unofficial) nervous breakdown two years ago. Rumour was, according to Helen, that Kevin was screwing around. Who knows? Maybe he was, but it doesn't matter. It fucked Tam up anyway. Kev's sexy if you get off on feeling like someone's prey, but when a friend's husband makes a pass at you within earshot of his wife, it's time to look elsewhere for cocktail banter. I don't need Tam to think I'm into her husband. Because I'm not.

After that, Tam went on to Prozac and lost all that weight. Ereka jokes that she should try it—she's been battling to lose the equivalent mass of seven newborn babies for the last six years since Olivia was born. But she won't. She's committed to dealing with her life in all its shitty reality, and to make peace with it. Tam, who is generally so anti-drugs, doesn't see the hypocrisy in it. It's all part of her altruistic persona—she's only popping pills because it makes her a better mother. The motto of her girl-scout parenting is 'being there for my boys'.

I reach the door just as the bell goes again. 'I'm coming,' I say and giggle as I think to myself that if I had to come up with a motto for Helen's and my parenting it would probably be, 'Mummy's going out now'.

the velcro of our maternal condition

At the door is Liz. She looks tired, but glamorous. 'How are you?' she says, pecking me on the cheek, not waiting for my answer. In her hands is a huge vegetarian lasagna. Homemade, but not by her. Under her arm is a bottle of red wine. 'Stunning vintage,' she says casually, gesturing for me to take it from her, which I do. She is pulling a stylish little maroon suitcase on wheels. She flounces in wearing an outfit. Not trackies, not jeans, but a classic silk-chiffon suit with matching pants, which on me would be 'grey' but on her is 'charcoal'. Around her neck is an expensive tangle of baby pink, peacock and snow white pearl necklaces. The last time I was that dressed up was at a relation's son's bar mitzvah a year ago. Liz always dresses like she's expecting the paparazzi to turn up at any minute. Next to her, I feel pretty frowzy in my jeans and jumper.

Liz is the high-powered businesswoman among us—an anomaly in this group of full-time, or at least part-time, mothers. While the rest of us have to be satisfied with a life's purpose of successfully running our own homes, Liz runs her own advertising agency.

People call her 'boss' and she hires and fires. She is one of the smartest women I know. Her and Fiona are childhood friends and it's mostly because of Fi that Liz is invited to our get-togethers. I'm always surprised when Liz actually turns up—surely a mover and shaker like her must find our conversations as boring as a marathon Snakes and Ladders tournament. But interestingly, Liz does often come, unless she's overseas on business. And she's always good value, if a little opinionated. I respect her opinion on just about every topic from the state of the stockmarket to whether the media killed Princess Diana. Mothering is the only issue on which I steer clear of her razor-sharp judgments. 'Juggle, darling?' she once said to me. 'Only clowns juggle. You want to be the clown or the MD? It's simple—you want to have a career, have a career. You want to be a mother, get someone to do the job.'

Liz told us that the only reason she had kids was because Carl wanted them—probably the only deviation from her otherwise flawlessly self-centred existence. I've heard her deride maternal instinct as a load of 'misogynist propaganda designed to keep women at home'. She handles her kids Chloe and Brandon like disgruntled employees requiring managing and mentoring. She holds them accountable to a minimum code of conduct which she has printed out, laminated and tacked on the inside of the bathroom door. Her mothering is based on the sound business principle that familiarity breeds contempt. Her kids have got the message (they're not retards): be independent. Chloe and Brandon can both feed, dress, entertain and put themselves to sleep if they have to. But Liz's also got an insurance policy.

What's it called? One beautiful four-letter word: Lily. Lily is Korean and has a heart (and girth) the size of a whale. All children light up in her presence, even though she speaks in broken English and it's sometimes difficult to work out whether she's offering you 'tea' or inquiring whether your child is 'three'. I once managed to ask her if she had kids of her own and had to turn away lest she see the tears in my eyes when she told me she has a five year old and seven year old ('beautiful babies—mine') in Korea being cared for by her mother. Her husband abandoned her during her second pregnancy and she left her three-month-old daughter and her two-year-old son to come to Australia to earn money to send back to them. She hasn't seen her children since. In relaying this to me, she proudly retrieved a tatty photo of a newborn from her blouse pocket, 'See, but she big now.' I despised Liz in that moment.

Lily lives in with Liz and Carl to accommodate their lifestyle. She is at their beck and call twenty-four hours a day, though Helen's told me that Liz pays her well. Liz insisted that Lily learn to drive, paid for a course of driving lessons, and then another course after Lily failed her driver's licence and when she finally passed at her fourth attempt, Liz bought a brand new third car, air-bagged and with every other safety feature on the market. Lily now drives the kids to and from all their extra-curricular activities: cricket, ballet, music, chess and swimming. I suspect not all the income is finding its way back to Korea—I once saw Lily with a Louis Vuitton handbag, but maybe it was a hand-me-down from Liz. Lily is blindly loyal to Liz in that ingratiating way that slaves are indebted to their masters and thinks the sun shines out her arse. It may well do. Liz is one of those enviable achievers who have it all. But I'd hate to have her as my mother.

Liz works like a demon. Most days she arrives home too late from work to see her children, awake that is. But Carl fills in for Liz and Lily fills in for both of them. Liz is clear that her wellbeing and sense of self pivot on the fulcrum of her successful career. 'I'm role-modelling for my daughter what a woman can do,' she says. Helen and I joke that Chloe will probably get married at eighteen and have six kids and be a stay-at-home mum. I'm convinced that kids absorb our deepest insecurities and convert them into diesel to fuel the inexorable revenge they're all programmed to exact upon us. Liz's in for a nasty surprise when the mathematics of parenting don't show an appreciable return like a bonus-worthy balance sheet. But in her favour, Liz is brutally honest. Most of us are too nappy-whipped and guilt-ridden to pursue our own careers, let alone with the drive she has which, let's face it, could launch a rocket ship. But she says, 'I spent ten years of my life building my company, making a place in the world that was mine and that I was proud of. I wanted kids as part of my life, but I was not prepared to give up everything to be a mother. They had to fit in with me, not the other way around.'

Liz parks her little suitcase at the foot of the stairs, slinks into the lounge room, slides the lasagna on to the coffee-table and sinks into the nearest chair with the practised grace of one accustomed to the observational nit-pickings of underlings. She is the least self-conscious person I know and if her stocking happened to have a ladder all the way from the heel to the crotch, she'd exude the aura, 'it's *meant* to be there'. She exhales deeply. 'God, get me a drink someone,' she says as Helen and Tam come in from the kitchen, Helen carrying a tray with eight glasses of strawberry daiquiris.

'You look like you need one,' Helen says, passing her a glass from the tray.

'No, I won't have that,' she says, 'it's the sugar. Just a glass of red. Fi not here yet?'

'Not yet, she's probably cleaning her stove top with a toothbrush as we speak . . . but she'll be here, she's confirmed,' Helen says. 'Oh go on, have a daiquiri—it's good for you.'

'I'll skip it and have some wine thanks,' she says, pointing to me, still holding the bottle.

Helen just shrugs as she takes the bottle from my hand and toddles off to open the red wine.

'So have you heard what our Fi's up to these days?' Liz inquires.

'No, what?' I ask.

'She's taken up kickboxing!' Liz laughs.

'Fi?'

'Yep, and she's loving it by all accounts.'

'I can't imagine Fi doing such a violent sport,' Tam says.

'It's not really violent, it's in a very controlled environment. She says she wishes someone had told her ages ago about the satisfaction you get from kicking and punching the shit out of those bags,' Liz says.

'She's full of surprises, is our Fi,' Tam responds. 'A whole secret life we don't know about.'

'We're all entitled to a little mystery,' Liz replies.

'So what's your secret?' I ask Liz.

'Got none,' she answers airily.

'Forget the secrets, just tell us how you are, Liz,' Tam says. 'Long time no see . . .'

'I've had a bugger of a day,' she answers. 'Don't ask me the details—they are too boring for words.'

'What multi-million dollar slogan did you dream up today?' I ask her, lifting the foil off the edge of the lasagna and pinching off a corner of dried cheese to taste.

'How do you make tampons sexy?' she asks.

'I give up, how?' I reply.

'Don't hide them. Make them an accessory,' she says. 'Get boys to sell them, because all boys want to go where tampons go . . .'

'That's quite clever,' Tam says approvingly.

'Quite?' Liz asks, raising a finely shaped eyebrow.

'Very clever,' Tam revises.

'Who made the lasagna?' I ask.

'Who do you think?' she says. 'My children's mother.' She laughs as she rakes back her meticulously cut blonde-to-the-roots blowdried hair.

Apart from being a scrupulous housekeeper, Lily is also a superb cook. Liz sent her on a Donna Hay cooking course to master the secret art of spaghetti bolognaise, lasagna, roast chicken and lamb chops with mash. Staples in her kids' and Carl's diet. Liz herself only eats takeaway sushi and salad—without the dressing. If there is anything about her that I find despicable, it is her attitude towards food. To Liz, food is perfunctory, must be able to be eaten on the move, with maximum efficiency, zero sugar and no mess, and to fill a space so she can concentrate in the next meeting. She is entirely unmoved (and therefore slightly psychopathic, in my estimation) by more joyous foods like mangoes and lychees and unshelled prawns drenched in garlic butter.

'If only you could get her to fuck your husband, you would be off the hook entirely,' Helen says, handing her a glass of red wine, which Liz takes gratefully.

'If only I could . . .' Liz laughs, taking a regal sip.

•

The phone rings. 'I'll get it,' I say, not that anyone else was offering.

It's Ereka. 'Look, Jo,' she says, 'I'm in a foul mood. I'm thinking of taking a raincheck tonight, is that okay?'

'That is absolutely out of the question,' I tell her. 'Hey girls,' I say aloud, 'Ereka is blowing us off. What do we think of that?'

'No way!' 'Don't stay away.' 'Please come.' 'Just get here!' is the chorus that rings back.

'Hear that?' I say.

'I've had a horrible afternoon with the girls, Olivia's been wild, and I am tired and just want to get into bed,' she continues.

'It's no good,' I say. 'You have to come. We have the most gorgeous food, and you can just chill out here. Come on. How can you miss the sleepover?'

She sounds reluctant. I hand the phone to Liz. 'You'll feel better once you get here,' Liz says. 'You need to get away, just tell Jake you are leaving, just get into the car and come. Don't think, just do it.' She pauses for a minute to hear Ereka's response. 'Talk to Tam,' she says, handing the phone on, her patience for pandering spent.

'Hello Ereka,' Tam says gently. 'Had a bad day?' She listens for a while, but we start hollering in the background, 'just tell her to come', until Tam says, 'Ereka, why don't you just come for a little while? I can't sleep over either—you can stay for an hour, and then leave when I go ... Okay?'

Tam smiles and says, 'See you soon.' She hands the phone back to me. 'I think she'll come. Poor thing. God knows she needs to get away. More than any of us.'

•

CJ and Dooly arrive together. They are deep in conversation by the time I open the door. '... so apparently Celine loved the house, but it has one bedroom too few, so they are thinking about getting a quote for a renovation ...'

'Come on in, girls,' I say. I give each one a hug. CJ hugs back, Dooly does not, uncomfortable as she is with public displays of affection.

Dooly has a furry orange scarf looped around her neck and is apologising. For being late, for not making anything, for not having returned my last two emails. Her stooped shoulders, scraggly hair scraped back in a ponytail and 'ACF Medical Aid You Can Trust' jumper are a pallid mosaic of the garish domesticity of her life. She could really do with a makeover, some Queer Eye tjuzing and a decent haircut and facial. I always get the sense that, unlike Helen, who doesn't give a damn about her appearance, Dooly does mean to get to herself, it's just that time always runs out before she does. Juggling her four-mornings-a-week social work job with aged people, her two boys, bi-polar Max and all those bloody unnecessary pets makes her the busiest person I know. She is never able to return calls, meet for coffee, go for a walk, take in a movie or do anything for herself. She is also the worst cook I've ever met. Accepting an invitation for a meal at her place is very stressful for me—she doesn't use salt and unless something is dry and leathery, she assumes it's 'underdone'. When we do go to her place I often offer to make at least two of the courses and, blessedly, she usually agrees.

Her husband Max is a lawyer (or perhaps more accurately *was* a lawyer). His bi-polar condition was diagnosed I think before they got married but, like the rest of us, she either chose to attach no relevance to objective evidence that her life was not going to be lived out happily ever after, or she implicitly consented to her role as his caretaker from the start. It's hard not to feel sorry for her, but she's kind of made her bed.

Sometimes Max is so bad he can't even get out of bed let alone make it into chambers. And it's kind of a snowball effect—the blacker his dog and lower his confidence, the fewer tax-evaders, maintenance shirkers and petty criminals looking for kick-arse representation flock to his door. Dooly and Max are financially very strained, we all know that even though she never talks about it, and so I feel awkward about the size of the vat of chocolates she has brought—fifty dollars' worth at least. A while back Tam told us about some research indicating that chocolates release endorphins, which make us happy. Since then Dooly has been eating chocolate as a staple, which explains why the Prozac hasn't whittled her slender. I don't know how happy all that chocolate has made her. I don't think she can get over the shock of last year's episode. I remember sitting holding her hand in hospital the day after it happened, and all she could talk about was who was going to clean out the mice cage. The tears never stopped flowing down her cheeks as she asked over and over again, 'Who will think to clean out that cage?' I feel a bit bad that I didn't offer, but I really have an aversion to vermin, even the domesticated sort, and I did bring her an asparagus tart with rosemary, glazed onions and pecorino cheese, which she really enjoyed.

If she had the courage, she'd be better off divorcing Max, but that good old superglue of relationships 'GUILT' keeps her there, stuck by his side like a tacked-on appendage. She seems to be atrophying, like the stronger Siamese twin, and perhaps she's afraid that separation, even in the interests of the one more likely to survive, will endanger both their lives. She carries her grief in the exaggerated efforts she makes at conversation. When she talks, it's like she's having two conversations—the one we can all hear, and the small interior whispers she is mouthing to the part of herself she is mourning.

Her boys Luke and Tyler are both nearly the same size, even though there are three years between them, and well-meaning strangers often blunder in with 'Oh, you have twins!' which of course just exacerbates Dooly's anxiety. Luke, her eldest, has some kind of food allergy Dooly has been trying to pin down for years,

but I think she has just given up and is hoping Mother Nature will take care of it. Tam has been on her case about gluten, and once suggested that Luke's allergies are all vaccination-related. You'd think Tam might have bitten her tongue, knowing what a prime candidate Dooly is for guilt, but no, she *had* to say it.

I feel protective towards Dooly like I do towards disabled people. I always offer the patently afflicted a kindly glance, an offer to carry a parcel or assist them across the road. Dooly brings that out in me. But in a different life, having made different choices, she would have flourished, maybe. I suspect she is a deep thinker and has a latent sense of humour that we seldom see, but which is there buried under the burdens of her existence. She doesn't expend any energy hiding the strains of her life, and there is something so compellingly sincere about that.

CJ arrives complaining—of a headache, of nicotine withdrawal, of needing to use the loo before she has an accident. But she clutches a cheap bottle of white wine in one hand and a bunch of heavenly saffron coloured tulips in the other. I adore her for bringing flowers, flowers without an agenda. Not perfunctory Valentine's Day tokens. Not because a birthday's been forgotten. Not for any one of us in particular, but just for the table and in honour of this feast. Over her shoulder is slung a huge Puma sports bag. She too looks drained, strung out, but I guess all single mothers are—even more so than we married ones who have at least the illusion of help in our husbands. She is another 'professional' in our ranks and the stress shows; despite being in her early forties, her once-ebony shoulder-length hair is greying considerably and lines are etching her face with undeniable character. Those little crinkles of personality that gather at her temples when she smiles her toothy grin are incredibly endearing. She has one of those faces you don't get tired of looking at, with a little mole above her lip which, in her youth, must have driven men delirious with desire. Unlike Tam or Dooly, CJ is full of sex appeal, even if she can't see it.

CJ has a decent job at an average law firm. She does around thirty 'nasty, vicious, acrimonious' divorces a month and is the only one among us who is 'on the market', officially that is (for who among us wouldn't give a small limb for our 'real' soulmate to come along, and drop our comfortable husbands like prickly pears?). And what a dastardly place 'the market' is, given CJ's accounts. She's had a couple of dates in the past four years with men who are either divorced and 'pickled with ex-wife rage', as CJ puts it, or who are 'hard to find under all the baggage they're carrying'. Available men are either after quick sex, a midnight departure and no follow-up calls. Or they want to cuddle, move their furniture in and open a joint bank account on the first date. With three small kids at home, a babysitter who charges by the hour with Swedish precision (even two minutes into the hour) and a belly scarred and stretched from her pregnancies, she explains it'd be easier to win a triathlon than to muster up romance. But we all nag her for stories—of sex in restaurant cubicles, premature ejaculators, anal-sex fetishists and porn-charged strangers. We live vicariously through her, and she through us. Most of the time, she says, being single is just plain lonely and desolate. What she would give for some uncomplicated male companionship on a night when she has a headache, or when one of her kids is running a temperature. She once confessed that when she's really lonely, Liam comes and sleeps in her bed with her. I don't think I let on how weird I thought that was. An eight-year-old kid is no substitute for a lover. Though comfort is comfort, I suppose.

•

With their stems cut the tulips loll in a vase in the centre of the table by the time Fiona arrives ('Sorry, just needed to do a quick tidy of the house before I left, I hate coming home to a mess'). She smells of lavender and has a moist glow about her as if she has spent her day soaking in natural oils. Her long tresses of wavy auburn hair look glossy, her face is clean of makeup but has a brownish sun-coloured glow to it (which in winter months is something of an enigma) that makes her green eyes all the more translucent.

'So have you knocked anybody out yet?' I ask as I hug her and nestle my face in her hair. The aromas of citrus, tea-tree and chamomile rush at me like a throng of welcoming arms. She is an enchantment to the senses in a loose turquoise Indian-cotton shirt, without a bra underneath—though her breasts are so small, a bra is wasted on them—and large flowing purple cotton pants. She wears thongs despite the weather and her feet look healthy and strong like she's just hiked the breadth of Australia.

'So Liz's already spilled the beans about my latest obsession?' she laughs.

'There's no secrets here, Rocky,' I say.

'You should come with me one morning, it's great fun,' she says to me. 'It's a great release for aggression.'

'I've got no time,' I say. 'And besides, I can always be mean to Frank if I need to get out some pent-up anger . . .'

Under her arm she carries a little wicker basket, its contents wrapped up in a shawl of fuchsia and crimson. 'Oils,' she says, pointing to it. 'I figure we all need a little pampering tonight . . . Am I wrong?'

'So right,' I say, ushering her in. Fiona has a containing presence to which the bedlam of my impulsive inclinations is drawn for settling. Though she has a degree in microbiology, two years ago she became an aromatherapist and now runs a very successful little business from home that she charmingly calls 'earthtouch', small 'e'. Despite her healing persona, she has a slight aloofness that is alluring. Her son Gabriel is an eccentric but adorable kid who carries a harmonica around with him at all times and insists on being called 'Norton'—his self-declared nickname, which Fiona suspects he's lifted from her antivirus software box in which he's been breeding generations of silkworms. Fiona also has a seventeen-year-old stepdaughter from Ben's previous marriage. Her relationship with Kirsty is ideal. Any woman who can win over the heart of a stepdaughter is a genius, period. Stepdaughters are generally spiteful, wicked little nymphs who plot revenge on the women who have 'taken their fathers away'. Not Kirsty. She adores Fiona, they go shopping together, spend the day at health spas, have their hair blowdried and their nails French manicured as they sit side by side sipping their pineapple, watermelon and mint juices. Ben, Fi's husband, sources and sells antiques and spends more time on overseas trips than at home. But Fi releases him without complaint or calculating payback. Of all of us, she seems the most self-preserved, despite her obsession with keeping her house clean and tidy. And now this new kickboxing fad.

She often sits silently among us, rarely talking about herself or her relationship with Ben as we gab away, overreaching with vulgar regularity the respectable limits of 'too much information'. I have sometimes, in the quiet reflections of internal retreat, fidgeted with the discomfort of having revealed too much of myself to her, without reciprocation. And it's not like she's judgmental per se, but her silence suggests reproach of my gut-splurging disclosures.

'God, Fi, you smell good enough to eat,' I say.

She laughs. 'Ben hates the smells of these oils. He says it masks my natural smell . . .'

'Good on him,' I say. Any man who loves the smell of a woman's body is a prince in my eyes. And momentarily there, I have a flash of Ben going down on Fiona. I've never thought about Ben in a sexual way before (he's sixty-two for godsake) and I feel slightly hot with a sensation that's either titillation or embarrassment.

•

Ereka arrives an hour late. With an overnight bag slung over her shoulder (just in case). What a trooper. By the time she waddles in, wrapped in a lavender pashmina, which inflames her glorious red hair with colour, everyone (other than Tam and Liz) has at least two daiquiris in them. She looks bewildered and strained, but is ajangle from her ears to her fingers, thick wrists and neck with beads and silver, an artist even in annihilating weariness. She heads straight for the table laden with food, and is almost in tears when she takes in the spread that has been laid on. 'Oh, wow,' she says. 'I always forget how divine it is to be with you all ...' And she pops a sushi roll into her mouth. She is folded into our midst like a long-lost lamb and soon the laughter, the teasing, the shrieking and the silliness has washed the shadows of fatigue from her eyes. Within twenty minutes she is outside on the balcony, a joint in her hand, and the evening breeze is blowing her copper hair around her face in seductive wisps. She is young and free and beautiful again, not the mother of a brain-damaged child. Not nursing an almost five year old from her breastfeeding-worn nipples. She's just a girl, with hopes and dreams, unpunished by life's cruelties.

•

How did we all meet? It's not a very glamorous story. We met at our kids' preschool, making these all relatively new relationships. No one ever told me before I had kids that it would be through them that I would meet some of my nearest and dearest. Preschools are incredible reservoirs of women's friendships and are a much underrated source of connection. The same lassitude binds us all. We are all equally saddled with the exponential trivia of caring for little people. The same crippling sense of failure as mothers, when our children steal or bully or seem genetically incapable of moving beyond the tantrum stage, feeds our deteriorating self esteem. We are sisters involved in one struggle, silently and individually braving it out alone. Behind each of our closed suburban doors, echo the same battle cries for gender equality and recognition of our worth as people.

Through my associations with other mothers, I have garnered comfort from the knowledge that though at times I feel devastatingly alone in my nuclear family, burdened by the unshirkable responsibility for my children's welfare, nutrition, emotional, spiritual and moral upbringing, I am not alone in my loneliness. I now know that our personal traumas, which isolate us and make us feel cut off from the world, are universal conditions experienced by others, and that it is only closed doors that keep us from a sense of community and from the awareness that we are all linked by the Velcro of our maternal condition. I now understand that motherhood is a politically charged place where many of us unwittingly but incontrovertibly reinforce the myths of motherhood. But I also know that we each privately dream of bludgeoning the injustice out of them with a sledgehammer. Or chopping them up into little bits with a scalpel-sharp Victorinox knife, that slices like a dream.

CHAPTER 3

for the sake of the kids

In the centre of the dining room table, which is bedecked with one of my fuschia-coloured saris, is a *fayanza*. What the hell is a *fayanza*, I suspect you're thinking. A *fayanza* is a magnificent symbol of generosity and hospitality, invented by the Greeks. It is an enormous platter, the kind you use when you are entertaining by the dozen. The sort of platter used by caterers and brought out for weddings and bar mitzvahs. Liz and Carl gave this gorgeous white platter to me for my wedding. Carl is Greek, and apart from importing his exotic surname into his children's lives (Chloe and Brandon Stern-Nikolaos), he has also brought a touch of the Mediterranean to the crockery in my kitchen. Apparently every good Greek wife has a *fayanza*. 'The six I got for our wedding are at the back of the pantry collecting dust,' Liz once confessed to me. But she never offered to give me any, even though she knows they'd get a workout in my kitchen.

Tonight, my *fayanza* is the canvas for one of my salad masterpieces. I'm coy about some things, but I never allow modesty to interfere with my concession that I don't know anyone—not even Helen—who can make a better salad than I can. The bottom line with salads is that you've either got it or you haven't. It's like blue eyes. Skinny genes. Rhythm. You cannot make a salad by following a recipe. Like maternal love salads are pure instinct. If I tell Helen 'a dash of paprika' she asks, 'a teaspoon?' 'No, a dash,' I say. And then she puts her hands on her hips and gives me that look. 'You're being very uncooperative,' she says. She only understands the world in measurable quantities, doesn't believe in God and thinks astrology is a load of bollocks. She has officially delegated the spiritual education of her children to me. 'Just don't tell them lies,' she says.

'Telling them God exists is not a lie,' I say.

'If you can't prove it, it's a lie,' she says.

I've still not forgiven her for telling Nathan that the tooth fairy doesn't exist when he asked. 'What was I supposed to do? He asked me to tell him the truth,' she said, as if that was somehow excusable. Coupled with her coriander aversion, her quirky sense of what is right and her ability to reduce the world to four-cornered precision are just about her only failings.

In the centre of the *fayanza* sit fifteen plump, berry-coloured baby beetroots. Fanning out around them are thinly sliced avocado crescents. To make it into one of my salads, an avocado cannot concede the slightest mooshiness, but must maintain a firmness and that nutty-yellow aloe colour. Anything less and an avocado can expect to come to a guacamolean end where all imperfections are easily forgiven. Then comes a circle of slightly browned roasted pumpkin, which has been drizzled with extra-virgin olive oil, and some fresh lemon thyme. A ring of carefree and peppery rocket, flouncing its leaves in all directions' is next. Across the whole salad like wind-tossed blossoms are perfect rings of purple Spanish onion, fresh shavings of parmesan cheese and roasted pine nuts. I have also—in a moment of decorative extravagance—scattered a few yellow, orange and red nasturtiums from my garden. Finally, the dressing is homemade (forget Paul Newman's balsamic efforts at $4.50 a bottle). My salad dressing recipe is a secret. Helen has tried—on more than one occasion—to squeeze it out of me, but I prefer to make a bottle for her without revealing too much, and I've promised to leave the recipe to her in my will. Suffice to say it has thirteen ingredients including reduced balsamic vinegar. In cooking, 'reduction' magically diminishes the volume but enriches the substance. My salad dressing is laced with a good few glugs of thick, delicious balsamic syrup.

'God, but there's a lot of food,' Liz says from her seat, straining to look at the table where I am pottering with last minute preparations, just waiting for the timer to ring on the oven where the lasagna is warming.

'What do you care?' I quip back. 'We'll be lucky if you nibble on a lettuce leaf before midnight.'

'It's a bit over the top,' she retorts.

'That is the idea,' I say, folding some teal- and amber-coloured serviettes next to the fan of knives and forks.

'Does anyone have headache tablets on them?' CJ asks, sitting up from the sofa. 'I've got a bugger of one.'

'I'm sure my folks must have some in the medicine cabinet,' Helen says, making to stand.

'Don't worry, I've got some codeine somewhere in my bag,' Dooly offers, ferreting in the caverns of her enormous Mary Poppins handbag—from which she once brought out an entire toolkit when we were at the park and I jokingly asked if anyone had a screwdriver to tighten Aaron's training wheels. She flicks the tails of the orange scarf over her shoulders. It is appallingly knitted, with large holes and uneven edges. It can't possibly be a fashion statement. I don't know why she didn't hang it up with the coats in the hallway when she arrived.

'Brilliant,' CJ says. 'I suppose there's no chance of a cigarette?'

'No, but I've got a Tampax you can try,' Dooly says, handing over the tablets.

'No thanks, cotton wool is no substitute for good old nicotine . . .' CJ responds.

'I also brought some trashy magazines that I'm done with,' Dooly says, hauling out six well-thumbed ones that look like they've just spent the last month in Dooly's bathroom. They're full of trivial entertainment, with glitzy celebrities sprawled on their covers, a veritable feast of gossip about Brad and Jen's break-up, Angelina's latest adoption, Russell's most recent temper tantrum and Paris's hottest pair of sandals. Dooly tosses them onto the floor between the sofas. *Star Wardrobes: Who has 4000 Pairs of Shoes?* I read on the cover of one and, despite how I despise myself for it, my curiosity is piqued. Though I'd never actually buy them myself, like a social smoker who bums cigarettes off everyone else, I gladly accept pre-owned magazines. No one else rushes for them. It's only Dooly and I who confess to wallowing in the trough of celeb gossip.

'Once you've had something to eat you'll feel better,' Fiona says soothingly.

'And you won't be short of choices,' Liz says, fingering her pearl collar.

'Personally, I don't think there's enough food,' Helen says, winking at me.

'I mean how much can a person actually eat before it becomes unpleasant?' Liz continues, sipping her wine.

'Being full is never a reason to stop eating,' I say, pouring out a tube of water crackers to surround the smoked salmon dip.

'Are you going to bring your daughter up with that philosophy?' Liz asks, blinking her bright blue eyes in my direction. With irises that colour, she really doesn't need all that makeup.

'I sure am. Food is one of the great consolations of post-Neanderthal civilisation,' I say, speaking with a mouth full of biscuit covered in mascarpone cheese. 'God, but this is divine...' I mutter.

'Well that's a formula for an overweight and depressed teenager,' Liz says pointedly, smoothing down the pearls on her matching bracelet which sits large on her slender wrists.

'At least she won't be an anorexic food-a-phobe,' I say, moving from the table of food back into the open-plan living room, and passing around a plate of canapés of bocconcini, fresh basil leaves, slivers of sun-dried tomato and a caper or two all held together with a toothpick. 'Food is friend, not foe,' I say, paraphrasing a line from *Finding Nemo*. The allusion is lost on Liz—when would she have seen *Finding Nemo* with her kids?

'And fat is sad, not happy,' Liz comes back to me, taking a bocconcini skewer in her maroon-tipped fingers. 'How the hell do you make these?' she asks, examining it.

'With great love,' I say.

'I'd prefer it if you don't let Nathan hear your philosophy on eating,' Helen says to me, taking three canapés at once.

'Are you still worried about his weight?' Tam asks, holding a skewer she will soon scrutinise for hidden gluten.

'It's just that other kids are noticing now and are starting to tease him,' Helen says with a mouth full.

'Poor bunny,' Dooly says. 'These look very interesting,' she says to me, but doesn't take a speared mozzarella ball. 'But I'm saving my appetite...'

'What for?' I ask. 'A rainy day?'

She chuckles. 'I don't want to fill up on healthy food, when there's all that chocolate . . .'

'Why don't you take that scarf off?' I ask her. 'Aren't you hot?'

'I am but I promised Luke I'd wear his scarf all night,' she says goofily. 'He knitted this all by himself . . . Well, I helped him a bit.'

'Well, he's not here to see,' I say. 'He'll never know—just tell him you wore it all night.'

'I couldn't do that,' Dooly says.

I shrug. 'I'm sure there's a medical term for your condition,' I say to her. 'Compulsive integrity or irrational truth-telling.'

'I wouldn't worry about Nathan,' Fiona says to Helen. 'He'll grow out of it—it's puppy fat.'

'Which is turning into doggy lard,' Helen says. 'You should see him on the soccer field with his tummy wobbling and his thighs rubbing together, it's pathetic.'

'Sounds like me,' I say.

Tam excuses herself and goes off into the kitchen in search of a clean glass.

'Everyone thinks it's only girls who have to worry about getting fat, but I tell you, boys can be cruel too,' Helen says.

I give Helen a grim smile—Aaron, my son, is one of 'those boys'. It is a shame I cannot evade, despite my competence in the art of denial, that I have spawned a child who is (forgive the labelling) a menace and a bully. I console myself with Discovery Channel documentaries. Lions stalk fawn. Crocodiles devour giraffes. Cruelty is survival in nature. My son is a hunter, sniffing out and swiftly culling the meek and the mild, the kids that never cause any trouble, who do as they're told, have impeccable manners and share their chocolate with whoever asks. Explanations about 'unacceptable

behaviour' are lost on Aaron, much as I suspect a stern lecture to the cat for killing that bird would be a waste of breath.

A few months ago Gretchen Oates, his preschool teacher, called me. When my heart had stopped pounding (it wasn't a 'we-managed-to-retrieve-his-finger' or a 'don't-worry-he's-still-breathing' call) she asked me to 'come in to have a little chat about Aaron'. That afternoon, after ten minutes of preamble on 'what a delightful, spirited, clever and confident' child he is, which just served as a drumroll for my anxiety, she broke the news—he teases and jibes other less confident children and 'delights in their misery'. I must have blushed crimson. I listened as Gretchen outlined his insolence, tantrums, explosive temper and nasty little ways and I suddenly piped up, 'That's exactly how he treats me.'

'Well, he's bullying you too,' Gretchen said. 'Now, who is the boss—you or your four year old?'

When she put it that way, I desperately wanted to feel a potent resolve in the wake of this humiliating realisation. And so I confidently asserted, 'I am, of course.' But really, a truthful squeak would have been 'my four year old'.

'Have you tried taking Nathan off gluten?' Tam suggests to Helen on her return from the kitchen holding a large glass of—can you believe it?—water.

'I've tried to take him off sugar and fat, but do you know how much food is made with hidden sugars and fats? He is so miserable. It's not just the ice cream, chocolates and chips. It's all the so called "healthy" stuff too—the muesli bars, the fruit sticks. He's feeling very hard done by at the moment,' Helen says, wiping her lips.

'What about taking him to a dietician?' Tam asks. She sips at her glass like it's a fucking martini.

'Naah, that's overdoing it. I've just got to persevere with the healthy eating and exercise,' Helen says. 'Is anyone going to have another of these gorgeous thingies?' she asks, gesturing to the plate of canapés.

'All yours,' Liz says, still holding her uneaten one in her hand. 'You need to nip it in the bud now,' she continues. 'He'll grow up to be a plump teenager and then your problems will really start.'

'I know, that's what I'm anxious about,' Helen says. Only two canapés left.

'Every time he wants seconds or to eat crap, just tell him he's going to grow up to be fat and miserable,' Liz says. I look at the balcony door, relieved that Ereka, who would never shirk the label 'fat', is out of hearing range.

'Oh, come on, Liz, that's very harsh. He's only five, for godsake,' I say.

'Six,' Helen corrects me.

'Five, six, he's still a baby,' I say.

'Good habits start young,' Liz asserts.

'You're a food Nazi. And I'm keeping these last two for Ereka,' I say, looking at Helen, who would eat them all if I let her.

'But I don't have fat kids,' Liz says.

'Neither do I,' I say. 'And I don't pound their heads with anti-food talk.'

'Yeah, but your children don't eat,' Liz says.

'Only Aaron,' I say defensively. 'And he *does* eat. Only two things and quite infrequently, but he does eat.'

'I was a fat kid,' Tam says.

We all look at her.

'That's hard to imagine,' Dooly says tenderly, perspiring on her forehead and upper lip. I wish she'd just take off that goddamned scarf.

'I was never picked for the teams, never had boyfriends at school. My nickname was Stump—as in tree stumps for legs. It was excruciating to be me.'

For a moment I feel something bordering on pity for Tam.

'See?' Liz says.

'And then what happened?' Helen asks.

'I developed a bit of an eating disorder in my teens and lost a lot of weight. I put it all on again after the kids were born, and now I just eat enough to keep healthy,' she says. She doesn't mention the nervous breakdown, the Prozac she's still on that makes weight just fall off you. But I guess no one's got to point out when an elephant's farted—it's obvious, isn't it?

'See?' I quip back at Liz, still slightly stunned at the revelation of Tam's ferreted history. How seldom we have visited the acres of one another's years that preceded our meeting at the crossroad of motherhood. What girls were we? What hang-ups propelled our teenage wretchedness? Were we luscious and seductive? Awkward and desperate? The queen of the prom or the wallflower no one asked to dance?

'That's a lot to have gone through,' Dooly says in her social worker's voice that tells the speaker, 'I've heard you, your pain matters.' She unfurls the scarf, so that it is now just draped around her shoulders.

'I'm okay now,' Tam smiles briskly. 'They were a dark few years, but I'm okay now,' the echo unsettling me with muted overtures of exaggerated protest. 'Anyway, the point I wanted to make about Nathan is that you don't want to pathologise eating. That's what my mother did to me—she made me neurotic about everything that passed my lips, and that created a huge psychological obstacle for me to overcome. Just reinforce good habits, and let Nathan have some junk every now and then.'

Junk? I can't believe I've just heard her advocate crap, even as a treat.

'Yeah, that's what I think I'm doing. But I have to bite my tongue every time he asks for seconds and thirds,' Helen says.

'You want to call him Fatty, don't you?' Liz says. She finally puts that canapé in her mouth.

'Don't you dare!' Tam says, indignant.

'I'm joking,' Liz says, chewing. 'I know I'm cold hearted, but plain cruelty is not my style.'

'Gluten,' Tam asserts again.

'Yeah, I'll think about it,' Helen says.

'If you all change your diet in the house, he'll have to get used to it. He may not be so quick to ask for seconds of lentil stew and steamed asparagus,' Fiona says. She has taken off her sandals and is pressing her toes, with learned reflexological precision.

'You don't know my son . . .' Helen laughs. 'But that's an idea. For his sake I would do it. Give up all my earthly pleasures . . .'

'Talking of which, who's having another strawberry daiquiri?' CJ asks, armed with the tub and an ice cream scoop.

'Fill me up,' Helen orders, holding out her glass.

'Drinking?' Tam asks, raising her eyebrows. Her glass of water now empty, ready for a refill.

'Fourth baby,' Helen says. 'It'll just have to cope.'

'You want to give it the best chance,' Tam says. 'At your age, it comes with a one in thirty chance of Down's syndrome.' She says this in a sort of whisper, even though Ereka is still out of earshot on the balcony being caressed by the wind and the night air.

'Oh, give her a break,' CJ says. 'Someone fill up Tam's glass before we get a lecture.'

'No, I'm fine, really,' Tam says, protectively covering the top of her glass with her hand.

'Shit, I heard a funny story the other day,' Helen says. 'It's probably an urban legend, but hell I laughed. A woman went for an amnio and was waiting for her results. She phoned the doctor's rooms and the usual receptionist was away, and there was a woman answering the phone, a foreigner, whose English wasn't good ...'

'Don't you hate that?' CJ says. I turn to her with a chilling look.

'What?' she says. 'I've got nothing against them. But when you've got to work with people all day who can't even speak English ...'

'Can I finish my story?' Helen asks.

'Don't start, CJ,' I say.

'Well, English is the language we speak in Australia, and if people want to come here, shouldn't they at least be able to communicate with the rest of us?' CJ asks.

'Yeah, I guess we should also insist that everyone is white and heterosexual—just like us,' I say sarcastically.

'Oh get off your high horse,' she says crudely, 'you bleeding heart liberal.'

And now I find CJ distinctly lacking in appeal, sexual or otherwise. Race politics are not her forte and I know if we are to have a reasonably pleasant evening together we will need to steer clear of the topics of refugees, illegal immigrants and the Arab-Israeli conflict. Unlike my university-forged friendships, these relationships with my children's friends' mothers come without a political history, denuded of the context on which we base so many of our intimacies with others.

I don't know on which side of the bra-burning issue any of them would fall; I wouldn't trust any of them (other than Fiona) not to have voted for Howard or even to support Bush. Our unity lies simply in our bond as mothers. In that we offer a unified front.

The rest is a minefield. I swallow my distaste at her comment like an unseasoned, overcooked mouthful of Dooly's cooking. CJ's a university graduate for godsake. You'd think she'd know better. None of the others rush to support me. Not even Fiona. Everyone here is so confrontation-averse. What's the point in doing kick-boxing if you can't use your moves in conversation to shut CJ up?

'So anyway,' Helen continues, 'the woman asks if her test results for the amnio have come back, and the receptionist says, "I'll just check on the computer". She goes away and comes back a few minutes later, and says, "I'm sorry, it's Down's". As you can imagine, the woman is distraught. She phones her husband and is in a terrible state. Turns out, it was the computer that was down. Her test results were normal. Can you believe that?'

'I'd have sued the pants off that doctor,' CJ says. 'Emotional distress.'

The rest of us are laughing. Dooly, not quite, her victim-endeared training only marginally wavering in the gale of our defiling witticisms. The daiquiris are starting to kick in. There is a freedom in our banter because Ereka is not here to hear us. But, even so, it *is* a funny story. Only if you are not the woman waiting for the test results. It is so pleasing, is it not, to have the freedom to laugh at jokes like these? I remember those anxious stretches of waiting in my first pregnancy during which suddenly my unseen baby became a potential statistic for Tay Sachs. Cystic fibrosis. Spina bifida. Even after all the tests were done and we held in our hands the paper assurances of a one in 283 chance of Down's and one in 528 for spina bifida, we never quite shook off the haunting prospect, the 'what if?' No number of tests deliver the unqualified reassurance that you are not the 'one' in the 'one in 283' part of the equation. Someone has to be. All of us are seeking the same outcome. A normal baby. With eyes that see. With ears that hear. Without a cleft palate. Perfect. The only sort of baby any of us want.

But we don't go there. Not in front of Ereka, anyway. Olivia, her eldest daughter, has some degree of brain damage, the full extent not yet known. Whenever I lie awake in the chilling hours of night, and the enormity of all that can go wrong in life keeps me sleepless, I think of Ereka. All she wanted was a home birth. She fought so hard to win Jake over. How could it all have fallen apart like that? Deprivation of oxygen, getting to the hospital too late to prevent permanent damage. With such frightening speed our fragile worlds can shatter.

Something unspeakably sacred is held among us all around this topic. A shared grief at how easily Humpty Dumpty can fall off that wall. And for those of us who escaped with healthy kids, a kind of survivor guilt. A guilt borne of our unutterable relief that it was not us.

•

Ereka soon returns from outside. She is smiling. She looks demure and windswept. 'It's gorgeous out there,' she says, and there is a slight hum in her voice. I try to imagine who she was before Olivia was born. Did she laugh from deeper in her belly, or always from the shallows? I wonder whether the unknown terrified or intrigued her; and whether as a gum-blowing schoolgirl, a gypsy tie-dyed teenager or funky paint-spattered artist she ever just stopped in her tracks, the premonition of a life tethered to a 'disabled child' casting its shadow on her youthful happiness. I only met her two years ago, when Olivia was already four. In a moment of rare authentic intimacy, she once let me peek at some of her paintings— mostly self-portraits and one startling one of Olivia in blues, 'because she was so blue at birth', chilling and strangely beautiful. Very Frida Kahlo.

'I saved these for you,' I say to Ereka, pointing to the remaining canapés.

'Thanks a million,' she says, gratefully picking them up, one in each silver-weighted hand. 'So how're you feeling, Helen?' Ereka asks, the song of the wind still in her voice.

'Remotely better,' she says. 'I'm not only eating nougat and cheeseburgers. I've progressed on to Kentucky Fried Chicken and pineapple pizzas.'

'You're looking well,' Ereka says.

Helen smiles broadly, incapable of guile or sentimentality. 'Someone's got to,' she laughs.

Ereka smiles too, but finely. 'Gosh, these are divine,' she says, chewing and swallowing. 'I sometimes forget how delicious things can taste . . .'

'Who's going to eat with me?' Ereka asks heading for the table, jingling as she goes.

Both Helen and I answer, 'We will', and we join her at the table.

'Hey girls,' I say, attempting a roundup. 'Anyone for a bite yet?'

None of the others takes the slightest notice of me. Fiona is massaging CJ's left hand looking for 'pressure points' to relieve her headache, Liz is paging through *Glamour* magazine, Dooly, sitting next to her, is licking her glass for the last traces of strawberry daiquiri. My friends are all stretched out on the couches in Helen's folks' lounge room overlooking the water. Crepuscular light is starting to touch all the eye can see.

It is precisely this oceanic vista, the vast expanse of water reaching to the horizon and dipping beyond that has kept me calm and centred on many days when I have felt myself slipping into a deep and dark place when my longing for home is more than I can

bear. These women have become my replacement family since we left South Africa three years ago. These friendships are all that hold me from total isolation and blistering loneliness. I am washed with a warm feeling of comfort by their presence

'So I finally relented and bought Tyler a plastic machine gun,' I overhear Dooly saying to Liz. 'He's been running around the house rattling it off at everything.'

'It's not going to do him any harm,' Liz says, lazily closing the magazine. 'Let him get it out of his system now, and he won't end up in McDonald's with a real machine gun later.'

Dooly sighs, unconvinced, and twirls the end of the scarf around her wrist. 'The noise drives Max crazy, though. You know his medication heightens all his senses.'

'Get one for Max,' Liz says, taking a drink from her glass. 'He'll probably find it very therapeutic.'

Dooly gives a little laugh. 'Yeah, that's an idea . . .'

Liz is utterly self-possessed. Next to Dooly it is starkly evident. When Liz speaks, she commands 'listen to me', exuding an expectation of compliance. I suppose spending all day in an environment of unequals, where your every word makes it into shorthand, where your every whim is obeyed and your every snarl ruins someone's week, is amniotic fluid for the ego. Liz is preened on affirmation. She exists loudly, people talk about her, agonise over how to approach her, fear her censure, crave her approval. She needs self-justification like a fish needs a bicycle. Every thought that wafts through her head is a potential moneyspinner.

Dooly, on the other hand, natters falteringly, as if awaiting contradiction, anticipating negation. Her ideas she keeps largely folded away from scrutiny, though when she does share one it's usually profound, like a rolled-up masterpiece she's been quietly working on for years. It's like she's afraid of letting out the riches of her mind, lest they get plundered and snatched away. I can understand it after all she's been through. The last time we chatted on the phone, which was two months ago, she confessed, 'If I didn't have to worry about the kids . . . I'd love to just disappear . . . I know Max needs me, but he'd be okay. But you can't run and hide when you've got kids, can you?'

'You mean divorce Max?' I'd asked.

She couldn't bring herself to say the word. 'Something like that,' she'd sighed.

'Isn't it better for kids to have two happy homes than one unhappy one?' I had asked.

'No. At least I can pretend to be happy, but we can't pretend to be a family if we're apart,' she'd said. 'I'll stay with Max for the kids' sake. For now.'

A happy marriage—what is that, really? We fall in love with someone at the epidermal interface of knowing who they—and we—are. Six years later, you've got two kids, and a habit you call your husband. I know Ereka and Jake have something different from the rest of us, love maybe. I think Helen and Fiona are content. Liz, I am not sure about—Carl is part of the machinery that makes her life work. And her life *is* work. And we all know that Tam just stays with Kevin for the kids' sake too. He is a great breadwinner. And she's got big plans for her boys.

From my place at the dining room table, I hear Tam in the lounge room launching into one of her monologues about brain tumours. CJ must have prodded her for the latest on migraine headaches. To Helen, both CJ and I are 'whiney hypochondriacs'. Maybe I am—a hypochondriac, not whiney. But at least I have an ally. CJ and I share a common dread of the big C. It is a phobia so paralysing and consuming that we are both regular doctor-frequenters, always aiming for reassurance that the nosebleed, the bump on our upper arm, the irregular bowel movements or the stomach cramps are not 'It': The Dreaded Illness That Will Cut Short Our Lives and Leave Our Children Motherless. I know what CJ secretly thinks is wrong with her. That the migraine headaches are some symptom of brain cancer and that she is going to die before her forty-third birthday. I rally to her side, clutching my plate in my hands.

'Do we really need to talk about brain tumours?' I interject. 'When there is so much else to talk about, like the prawns, the sushi, the salmon dip?'

'You'll find this interesting, Jo,' Tam says.

'I have no doubt that it will keep me up at night,' I say, but I am drawn nonetheless to listen to what she knows about brain tumours. I am insatiably curious and equally paranoid, a phobia-addict unable to refuse a line.

'They've isolated three factors that have been scientifically proven to cause brain cancer,' Tam continues. 'First, mobile phones.' I mentally make a note to self: 'Get hands-free as matter of urgency'.

'I always thought those phones must cause cancer,' CJ says, her right hand now in Fiona's therapeutic grasp. 'And I live on mine—I'm sure it's done damage.'

'Yeah, they really don't do your brain any favours, all that electromagnetic radiation,' Tam confirms.

'That's still controversial,' Liz pipes up.

'What's the second and third thing?' I ask.

'The second is not drinking enough water. They say you have to drink loads of water to make sure your brain is washed in spinal fluid.' I guess that explains Tam's foray to the kitchen. I suspect we'll see a few more of those trips over the course of the evening. Maybe I should join her. I'm always hoping someone will come up

with something more inspiring like: eat more chips or drink more red wine. A strawberry daiquiri a day keeps the doctor away. 'And number three?' I ask, hoping for some magnificent revelation.

'No artificial red food colouring,' Tam says, delivering this with an air of serious iteration.

'You must be joking,' Helen interjects, holding a plate laden with food in one hand and a fork in the other. 'Who could consume enough red food colouring for it to make any difference at all?'

'Why only red?' I ask. 'What about the blue and yellow and green Smarties?'

'My kids drink bucketfuls of that red cordial stuff,' Liz says, picking up on the conversation.

'It's no good,' Tam says. 'That stuff is poison.'

'You are not seriously telling me that amidst the MSG, the preservatives, the passive smoke, the pollution, the radiation, the environmental pollutants, and every other bit of crap our kids come into contact with, the one thing I need to worry about is how much red cordial they drink?' Liz snorts in derision.

'It's been proven,' Tam says. 'And at least it's something you can control.'

'That's just bull, Tam,' Liz says. 'We're not in control. Control is an illusion. It's something you might want to explore. And you too, CJ,' she says, nodding in CJ's direction. 'Migraines come from wanting to control too much. You've just got to let go. Our kids are going to grow up one way or the other, and we have very little say over that process.'

Liz's comment comes from either a profound insight into the maternal relationship we create with our children or from the convenience of her self-centred psyche. She flaunts her liberation from her children 'by throwing money and nannies at the problem', as she puts it. Unlike the rest of us, she carries herself with an enviable confidence borne of one unenslaved to the unglamorous demands of small people. While the rest of us are buckling little bodies in and out of car seats, fetching and carrying, cutting fruit at preschool, exacting discipline and small hugs, reading about 'Sam I am' who loves green eggs and ham, she chairs meetings and designs campaigns to get people to spend more money on bathroom tiles, pantyhose and disposable razors. She claims success is about identifying the right person to whom to delegate.

She once even squeezed her narcissism into the overcrowded window-box of maternal magnanimity. 'If I didn't follow my heart and my passion,' she had said to me, 'I'd be a depressed and unfulfilled human being. What sort of mother would I be then?' The rest of us are quietly envious of her choice. An envy we brandish from our moral high ground. *We* are Real Mothers. *She* gives Lily money to buy ready-made catering and party entertainment for her children's birthdays. She wouldn't know the inside of a baking tin or a homemade meal if it pooed on her footpath.

But her logic is faultless, she is so perfectly rational about it all—motherhood is the antidote to all delusions of control. As Robbie Williams so urgently puts it, 'Watch me come undone' (any day, Robbie).

'We may not be in complete control,' Fiona says, 'but don't we have a responsibility to try to create the best environment for our kids?'

I nod. So does Tam. Responsibility. Cancer is the only other word that curdles my insides more efficiently. Responsibility for our children's wellbeing. Their safety. Their mental health. If our children have a life-threatening illness, we'd better be there to notice. Actually, it's best to get a head start by detecting the early signs. It is up to us as mothers to attend to the fevers, the rages and the hurts the world will inflict on our babies. If we are remiss or distracted by anything ranging from a rude bank clerk to a best friend's marriage breakup, our children will suffer. They may even die. CJ's Liam nearly choked to death at five months when she left him lying safely on a floor with a baby-gym hanging overhead for him to look at. She was in the shower when she heard a garroting sound and rushed to find that he had lifted up one of the legs of the baby-gym and jammed it in his mouth. Our children's lives and everything the promise of their innocence holds depend on the vigilance of our attention and the choices and sacrifices we must make for their sake.

At times I feel an almost suffocating pain in my chest when I think of the biggest decision we ever made. The life-changing moment of clarity that looped all our fates and changed the course of our lives. Jamie was only 18 months old at the time. We knew how prevalent rape was in South Africa, just not how close it hovered. Moments after hearing the news that Leah, my best friend, had been attacked and gang-raped, I stood over Jamie's cot, heaving with sobs I could not hold back. Every time I changed her nappy and wiped her tiny little vulva clean, I was overwhelmed with grief at what had been taken—not only from my beautiful friend, but from all the blamelessness and purity in the world. Three years later, Frank and I were on a plane to Australia, numb from thwarted hopes that 'things in South Africa would get better'. Frank had come home too many times to find me crying because of a headline that another baby had been raped. 'You can't take it so personally,' he'd say, straining to comfort me. I whispered to Frank late at night, when the fear was worst: 'Get us out of here.' And so he did.

We chose a life for our children, one bereft of grandparents, aunts and cousins because I could not live with my fear for their safety. Despite our overwhelming love for the place and its people, the violence in South Africa was too much of a risk—to my children or to the vestiges of my sanity, I could not quite tell. In grief, from which I thought I would never emerge, we packed up our lives, gave up our high-powered jobs, our beautiful nanny (and her entire extended family that we supported), our country, our national anthem and our homeland. For the sake of the kids.

No one warned me of the depression that would overtake me as a new immigrant living in a foreign country, despite the comfort of its safety. To come here, I forfeited a self hard-won as a respected advocate in my field of work in gender equality and women's rights, to bring our children to a promised land of little violence. Africa was my home with all the ravages of HIV, poverty, and its tormented history of Apartheid. And like a child snatched from the depredations of an abusive family, I still longed for the familiarity of my dysfunctional cradle. My well-adjusted, soft-spoken foster home only highlighted the brutality of my alienation.

I became utterly reduced (but not in the enriching cooking sense). I was a sliver of my former self. A shaving. Joanne Julienne, denuded of the chunkiness of my accumulated identity. The implications of self-sacrifice began to sink in—the loss of my history, status, position in the world, friendships, networks, unarticulated attachments to people, places, smells. All that was left was the mother in me.

There were days when I would sob inconsolably for no reason I could articulate. I *had* to be a good mother. It was all that remained. I strove to impart to my children that their lives were *rich* and *full* and *glorious*, that it was a privilege to be living away from the high walls, the injustices of Africa. But most days I failed, because my own desolation spoke more directly to those little faces than the empty words that left my lips.

Despite my numerous degrees, I was not qualified to do anything in Australia. Frank rewrote his law exams. I shopped, cooked, cleaned, mothered. At times our relationship strained at the seams, each of us feeling it was he or I who had given up the most and was bearing the burden of our immigration. On nights when heated acrimony gave way to moments of reconciliation, he would gently lead me by the hand and we would steal into the children's room and watch them sleep. 'This is why we came here,' he would remind me. And in the simplicity, the rightness of that, I would take comfort. What was my own happiness when weighed against my children's safety?

My children will never know the joy of being picked up from daycare by a grandparent with promises of ice creams and feeding the ducks. Perhaps Frank and I will survive without romantic dinners for the next ten years, because our budget won't cover babysitters and there's no grandparent to fill in the gap. We'll celebrate birthdays anyway, even if we have to rent a crowd of friends. We'll look forward, not back, focus on the positive and not dwell on the losses. Party face. For the sake of the kids.

I am deep in nostalgic thought when I feel Fiona's firm hands on my shoulders.

'Are you okay, Jo?' she asks. The others have all moved from the lounge room to the dining room table, without me.

'Terrific,' I say. 'Can I get you a plate? Please won't you eat?'

'I will certainly eat. What do you recommend?'

And with that, and the distraction of our banquet, I am able to ease myself out of the grasp of my self pity and into the open-handed delight of my friends and food.

CHAPTER 4

the plate reader

I survey my kingdom. From the head of the table, I can observe all seven of my friends and their plates. Some have not held back and have heaped their dishes with mounds of food as if it's the last supper. Others, more tentative, calorie-conscious, have frugally transferred tokens from the serving bowls to their own dishes, only half-heartedly participating in the ancient ritual of feasting. I know I can be an irritating nag when I want to feed people. I plead identity: I am a Jewish mother. My marrow dictates I must make people happy through food.

However, not everyone gets the same satisfaction from eating as I do. Some people treat it with as much excitement as they do an ablution. Like Liz, for example. It is truly a personality flaw, in my opinion, that when it comes to food she can take it or leave it. I nurture suspicions that a lukewarm response to my cooking translates into deeper and far more sinister shortcomings. A stinginess of the soul. A sensual meanness. I am always on the lookout for these unforgivable failings in her. My intellectual understanding and even grudging admiration of her ability to put herself first and keep her kids well and firmly in their place is outstripped by my silent judgment that she is unable to open herself fully to the task (the joy and the terror) of loving them completely. All this I can see in the single sushi ring and blob of dip on her plate. I am a plate reader, after all.

Then there is Dooly, still wearing the ridiculous scarf—how can anyone eat freely trailing two woolly fringes? Her plate is a haphazard mess of scoops she has quickly dished up without considering where on the plate they will go. The Thai curry is running into the dip, and the salad is an unrecognisable scattering over her plate. She eats in a hurry, the scarf clearly getting in her way, and as soon as she's had a few bites she fills her plate again, warding off its emptiness. And I know this about her—she will leave everything half eaten, as if she just simply cannot bear to see it all gone. She is a silent eater, the occasional murmur of contentment peeping out between bites. But whether she really tastes, through the wire-mesh of her distraction and insecurity, how utterly divine this food is compared to anything that emerges from her kitchen is anyone's guess.

'So how's Luke's arm healing?' Helen asks Dooly.

'The plaster's coming off in about five days' time,' she says, swallowing a mouthful of curry.

'And this is the . . . second time he's broken a limb?' Ereka asks.

'Third,' she says, nodding. 'He is the most accident-prone child. You know he dislocated a shoulder when he was born, just trying to get out in one piece. He also tore me from one side to the other—it was the episiotomy of the century.' I shudder, imagining Dooly's perineum stitched back together like a patchwork quilt.

'You must have shares in the Children's Hospital,' Fiona says teasingly, standing back and watching us all eat.

'They see us coming there at casualty, and they send out a welcoming party, with banners,' Dooly says, grimacing. And whoops, yes, there goes the scarf fringe into the Thai curry. Dooly quickly lifts it out and wipes the ends with a serviette.

'My kids have never broken any bones,' Liz says.

'What sort of a mother are you? Bringing up kids without any breakages?' Helen teases.

'You're lucky—I thought boys were genetically hardwired to break a few bones,' CJ says. 'We've had a broken tibia and a broken toe,' she says, taking a huge mouthful of lasagna.

'Broken bones are better than broken teeth,' Liz says. 'Chloe fell and broke her permanent front tooth at her sports day last month, and I'd much rather she'd broken an arm or a leg, at least that can heal. But a tooth—it's so evident, so difficult to conceal,' she continues.

Our incredulity encircles Liz in a spotlight.

'You'd rather she broke a limb than a tooth?' Fiona asks.

'Absolutely,' Liz says. 'Limbs heal. We had to get a cap for her tooth and it's still not perfect, you can see it's not.'

Fiona just shakes her head. Not even a small jab back at Liz. Where *is* that killer instinct of the kickboxer?

'So what?' Helen joins in. 'Perfect shmerfect, at least she wasn't in pain.'

'Pain passes. She's going to need a winning smile for a long time to come,' Liz says, lancing her sushi roll with a fork. For all her breeding, she still eats sushi like a novice.

'Isn't that a bit . . . shallow, Liz?' Fiona asks. But the sting of her words are rendered lame by the disclaimer that follows: 'I don't mean to be rude or anything . . .'

Liz chews completely and swallows before answering. 'It's honest, is what it is,' Liz says. 'We all go on about how looks don't matter, and as long as our children don't suffer, it's okay. I'll tell you how children suffer—when they don't fit in socially as teenagers. And they spend all their time agonising over how they look. Beauty is a great advantage when they're that vulnerable.'

We all absorb this diatribe. It's hard to win an argument with Liz. She's pretty much thought it all through.

'I'd rather spare my kids the harsh reality of life, they're so little and innocent, why spoil that?' Tam suggests.

'Some kids are born into the harsh realities of life,' CJ says bitterly. 'Mine have no illusions. Their father has seen to that.'

Their 'father', CJ's ex, is the demon we all love to batter with anti-male ire. None of us has ever met Tom, but that does not inhibit the avalanche of our invective against him; he's a bastard, prick, arsehole, pig, and whatever other slur we can concoct as a chorus-line of support for our friend CJ.

Together with Ereka, Helen and I, CJ could help us make up a world-class team if eating were recognised as an Olympic sport. Of the four of us, CJ is the only one through whom food passes without leaving those padded trails on the buttocks, inner thighs, and belly declaring *I once was here*. Sheer adrenalin must work on her fatty stores like corroding acid.

CJ sometimes 'pops in' to our house at that unmistakably dinner hour with all three kids, just to sneak in an invitation to stay for some home-cooking, a term which embodies all the longing and disappointment she feels about the way her life has turned out. It's like she's incapable of cooking a decent meal at home, without the husband, the assured rent money and the whole happy family caboodle in place. For CJ, cooking is a malicious bastard of a chore at the end of a long day, when there are papers to prepare for court tomorrow and hungry children shrieking like a trio of rabid monkeys. Under these circumstances, even Nigella Lawson would dial a pizza.

CJ and her kids mainly live off the consoling conveniences of takeaways and toast. There's not a McDonald's toy her children don't possess, nor a culinary tolerance beyond fries, burgers and chicken nuggets. She is the queen of the quick fix, and once boasted, 'I can whip up a meal in four minutes for my kids, thanks to my microwave,' which sent me into a spiral of vicarious depression. Last year she got all excited about writing a cookbook on quick and easy recipes for working mothers that even Liz said was a good idea and would sell millions. Each recipe was designed around a tin of something—creamed corn, chicken soup, baked beans, combined with potatoes, sausages, pasta, cheese or eggs. But she never got round to it and now it's just been shelved with all her other dreams of regular sex and happily ever afters.

When I remember, during my freezer-packing marathons on the first Sunday of every month, I make an extra tub of homemade bolognaise for CJ. It's a five-hour simmering epic involving lean mince, freshly juiced carrots and celery, tomato puree and a splash of Worcestershire sauce. A bugger to make but sublime to eat.

CJ, entangled in a maypole of frustrations, is a picker; unable to focus on the full plate in front of her, she intermittently reaches out and stabs her fork into the communal platters on the table, lifting a beetroot from the *fayanza*, a slice of avocado, or a piece of smoked salmon peeking out of the dip. She eats like a camel at an oasis, filling up for the waterless days ahead.

'My kids have had to build up a resilience,' CJ continues. 'I don't know if that will make them better able to cope later in life. Liam's the only one who can really express his feelings. And judging from the way he's been expressing them at school, he may have to go on Ritalin.'

'Don't put him on Ritalin,' Tam says to CJ.

CJ shrugs. 'I'll see . . .'

And Tam starts a private exchange with CJ about the dangers and long-term implications of drugging kids.

'At least our kids are all at an age now where they can talk. When Gabe was little, it used to freak me out that I couldn't figure out what he needed. Both of us used to get so frustrated with the other,' Fiona says. I look up at her and nod. When Fiona speaks I pay special attention, since it's not all that often that she ventures an opinion. She is usually content to sit quietly alongside all of us, a serene and unambitious presence.

Dooly also nods. 'You know what a whinger Tyler is, well he's always been like that. When he was about fifteen months, before he could talk, it took me two hours to work out that he had burned his hand on the iron, and wasn't just having one of his usual screaming fits.' She spoons some more lasagna onto her plate, fishing for the eggplant. The scarf now sits on her lap, coiled in an orange heap. I don't get why she had to wait for it to get dirty before she took it off. Now Luke's going to smell like coconut milk all winter.

'I still have to be a mind-reader with Olivia,' Ereka says. 'But,' to deflect the comfortlessness of what she has just said, she adds, 'I'm getting pretty darn good at it.' She helps herself to more salad, fossicking in particular for the inky bulbs of the beetroots, which have stained the rocket and parmesan to a gorgeous fuschian colour. Ereka once told me she had made her own watercolour from beetroots and used it in some of her paintings. She and I aren't all that different in the way we look at the world—she assessing everything for a canvas, me for a recipe.

'I don't want the added pressure of needing to have an intuition or a sixth sense to work out what's troubling my kids,' Liz says. 'I always tell Chloe and Brandon that they *must* use their words and tell me what's the matter, because you can call me lots of things, but a mind-reader I'm not.'

There is a general murmuring of consensus around the table that this is probably a sensible approach. Tam, having completed her discourse on hyperactivity drugs, excuses herself to go to the kitchen to ferret in the bin for the cream cheese tub to check if the cheese has any traces of gluten in it. When she returns to the table, with a fresh glass of water, she helps herself to the salad, and why she is so carefully avoiding any parmesan shavings is anyone's guess. Isn't parmesan dairy, not gluten? She takes some of the vegetarian lasagna, and mutters her gratitude for the eggplant instead of lasagna sheets, 'which are killers on the stomach'. To Tam food is a minefield to be navigated, not a bath of milk and rose-petals in which to immerse herself. It is so hard for her to have fun—how can your taste buds party if anxiety about the rash, the lactose, or God forbid the red colouring keeps on gatecrashing?

'How did you know to take Kieran off gluten?' Helen asks Tam, eating leisurely from her unabashedly laden plate. Hel is just about the only person I know who can, without a trace of guilt, scoff slices of smoked salmon, devour huge spoons of Nutella straight from the jar and pick the prawns out of the curry, instead of diluting them, as civilised decency dictates, with the requisite slice of bread or rice.

'Trial and error—I just eliminated different things until I could see a radical improvement in his overall wellbeing.'

'You've got the dedication and patience of a saint,' Ereka says with genuine admiration. Tam shrugs but glows at this compliment nonetheless.

Ereka is generous in that way, her own pain has resisted the alchemy into bitterness. Her size seems becomingly appropriate on her, generosity does not anthropomorphise into skeletal angularity. She oohs and aahs at every dish, commenting on the exquisite colours, the smells, the presentation of each. It is for people like her that I labour over a hot stove all day. As a teenager, my obsession to find my soul mate propelled me through the rapids of disappointment, as I encountered boy after pimply boy, not one of whom liked ABBA, read Rilke or could guess my star sign. Epiphany dawned in the shallows—each discarded candidate brought me one step closer to The One For Me. Kissing an entire wetland of frogs was indispensable to the process of elimination. Likewise at the dinner table, all others' indifference I can weather with good-natured resignation, for there is Ereka who puts the search for the perfect guest to rest. She is the ultimate sensualist, closing her eyes to truly taste the silky texture of the beetroot in her mouth, the cool chalkiness of a raw mushroom between her teeth, the pop of a snow pea being chewed. To those like Liz who think fat cannot be beautiful, watch Ereka eat.

'Are you still breastfeeding Kylie?' Tam asks her.

Ereka nods, wearily.

'*You're* the saint,' Tam says. 'That is amazing.'

'It's enough, I'm getting tired of it,' Ereka says.

I remain silent. If it were any other among us still breastfeeding a preschooler, I'd have plenty to say. When a kid can articulate, 'Mummy, would it be a suitable time for you to take out your breast and give me something to drink?' it's time to stop the titty. But in Ereka's case, different standards apply. We all silently withhold our censure. Who are we to judge? Among us, we privately feel that Ereka is above the laws of motherhood that apply to the rest of us.

Fiona, after holding back and waiting for everyone to help herself, finally ventures near the food. She has a graciousness, a

sense of her own abundance that dignifies her lack of urgency to rush to get to the food before it is all gone. It is either the restraint of well-bred moderation or self-control cloaked as courtesy. She will never be the first to slice a cake or break the surface of a piping hot pie. She exudes an aura of 'there is always enough', a trait I'd love to borrow to temper the impulse of my *carpe diem* appetite, goaded to overindulgence by Helen. Fiona takes good-natured pleasure in watching us all assail the food, and asks our advice about what is 'divine', 'diviner' and 'divinest'. When she helps herself, she does so like Baby Bear, not too much and not too little. A portion that is just right. And she does not forget to thank both Helen and I for all our hard work.

She is the only mother among us who has chosen to have a single child, and she insists he is a 'single' not an 'only' child, a term that has overtures of threadbare desperation. While most of us rushed to get the second and some the third, and in Helen's case now the fourth, one out 'before the oldest goes to school', 'before the youngest is out of nappies', 'before the ovaries give up the ghost', 'before menopause, old age or death', for Fiona, Gabriel alone was sufficient.

'What if he died?' I once asked her. 'Wouldn't you be sorry you hadn't had another?'

She had looked at me with a mystified frown. 'I don't think having another child would make it any easier for me to get over his death, do you?' she had asked.

No, of course not. We're not turtles—needing to breed in excess to ensure that one or two will make it to the water's edge. Fiona's right. You cannot replace a child. And yet one is such a vulnerable number. Fiona seems happy with what she has. She doesn't grasp after insubstantials, or give the impression that she is missing out. She is content and contained, only her masochistic preoccupation with the cleanliness of her house and her sometimes stark passivity in big groups a give-away that she is anything other than enviably sane.

And what of me? I adore the task of nourishing people I care about, of preparing a feast for my friends. It seems so magnanimous, doesn't it? It's just that when people don't appreciate my food, I curl into melancholic self-pity. I feel unvalued and unloved. My self-worth depends largely on the successful rising of my soufflé and the perfection of a leg of lamb, crispy on the outside and pink and delicate within. I'll stuff a quail with walnuts and sage, whip up a fig puree for a lamb chop or mango salsa for a corn and rocket patty mid-week. I always go to trouble, even if I am the only one eating.

I have been branded 'intense', 'consuming', 'over the top' and 'a perfectionist', by those most unrelentingly affected by my idiosyncrasies. Frank's recurring relationship complaint is that no matter what he does or gives, 'it is never good enough'. That's not strictly speaking true—I am happy with toasted cheese and tomato, but if there's fresh basil and wasabi mayonnaise to go with it, it seems imprudent and truculent to hold back.

Frank and I often fight about the small things. Like whether to eat the takeaway sushi from the plastic takeaway container, or to lay it out on one of my exquisite sushi platters and eat it with the wooden chopsticks with tips of inlaid mother-of-pearl. The way Frank sees it, eating it out of the container means there is one less thing to wash up. The way I see it, I would rather go hungry than eat sushi out of a plastic container. I want the floating candles and the frangipani blossoms. They make the sushi taste better. Frank would rather get out of washing a dish. Every time we get takeaway sushi, I hold out with hope that this time it will be different. He will just look at the sushi all squashed up in that tub and think,

'How beautiful this will look laid out on the emerald-green leaf plate . . . or perhaps the stone-white rectangle plate . . .' But I watch from the corner of my eye with mounting distress as he picks up the sushi in his fingers (that way he won't even have to rinse a dirty chopstick), as I helplessly witness the dashing of my hopes, plagued by the thought that I may have made an error of judgment on the soulmate question. I will at this point be rigid with certainty that Robbie Williams does not eat sushi from the takeaway container.

I sense that storm brewing in me. 'Walk away,' I tell myself. 'Forgive him, for he knows not what he does.' But it is no good. I blurt out something nasty and vindictive and accuse him of the unpardonable transgression of cutting corners and taking the easy path. Of deliberately avoiding the beauty in life. Of only perceiving function, not poetry. Then, bewildered, he hurls accusations back at me. 'How can you say I take the easy road? I married you, didn't I?' I snarl that I don't think the relationship is working. He trudges off in a huff to watch *Seinfeld*. And when the emptiness and longing inside me feel everlasting, and I wonder why I didn't marry my first love Eitan the artist, or Francesco, my Italian lover, or just bloody stayed single (I was happy wasn't I?), and I've planned the divorce and even distribution of our joint possessions, he comes back into the room (Jerry and George's inane paranoias have cheered him up) and he says (he always says), 'I am sorry, I don't want to fight with you. I love you and I want you to be happy.'

In generous moments I'll tell him 'come here', and he will kiss my hand and then my neck and then climb on top of me and I will nuzzle his neck and we'll end up having make-up sex. But if the dishwasher is not working, or I have not heard back from my agent about my next book, or Aaron has driven me to red wine at four p.m., I will look at him over the top of the book I am reading and say, 'Fine, good night.' Then I will mark my place with Jamie's

laminated 'A Poem to My Mother' bookmark, flick off the light and leave him standing there. Confused and lonely. Just the way he deserves. Fucking sushi-from-a-plastic-container-eater.

Believe me when I tell you that I never used to be a bitch. Before I had kids, Frank fondly called me a 'sexy bitch', but that is different from being a bitch. The incorrigible flirtatiousness of my youth was always balanced by my immaculate diplomacy. Even before the condom was unwrapped, to avoid any post-coital misunderstandings, I would inform all my lovers that they would be leaving after sex. Those I led on for sport, I let down gently. I never humiliated, swore at or intentionally hurt anyone, even though men give one countless opportunities to do so. Many of my ex-boyfriends are still close friends. Others flick me a titillating email every so often, which keeps me going for weeks, charitably indulging my need to believe I still have some sex appeal somewhere on this sagging overcoat of flesh I once called my body.

The truth is that after I had kids, something happened to me. Wrinkles in my personality emerged, along with the stretch marks and the grey hairs. Pre-motherhood, apart from intermittent road rage and feminist indignation, I never lost my temper or believed I was capable of spitefully and intentionally wounding a person I love. But three months after Aaron was born, I realised I was being stalked. My motherhood performance was hosting another personality in the wings. Jamie was grappling with the Galilean horror that the planets did not revolve around her and one night just refused to go to bed. My pleading and begging only aggravated matters. At what particular point the curtain on the chorus-line of my demons flew up, I cannot honestly recall. But I picked her up and I threw (yes, flung) her onto her bed. I heard a voice screech, 'Go to sleep now!!!!' Surely that wasn't me? In the mirrors of her terrified eyes I caught a glimpse of my reflection. And I was afraid too.

Admittedly, I was functioning on all of three hours of sleep a night, Aaron was colicky, it had been raining for two weeks solid and I had barely left the house. I was a little frayed at the edges. But those are just excuses, aren't they? Abuse excuses. Child molesters use them ('I was sexually abused as a kid too'); rapists use them ('my father was a cross-dressing homosexual who experimented on rodents'); women who kill their children use them too ('I was functioning on three hours of sleep a night, my child was colicky, it had been raining for two weeks solid and I had barely left the house').

Reprehensible conduct often does scuttle from a cockroach's nest of perfectly good excuses. And while excuses explain our conduct, should they also exculpate us? Motherhood, like the image of a beach at sunset on the glossy pages of a travel brochure, was such a perfect place of infantile cuteness and compliance. And then I got there, and the water was too cold, there were bluebottles swirling in the depths, and the sand insisted on getting in everywhere. When motherhood took on the contours of a real relationship with another person whose thoughts, wishes and personalities confronted my own, it all started to unravel. I watched in powerless horror as the person I had been began to erode.

My audition for the part had been impressive. I was confident I had it in the bag. But as the ensuing daily performances came and went, the role of 'The Perfect Mother' slipped from my grasp. I knew all the lines backwards. I'd rehearsed the mother's role, the one Cosette in *Les Miserables* describes in the song, 'Castle on a Cloud', who sings lullabies, and feels soft to the touch, and always says, 'I love you very much'.

On good days, I *can* be that mother. When the house is not strewn with Lego pieces, when Aaron hasn't tipped over heaps of once-neatly folded washing in his eagerness to grab the bottom t-shirt and the whine 'Muuuuuuumeee' is not on three-minute auto-repeat. I can do a convincing rendition of that role, even for a short while. First thing in the morning is usually my best twenty minutes. After I've woken, made a cup of coffee and checked my emails, Aaron rouses warm and toasty and snuggles in my lap for his cuddle. We call it 'the favourite part of the day'. I say adoring things to him, like 'who's the handsomest boy on earth?' and 'my eyes have missed your smile while I was sleeping', and he retorts, 'I love your face', and 'you're the best mum in the world'.

But as soon as he hops off my lap, my perfection, no longer weighed down by the gravity of his little body, slips from my fingers like an over-inflated helium balloon. I wonder how breakfast will go today. I consciously muster patience when he changes his mind from peanut-butter toast to Nutri-grain and back again three times. I eat the toast, mildly unhappy because I never give up hoping to start my day the Special K way (99% fat free, high in protein and taste, with apple and a hint of cinnamon). But I don't like to see food go to waste, not with Sansiwe's little face smiling from the World Vision photo we keep on our fridge. Aaron eats two spoons of the Nutri-grain before complaining he is full and has a sore tummy. I sigh and put the bowl down for the cats to drink the milk and I tell him to go and get dressed. He says he wants some juice. In a remotely strained voice I say, 'We can't have juice if we haven't had our breakfast, can we?' I inhale. I wait for it. And it comes. It always comes. His outrage. His vitriol. 'You are the worst mum in the world,' he declares. 'I hate you.'

I feel my voice, blood pressure and rage compete wildly for first place. I instruct him, 'Go. And. Get. Dressed.' He stands his ground, hands on his hips and screams at me, 'NO. I. WON'T.' I count to ten. I remember to breathe. I turn away. But what I really want to do is to grab him and shake him and tell him what a horrible little shit he is. But I don't. I close my eyes and think that in an hour's time he will be someone else's problem until three p.m. I say a prayer of gratitude for preschools which allow mothers like me to have a break from the irrational and unreasonable tyranny of four year olds.

I never tell Aaron 'I hate you too', but I think it. I think it over and over again. I think how I hate being verbally abused by a small person. I think that I should be more of an adult. I think about using that calm controlled voice Gretchen Oates uses: 'Now Aaron, let's use our words, shall we? Let's think about whether shouting and fussing makes us happy or gets us what we want.' I think how I hate that stupid word 'Let's'. The only way I want to use that word is in the following sentence, 'Let's get this straight: I am a human being. Don't speak to me like shit while I am folding *your* laundry, making *your* breakfast and packing *your* lunchbox with things in it that *you* will actually eat.'

I lose my temper at least three more times before we leave the house. Because Frank hasn't taken out the rubbish. Because Jamie didn't put the lid back on the toothpaste. Because *I* have to do everything around here.

Some mornings are better than others. They usually coincide with my having had a good night's sleep. Or not having my period. Or with something to look forward to in the day that is not about the kids—a massage, a haircut and, what the hell a blowdry, or a coffee with Helen in the park. Some days I actually do manage a full twenty-four hours without shouting, threatening or losing my temper. They seem to coincide with the days when the kids are not tired and ratty, and when they play together instead of trying to inflict grievous bodily harm on one another or the cats. Perhaps it's simply that they're calm when I am calm, and I'm calm when they're calm but neither of us is willing to go first.

But mostly, mortifyingly, I am not that mother in Cosette's song. I am a wretched, exhausted, irritable, shrill, nagging, perspiring almost-middle-aged woman, rushing to get Aaron's persistent cough to the doctor, Jamie's imperfect tumble turn to swimming lessons, both kids to school on time, a quick look through lost property to find Jamie's missing school cap (I am *not* getting her a new one—she loses everything and will never learn the value of anything), both kids back from school, dinner made (including something that Aaron will actually eat) and both of them to sleep (happy). It's a long 'to do' list each day. Calmness and gentleness often don't make the finish line.

Didn't I want kids? Anything but. I was nauseatingly maternal at a disturbingly early age—I bought and collected baby clothes with my pocket money for the babies I would one day have. I babysat without compensation—I just loved holding those little creatures, feeding them, sniffing their soft downy heads and singing them little tunes that peeped out of me involuntarily. In the tortured logic of childhood anxiety, I feared my longing to be a mother would be thwarted by barrenness (like Sarah in the Bible) if God really knew how much I wanted babies. But of this I was certain, like Sarah, I would wait till I was ninety, if only it meant I would be rewarded some day with my own precious darlings.

After each of their births, I was high with postnatal euphoria. I smiled at stony-faced strangers, finally able to muster patience with geriatrics behind the wheel, easily resisting that vindictive 'get a move on' or 'pick a lane pops' hoot, suffused with the sense that I had been touched by angels. Frank's comment that 'the tiger had finally been tamed' by a little person in nappies sounded like a

tribute. I wanted kids all right. And now I would not choose to live a single day without them in my life. My heart aches with unsolicited compassion for those who don't or can't have children. But seven years down the line, the romance has worn thin. Now that they are here, like that pamphlet come to life, my kids have brought out the mum in me, and she is not as lovely as I had hoped she would be. She's a bit of a bitch really.

When relationships are in trouble, I've heard it said that money is more wisely invested in getting domestic help than going for marital counselling. There is something so marvellously practical about that. Perhaps with a good dollop of domestic help, with a mothering mule to carry the burden of the domestic drudge, all my inadequacies and irritations would vanish, and I could become that Perfect Mother and could focus on nurturing, doing craft activities, reading library books and telling stories to my kids without always wondering when I was going to have time for me. Maybe Liz has cracked the code of motherhood after all.

Time for me. It seems such a small ask, doesn't it? In this group of schizophrenically alternating saints and bitches, we all have modest requests that would make us better mothers, nothing more ostentatious than an hour on a Saturday to go to a Pilates class, or the occasional movie with popcorn, a huge Coke and a bag of Maltesers.

I am awed by how much of the world women hold up—without fanfare, accolades, reward or gratitude. They just get on with it, prepare meal after meal, fold load after load of laundry, make trip after trip to and from school gates, anticipating hunger, exhaustion and illness with good-natured resignation and weary adoration.

The plate I am holding is empty. All day long in my fastidious preparations, I have been tasting food in anticipation of the banquet. Now that the feast is upon us my appetite has recoiled, the idyllic

panorama of delicious dishes somehow less than inviting. Still I cannot think of a single excuse not to eat wonderful food. So I dish up onto my plate.

But the anti-climax is devastating.

CHAPTER 5

the arc of the pendulum

'So, Helen, are you hoping for a boy or a girl?' CJ asks, leaning back in her chair. She has undone the top button of her pants. Her little tummy—the only squeezable flesh on her wiry, lean frame—protrudes roundly from between the flaps of her white shirt, revealing the silvery etchings of stretch marks from her pregnancies.

'If it's another boy I'm sending it back,' Helen says, unfixing prawn flesh from its shell.

I share her sentiment. I am a very proud mother of a daughter. When Jamie was born I flamboyantly celebrated her girlhood with a Girlchild Celebration to which only women were invited. Frank was only too relieved to be let off the hook. 'Whatever makes you happy,' he said, packing his golf clubs. Frank is tolerant of my rituals as long as they don't involve him—incense makes him gag and he's not interested in the 'properties' of my crystals because 'they don't have sea-views'.

Every woman that I invited to this special celebration brought Jamie a treasure of her womanly identity in response to my request

for a gift that cost her no money. One offered the first pot she ever centred on the pottery wheel—it was as big as a thimble. Another presented a tiny little pair of undies in leopard-skin design. Some bequeathed recipes handed down in their families. Another gave a sapling to plant in our garden which would burst with seasonal regularity into pink blossoms in April, around Jamie's birthday.

In a circle surrounding Jamie, my dearest friend Matty, an African sangoma, called on each of us to speak our names, the names of our mothers and the names of our grandmothers. She then invoked the spirits of all these women to protect Jamie as she grew into womanhood. It was a gathering of crones, mothers, young, teenage and girl children, in an ancient matriarchal ritual in honour of women who birth, nurture and love other women. It would have made Frank squirm.

'What's wrong with another boy?' Tam asks, wiping a food spot on her pink tracksuit. 'Boys are great.'

'I've got two already,' Helen says. 'I'll take another girl, thanks.'

Poor Tam. I secretly believe all women crave a daughter. I don't judge mothers with two and three sons who say, 'I actually wanted only boys'. Self-delusion is a legitimate form of solace. My heart goes out to Dooly. It can't be easy knowing she'll never get a chance to try again. I was just lucky. Jamie's arrival heralded relief from both Frank and me. In my case, anxieties about the sex of any future offspring vanished. And in Frank's case, because perhaps I might be satisfied and call it quits—was there any need to have more?

Pregnant for the second time, I broke into a cold sweat during the ultrasound. 'What were those marbles between the legs?' 'Relax, it's just a penis and testicles.' RELAX? I writhed with ambivalence for days, but finally made friends with the notion I was to have a son. Perhaps he'd be an effete poetry-reading bookworm. A lovable wimp. A tormented artist. Possibly gay with wonderful dress sense and flair in the kitchen. A kind of girly-boy. But I obviously hadn't filled in the forms right, and stated clearly what I could cope with. I got the other model.

I mother Jamie like I breathe—without thinking or effort. I sense her fascinations, fears, anxieties, without her needing to speak. I feel a bond with her that is ancient and abiding. I mother Aaron like I ride a bicycle—in great discomfort and wishing I could get off. I suspect I will die without knowing why he cries when laughter is fitting, and laughs when tears are called for. My calmness appears to exasperate him, my fury makes him chuckle. Apparently, head butting is a gesture of adoration; farting, a competitive sport to be communally enjoyed; hacking the heads off my delicately cultivated sweet peas with his sword, a legitimate 'outdoor activity'; and the gruesome monsters and beasts on his Yugi-Oh cards, 'cool'. 'Won't they give you nightmares?' I ask tenderly. He snorts in derision and clutches them closer. In fact, he can't sleep without them. Daily I grapple with the Rubic's cube of his rage when his peanut butter toast leaves traces of the sticky spread on his fingers. 'Lick your fingers,' I suggest. 'No! I don't want to,' he yells. I offer him a serviette. 'You do it!' he screeches. 'I think you can wipe your own fingers,' I suggest. 'I'm just a little kid,' he says. 'And I'm *never* eating peanut butter again!' As if that is somehow a punishment to me. Male logic.

There have been minor consolations in this school of hard gender knocks. I no longer take Frank's morning erections (pointing in *my* direction like it's *my* problem to sort out) personally—because Aaron wakes the same way. Walking around with hands in trousers fondling the crotch area seems to be instinctual for males and not just poor breeding on Frank's part. I finally concede that at a certain point with boys, talking is experienced as harassment. Only violence placates. Sometimes a boy just needs to be wrestled to the ground, have his face slammed, his stomach kicked, and everybody is happy. It's taken me this long to understand rugby.

'Boys are harder now, but easier later,' Tam says, her food spot worsened with the wiping. 'Girls may be a cruise when they're small, but just wait till they hit puberty...' I detect a thread of vindictive pleasure.

'Can you really generalise like that?' Fiona asks gently, holding a piece of roasted pumpkin with three fork teeth sticking out the top. 'There are so many factors that affect how our kids turn out—like whether they're firstborn, or middle children; whether their dads are around; what sort of mothers we are...' Her voice trails off. She sucks the pumpkin off the fork. It's a good point, I just wish she'd made it with greater conviction. Before Tam gets a chance to defend her 'boys are best' position, CJ jumps in, 'You know what I do?'

'Tell us,' Fiona encourages.

'I'm much harsher on the girls than I am on Liam.' She looks up at us. 'I don't mean to be, but they irritate me in a way that he just doesn't.'

There is a silence.

CJ continues. 'I'm much more critical when the girls are rude or inconsiderate, you know. But when Liam is, I just think boys'll be boys.'

'We've got to watch out for that,' I say. 'Expecting girls to be well-mannered ladies and boys to be brutes just reinforces those stereotypes and puts pressure on the girls and lets the boys off the hook.' Despite my poor appetite only minutes ago, I have managed to eat nearly a full plate of food.

'Yeah, but I can't help it,' CJ says. 'Feelings are feelings.'

'I know what you mean,' Helen says. 'Like I really get uncomfortable when Sarah touches her privates, but when the boys touch theirs, it's kinda cute.'

'That's very Freudian,' Tam says, tapping her fork on the table.

'What do you mean?' Helen asks, reaching for the salmon dip.

'Mothers are harsher on their daughters than on their sons because women project how they feel about themselves—their insecurities, inadequacies, frailties and hopes on to their daughters,' Tam says. 'Which is why mothers have a very close bond with their sons. It is the least complicated familial relationship.'

'Oh yeah?' Helen says, quite lost.

'You really should read Nancy Friday's *My Mother, My Self*,' Tam says. 'It's essential reading for mothers of girls.'

'Next lifetime,' Helen says.

I take a quick sideways glance at Dooly. It has only been a couple of months since her miscarriage. For all her equivocation, at one of our previous gatherings she actually articulated how desperately she was hoping for a girl. I'd done a spontaneous ritual—we all put our hands on her newly pregnant stomach and wished the baby well. Days later a bleeding started that nothing short of a radical hysterectomy could stem. And just like that, it was all over. I suppose just the knowledge that your womb is there, monthly shedding its walls of blood, is a source of comfort. Like that special treasure you put away as a child, waiting for the perfect moment to take it out, even if when you get to it, it is corroded and useless. But at least it was yours to discard.

Have you ever noticed how women carry the pain of miscarrying? It is in stark contrast to the exaggerations to which male frailty is prone, where a cough is 'pneumonia', and a hernia incision 'debilitating'. On the odd occasion, I have heard via Helen, that one of the mothers at our children's preschool has miscarried.

And yet I would have greeted her just that morning in the hallway, in passing at the children's lockers, exchanging weary smiles. Her pain undetectable, her loss never interfering with her pitching up to do the fruit roster on her appointed day. All mothers keep their children from too much knowledge, generously self-abnegating the private inner world of their pain. Like the father in Roberto Benigni's *Life is Beautiful* who, for the sake of his son, pretends that their internment in a German concentration camp is an elaborate game, we invent innocent scenarios to explain the world to our children. We cry in secret. Grieve behind closed doors. Plead for a better world when little backs are turned. Whisper 'cancer', 'war', 'terrorism'. Pray for their health and safety when they are asleep. No goddamned wonder we're all so exhausted. It is draining to have to lie all the time.

Now Dooly listens to our banter about the joys of raising girls, and Helen's pregnancy, holding the hope of another female life. She wears a pale smile on her face. She laughs when we laugh, nods and gestures as part of our conversation, but the trail of her loss divides her from us in a scorched firebreak of silence.

'I like the name Cassandra,' she says softly.

'That's a gorgeous name,' Helen says. 'Can I use it if it's a girl?'

Dooly hesitates, but only momentarily. 'Of course,' she smiles. 'I won't get to.' I try to catch Helen's eye. That was fucking insensitive.

'Just like that?' I ask.

'Just like what?' Helen says.

'Don't you want to think a bit more about the name?'

'Why? I like the name,' Helen says.

I shrug. Unlike Gwyneth Paltrow, I meticulously thought through the logical consequences of each name Frank and I considered for our children. The responsibility of choosing a name

for a person without her consent felt appropriately momentous, a name which couldn't be exchanged like an ill-fitting dress, and which she would be required to respond to in perpetuity, and which would some day be carved in stone on her grave. I liked the sounds of Opal, Willow, Amber, for girls. Frank shook his head. 'No minerals, no plants,' he said simply. 'Just a nice ordinary name. Nothing fancy.' Despite his denials to the contrary, he's still unresolved about his own name—Sinatra is to his mother what Robbie Williams is to me and I think he feels demeaned at having been unwillingly roped into the fantasy.

'My sister still hasn't named her baby,' Fiona says. 'And the baby is five months already.'

'What do they call her?' Helen asks, leaning across the table for the sushi platter. I pass it to her.

'The baby,' Fiona says.

'That's ridiculous,' Helen says. 'I don't see what the big deal is. Just pick a name you like and move on. Poor kid, growing up thinking it's name is "The Baby".' She puts three sushi rolls on her plate and hands the platter back to me.

'Do you want to know what it is?' Liz asks.

Among us mothers, we are either 'Need To Know' types or 'Don't Want to Know'. There are those who must plan ahead, and those who love surprises. It's like those magazine personality quizzes that Helen is so fond of. Do you prefer: a) a confirmed booking or b) we'll find something when we get there? Are you: a) anal and controlling or b) spontaneous and adventurous? A while back Tam told us about some research which links anxiety in children to mothers who opt for a conveniently scheduled elective Caesarean over the serendipity of Mother Nature's clock. But Liz just scoffed. If her kids are anxious, it's Lily's problem.

'I can wait,' Helen sighs happily.

Helen exudes a vast contentment with how things turn out. Apprehension is as remote to her as gratuitous grooming. She has a solid acceptance of life's ups and downs and avoids the self-indulgent invention of horrible scenarios to which I am notoriously drawn. Nothing fazes her. Even this pregnancy—unplanned as it is—she takes in her stout but sturdy stride. If it holds, she'll figure out how to love it later on. If she loses it, she'll handle that too. I provide her with endless amusement whenever Jamie complains of a tummy ache, and I become panic-struck. 'Just give her a glass of water, or some Panadol,' she says good-naturedly, while I am working out where to get an abdominal ultrasound and wondering if our bone marrow matches. While most of us shudder whenever our children complain of headaches, and rush them off for CAT scans and blood tests, she puts hers to bed early. 'Tired,' she avers. It is her consistent rejoinder to every child-related issue, and if there is anything ruthless about her, it is her staunch insistence that children have an early night. Her kids are all in bed and asleep by seven-thirty every night. Without her having to lie with any of them.

Yes, okay, I am a mother who lies with her children. Tam's research establishes it as one of the Top Ten Sins of Mothering. But it all started quite harmlessly. As a newborn, Jamie was so little she fitted on a pillow in the crook of my arm, from where she fed through the night at my nipple. But when she started to roll ('clever girl!') the edge became a precipice and so into the middle of the bed she went. Frank grumbled about the wedge between us, but to me she was 'the butter keeping the sandwich together'. Before long, she slept soundly in her favourite sideways position kicking me in the belly and Frank in the testicles while Frank and I clung to the edges. When Aaron was born, even our king-sized bed seemed too small for four. Frank, never fond of a crowd, found bed very stressful. He retired to the lounge room floor to get a good night's sleep. I did eventually manage to relocate the small people from our bed into their own. But the damage had already been done.

So it is no surprise, that though Jamie is now 7 and a half and Aaron is 4, I am still lying with them in their beds to put them to sleep. Most nights I cherish that time of closeness with them, as little arms creep around my neck and little fingers play with my hair and little yawns subside into deep breathing. It offers me a chance to redeem myself from all the mothering transgressions of the day. I can love them back to me, silently ask their forgiveness for all the wrongdoing I have inflicted on them. Hope they'll forget all the irritability, snapping and yelling for which they are blameless, and which has more to do with the accumulation of minor infractions like Frank coming home late last night, the latest white laundry load with pink streaks of godknowswhat on it, and the latest chapter I just can't get right. At least I know that as appalling as I have been during the day, my children have gone to sleep happy, knowing that they are loved beyond belief. But many nights, I would opt for the shortcut if there were one so I can get on with folding the laundry, writing a poem that has been playing over in my head, finishing my dinner, having that poo I have been meaning to have the whole day, making a phone call or acknowledging Frank's existence.

'I've got a very scientific method for finding out whether it's a boy or a girl,' I say to Helen.

'Tell,' she says.

I leave the table to find my handbag, from which I retrieve a little purple sequined purse—my Mother's Survival Kit, containing several bandaids, a needle and cotton, a Swiss army knife including tweezers for removing bee stings, a little bottle of tea-tree oil that

can be used for cuts, bruises or stings, small nail scissors for broken toenails and tangled yo-yo or kite strings. And a pendulum.

Frank calls my pendulum one of my 'New Age flim flam accessories'. Scoff if you will, but dousing is an ancient art that works on the same principles as kinesthetics: our body knowledge emits an energy that supersedes our rationality, interpreted through a pendulum, which swings in one direction in the affirmative and in another in the negative. This is a startling but irrefutable fact. Helen's body holds the secret of her baby's sex and with the help of the pendulum the eight of us will soon know too.

The pendulum is my party trick—one that does not involve the removal of any articles of clothing. I anticipate much derision. Especially from the likes of Liz. Helen will tell me to stick my pendulum where it fits. I return to the table carrying my little purple sequined bag.

'What have you got there?' Tam asks, leaning over to look.

I say nothing as I take out yet another little bag tied with a golden ribbon from which I remove my pendulum. I take hold of its string and let its fat bulbous body fall. It immediately begins to swing.

'What the hell is that?' Helen asks.

'It's a pendulum,' Tam says.

'What's it gonna do to me?' Helen asks, holding her hands protectively over her stomach.

'It's gonna hypnotise you into wanting sex with David again,' CJ derides.

'Take it away,' Helen wails.

'How does it work?' CJ asks.

I explain. Briefly. I keep my explanation scientific.

'What if Helen doesn't want to know?' Ereka asks. A tentative gesture in favour of surprise.

We all look at Helen.

'Do you want to know?' Ereka asks.

'I don't believe in that stuff anyway,' Helen says defensively, 'so whatever it says, it makes no difference to me.'

'It really works,' I say.

'It doesn't if you don't believe in it,' Helen says.

'Actually, it does,' Tam says. 'So don't do it if you're not sure.'

Now the shoe is on the other foot. A few months ago when she produced the shaving cream and razor and had me encircled by my girlfriends ready to shave my pubic hair, I could hardly be a spoil sport and beg, 'Do we have to?' I knew by the glint of that razor's edge that I was in for weeks of itching and scratching as the hair grew back. The pressure of wanting to please my peers and fulfil their expectations of that moment made me drop my undies and allow them to have their way with me. So that there would be a story to tell. So that we could all regale ourselves with the memory, 'Remember when we shaved Jo's pussy for her wedding night?' And it would become one of the tales of our abiding friendship. Of the love and the madness that holds us together.

Now Helen is on the spot. If she says 'No' it will ruin the moment. For the first time, in all the years I've known her, she looks unsure. And I'm not really enjoying the revenge as much as I'd thought I would.

'You can ask it what you like,' she says. 'It has a fifty per cent chance of being right . . . so that's quite good odds.' She's broken through. She's gonna do it.

'You have to lie down flat on the floor,' I tell her (I made that part up, but hell she had me flat on the deck of that boat, without any underwear).

'For crying in a bucket, Jo,' she objects, but she pushes her chair away from the table and stands up.

'Where do you want me?'

'Anywhere you're comfortable,' I say.

She moves into the lounge room, and we all follow. She lies down on the carpet. We all form a huddle around her. I hold the pendulum above her belly. I lift up her top.

She pulls it down. 'Don't look at my flap,' she says. Helen refers to that huge roll of fat and skin that hangs over our Caesarean scars as 'the flap'. The flap is to blame for much of our early retirement from sex appeal. Most of us have some form of flap, if not a pouch. 'I'm not looking at your flap,' I say. 'I'm just giving the pendulum the most direct line to your baby.'

'It can bloody well go through my clothes,' Helen says.

'I didn't know you were into all this stuff,' Dooly says to me, curious, uncertain. 'This sort of thing unnerves me.'

'It's not black magic, or anything like that,' I say, watching as the pendulum starts to move.

'What's it say?' Helen asks.

'First we have to find out what "yes" and "no" is,' I say. 'Show us what "yes" is,' I instruct the pendulum. It slowly stops moving, and then begins to swing up and down.

'Backwards and forwards,' Ereka says.

'Yep, it's up and down for yes,' I say. 'Now show what "no" is.'

The arc of the pendulum decreases; the motion slows, then begins an anti-clockwise movement.

'Round?' Fiona asks.

'Give it a moment,' I say.

In a few seconds, the pendulum is now moving unmistakably left to right.

'Sideways,' CJ notes.

The mood has become earnest.

'Did everyone see that?' I ask. I stop the pendulum with my free hand.

'*You* must have changed the direction,' Helen says.

'I did nothing of the sort,' I say. 'Here, you try it,' and I hand the pendulum over to her.

She takes it from me, and holds the pendulum over her belly.

'Ask it what yes is,' I say.

She looks sheepish, says nothing.

The pendulum starts to move backwards and forwards. We all sit watching her. She remains quiet. The pendulum moves in increasingly larger arcs, but after a few seconds it slows down, and makes a clockwise move, and soon it is moving right to left.

Helen's eyes widen. 'Oh. My. God,' she says.

I laugh. I have witnessed many a non-believer turn discernibly white at the shift of the pendulum's swing.

'You asked the questions silently,' I say to her.

She grimaces at me. 'It's freaky. I don't like it.'

The mood is now positively bristling.

'Ask it if the baby is a girl,' Dooly says.

Helen now holds the pendulum with new deference. And this time she asks aloud, 'Is my baby a girl?'

We silently gaze. Our eyes pinned to the pendulum. It does not move for a long time.

'Maybe it's not sure,' Helen says.

'Just wait,' I say.

We wait. And the pendulum starts to move, slowly but perceptibly. Soon it's swinging in enormous arcs. Side to side. Side to side.

'That looks like a negative to me,' Fiona says gently.

'Another boy,' Dooly says, exhaling, her baby's name 'Cassandra' now safe in the realms of all that could have been.

I feel a constriction, the pinch of regret. To betray a secret, let a cat out of the bag that did not want to be let out is an irreversible disloyalty.

'I'm sorry,' I say to Helen.

'Stupid fucking pendulum,' Helen huffs. 'I don't believe in it anyway.'

'Boys are great,' Tam enthuses.

'Yeah, yeah,' Helen says. 'I'm going back for more food.' She sits up and clambers to her feet, stretching her lower back before shuffling back to the main table. The others follow her, one by one.

I remain on the floor, the pendulum clasped still in my hand.

As Tam rises she says, 'Some things are better left unknown.'

Alone in the lounge room, I reluctantly concede that Tam is right. Not knowing is a kind of hope. All faith nestles in ignorance. And every ounce of motherhood depends on it. Who am I to burst bubbles that hold optimism intact, illusory as it is?

I'm an idiot. The only solution is to bring out the artichokes.

CHAPTER 6

a few of my favourite things

If beetroots are the most intense of vegetables, as Tom Robbins writes in the opening line of *Jitterbug Perfume*, one of my favourite books, artichokes are the least forgiving. They require commitment upfront. You have to be prepared to go all the way with an artichoke on the first date. I am not talking about the tinned, half-leaved, de-prickled kind pickled in brine. I mean the fresh rosy bulbs of the long-stemmed sort you can only purchase at the greengrocers. The ones that need boiling, but so much and no more (artichokes cannot tolerate a lack of attention to detail). Those that require the efforts of a dressing, inevitably involving garlic, a splash of balsamic vinegar, olive oil and perhaps a small smattering of chopped basil or coriander, or even an anchovy or two, if you're in that sort of mood.

Artichokes don't like to be rushed. One must have a patient desire to reach their tender centres. Don't be coming towards an artichoke with the intention of fumbling and faltering—have a plan in place. Each leaf of an artichoke can be savoured until its heart lies exposed, protected by a ring of thistley hairs which must be scraped out, leaving the most sublime little morsel of flesh, the virginal artichoke heart.

You will by now have guessed that I eat artichokes alone. Frank has not the fortitude to indulge this fussy petulant vegetable. 'Too much work,' he says offhandedly. 'They're all yours.' Oh yes, if I eat all the leaves for him, scrape out the choke and dip the heart in an exquisite sauce, he'll open his mouth and eat it. Let's face it, what man wouldn't accept an artichoke quickie? But he hasn't earned it, and thinks that just because he's married to an artichoke fanatic he can have one whenever he likes. Men can be so crass. To truly experience an artichoke, you have to put in the hard yards.

Artichokes are quite magical and worth every ounce of effort if you can hold back and delay gratification. They contain a chemical which leaves a sweetish taste in your mouth, enhancing the flavour of whatever you eat next. Isn't that a generous trait? I love artichokes for every reason imaginable, not least of which is that I ate them, fried in olive oil, in a sidewalk café in Rome many years ago, when I was in my early twenties and the world was filled with possibilities (not to mention Italian men) and I thought I had tasted heaven. Artichokes are divine. And tonight I have prepared them with a sauce of lemon zest, rosemary-infused sesame oil, capers, parsley, garlic and rice vinegar.

I have placed them like a flower arrangement on a platter, sitting between wedges of lemon surrounding a glass jug filled with the dressing. I arrive at the table bearing artichokes, a token of reconciliation. I aim for Helen. She smiles broadly. 'Oh, give us one of those,' she yelps. She is quick to forgive, as I douse hers with excessive lashings of my sauce. I grin, relieved, as she attacks its outer leaves like it's the first thing she's eaten all year. The girls are all huddled around Fiona (Dooly now with that orange scarf tied around her waist like a sash), looking at photos of Kirsty in her black and red formal dress which adds about six misleading years to her, and could easily excuse the mistaken assumption that she is fair game for male seduction. I shudder, Jamie is only . . . gulp . . . nine years from that, max.

'How do you eat those?' Dooly asks, looking up, fiddling with the small gold hoop in her ear.

'Pull each leaf off and dip it in the sauce,' I say. 'And with the back of your teeth, scrape off the soft part of the leaf.'

Dooly crinkles up her face. 'Too much work.'

'It is worth it, I assure you,' I say.

'It most certainly is not,' Liz says. 'Artichokes are overrated,' passing the photos on.

I clutch my chest. 'Forgive her,' I utter, 'she really is a nice person when you get to know her . . .'

'I heard that,' she says. 'She looks so grown up,' Liz says to Fiona.

'I know, it's scary,' Fiona says. 'Ben actually couldn't look at her.'

'Liz, let's be honest: have you ever actually eaten an artichoke?' I ask.

'Yes . . . once or twice,' she says, lounging back in her seat. 'They are messy and fidgety. I don't mind the tinned ones.'

'She wore the diamond earrings and pendant I had on when I married Ben,' Fiona points out. 'Her mum wasn't happy about it—she wanted her to wear pearls but Kirsty informs me "pearls are so not in . . ."'

'Teenagers!' Liz clicks her tongue. 'We really should just put them in charge—they seem to know it all.'

I close my eyes and sigh. I place my hand on Helen's shoulder in solidarity.

'Don't try and change the subject, Liz. You are anti-artichoke, fess up,' I say.

'I confess,' she says mildly.

'We feel sorry for you,' I say, 'missing out on one of the most glorious tastes on earth.'

'Yeah, artichokes are one of my favourite things,' Helen says, sucking on a leaf and then waving it at Liz.

Liz chuckles, bemused by our earnestness.

'I can't think of any food that makes it onto my list of favourite things,' Liz says. 'Weekends at health spas; two dozen roses; four weeks in Tuscany ... these are a few of my favourite things.'

'Don't get the pictures dirty,' Fiona says quickly, the swiftness of her unease a giveaway that mess is anathema to her. She tries to shoe-horn her foible back to insignificance. 'Ben hasn't seen them yet ...' Ereka slides the photos over to Fiona before reaching for an artichoke.

'But what about roast duck with pineapple and chocolate mousse with caramel?' Ereka asks. 'Christ, at this point in my life, anything I can stuff my face with constitutes one of my favourite things,' she adds.

I nod vigorously. Ever since I saw *The Sound of Music* as a child, I started keeping a list of my favourite things—it felt like a treasure to which I could intermittently return, a nugget of knowledge reminding me of the enchantments of the world. It was my balm against my sporadic misgiving that there was nothing beautiful that moved me any more.

I began my first list, entitled 'Boys I Want to Marry', when I was six. Norman Forman's name was top of that roll (I loved how his name rhymed). He was one of the two elves in our school play 'The Elves and the Shoemaker'. I adored his lisp. I was captivated by his legs in his little green stockings, and his gravelly voice that sang, 'by night, by night, we sew by candlelight, every stitch will make him rich, oh what a true delight!' Every year new names were added to my catalogue, and old ones crossed off. I'm sure if I did a huge spring clean, that list would turn up somewhere among my childhood belongings.

Then came 'Boys I have Kissed', more elaborate with columns denoting name and place. 'Nice' (tick or cross). 'Okay' (tick or cross). 'Gross' (tick or cross). A column labelled 'Tongue' was later added. In my teens I kept a list of fattening foods and those I could eat without worrying about how they affected the look of my legs in gym shorts. Next was my list of 'Blowjobs', inspired by my best friend Meredith, who'd been keeping a list for years before I had even begun and who could never understand why she was labelled the school slut.

When Jamie was born I began milestone lists: Jamie smiles (7 weeks); Jamie puts her hand in her mouth (10 weeks); Jamie tries to roll on her side (13 weeks); Jamie eats ——————— this much banana (13 weeks, 2 days); Jamie laughs out loud (4 months); Jamie says 'mamamamababababa' (7 months).

Helen is also a list maker, but hers are 'to do' lists and they record all the mundane tasks awaiting completion and dictating deadlines. I find these lists rebuking and dispiriting. I prefer historical lists of all the things I have done and completed. My lists are personal inventories of who I am, my way of holding on to things that pass. They are also my small concession to amnesia— life's anaesthetic, and motherhood's ally. Because let's face it—it is no small accident of nature that our memories of the nausea kick-started by the epidural, the pain of labour and the bilious exhaustion of waking (for the fifth time in five hours) to nipple a squealing rabbit of a person are wiped clean. Otherwise, would we ever find ourselves musing, that perhaps it would be nice to have another one? If we remembered, we'd all be like Fiona. Once is enough, thanks. Motherhood is predicated on the certainty, the commandment 'Thou Shalt Forget'. Forgetting is built into the design; as our love and attachment to these little bedbugs grow, the masochistic hurdles we have overcome fade into the haze of 'those early days'.

'So, artichokes aside, what's one of your favourite things?' Helen asks me, sucking on another artichoke leaf.

'I know what one of my *least* favourite things is,' CJ says, jumping in. She too has taken an artichoke, and is pushing it around on her plate, insecure about her introductory move.

'What?' Dooly asks.

'Grocery shopping with children,' CJ says. We all hum in accord.

She continues: 'I could almost put money on it, that as I arrive at the front of the queue I've been standing in for twenty minutes, distracting the kids with lollies, opened Rice Bubbles, letting them play with (and drop) my keys, wallet, tampons, Scarlett will say at the top of her lungs, "I need to make a poo. Now".' She attacks the artichoke, shearing its enclosing petals in large clumps. I can barely watch.

'Tam, isn't there some research to show that grocery shopping is a proven diuretic and laxative for kids?' I ask.

Tam grimaces. 'Actually, shopping is regarded as one of those "high risk" situations in positive parenting terms,' she says. 'You need to go prepared with a plan to pre-empt that happening.'

'Yesterday I was shopping with Cameron and at the top of his voice in a crowded food hall he shouted "I hate you, you are the worst mother",' said Helen. 'I had just told him he couldn't have an ice cream, and he was still holding half a hamburger and a toy from his McDonald's happy meal. The little bastard.'

'He was probably tired,' Tam says.

'That's my line,' Helen says to her.

'My worst is restaurants with kids,' Ereka says, deflowering an artichoke with practised ease. 'Because unless they've got enclosed play areas, away from roads, and serve chicken nuggets and chips for breakfast, lunch and dinner under four dollars, what's the point of even trying?'

'Restaurants are for beautiful people,' CJ says, 'childless, manicured, sparkling-water-drinking beautiful people. Not us.' She turns to me. 'Won't you just get rid of all these leaves for me, so I can try the artichoke heart?'

I want to tell her that she has butchered a perfect artichoke beyond recognition. I take her plate and gently remove what remains of the artichoke's encircling foliage.

'When I go into a restaurant I always pick the mildest, youngest waiters because I know I'm going to have to pull rank and make them believe it's completely normal to be called back every three minutes,' CJ says, 'once to change the order from scrambled eggs on toast to a muffin. The second time to change the order back to scrambled eggs. The third time to take the scrambled eggs back uneaten—"though we'll pay for them of course, can we get a muffin instead?"—and to order a hot chocolate—"just one in two glasses, please".' She watches my moves with a steadfast gaze.

'And lastly to retrieve the salt cellar from the hot chocolate,' Ereka chimes in.

'And bring a mop!' I finish.

We all titter.

'And I do so love restaurants . . .' Helen whimpers.

'Kids' parties. I just won't do them,' Liz says. She has refilled her wine glass and is gradually sipping her way through it.

'Your kids have parties,' Helen says, messily.

'I outsource,' says Liz. 'I won't do them at our house. It's not my idea of fun to host a crowd of small people, high on sugar and MSG, squishing chocolate icing into my furniture, spilling red cordial on my carpet, and complaining about the lolly bags at the end, because "Jasper got a red one and I want one like that".'

'I actually quite like having them at home,' Dooly says softly, her meandering gaze in search of—I bet you—chocolate.

'The endurance of the human spirit never fails to inspire me,' Liz says.

'Tired kids are my pet hate,' Helen says. 'My kids can actually wake up tired. And you know how I know? When they burst into tears when I say anything other than, "you can watch TV all day and eat junk".'

'Putting eyedrops in children's eyes?' Fiona says. 'Seriously, there has to be another way to fix conjunctivitis. You'd think by now someone would have invented a syrup that tastes like chocolate.'

We all chortle in assent. I pass CJ's plate back to her; the artichoke heart, scraped clean of its prickles, is ready for her.

'Thanks,' she says. She picks it up, dips it into the dressing and chews. 'Nice . . .' she says. With words like sublime and exquisite in our language, all she can squeeze out is a 'nice'?

'Try having a telephone conversation with a client at five p.m.,' CJ says. 'Thank you so much for calling me back will you please put the hamster back in its cage? Sorry about that, I have left a few messages, no you can't have an ice block now, can we talk about this later? Sorry, what was I saying? Did you get my email? Later on, I said, not now!' she mimics.

'Kids are just looking for your attention when you're on the phone,' Tam says, chasteningly. 'It's another high risk situation that you've got to prepare for.'

'Tam, I've got a life to live with no time for planning for every eventuality—fucking life is high risk,' CJ says grimly.

'I'm just telling you what the experts say,' Tam quips back. 'But if you're not interested . . .'

'Remember trying to get the lice out of Jamie and Sarah's hair last term?' I say, turning to Helen. It was an agonising fine-tooth-combing exercise that lasted for six months.

'God knew what He was doing when he included lice as one of the ten plagues,' Helen grumbles.

'God?' I ask. 'Did you say God?'

'I must be drunk,' she says. 'I need some more daiquiri,' and she leans over for the tub.

'I find being in a doctor's waiting room with kids very stressful,' Dooly says.

'Sick children should be drugged to a point of floppy manoeuvrability so they are easy to lug around,' Liz says.

'You're joking, aren't you?' Tam asks.

'No, I'm serious,' Liz replies.

'I'm with you,' CJ says to Liz.

'I always look forward to the receptionist calling me over and politely asking if my child could please refrain from dispensing water from the cooler and using up all the cups,' Ereka laughs. Her artichoke heart is almost within sight. She perseveres resolutely.

'Kieran is so into his reading, he collects all the information brochures from the doctor's rooms. When I'm tidying up, I come across all these pamphlets on vasectomies, genital herpes and weight control during pregnancy stashed next to his bed,' Tam says. 'The other day he went home with a friend, and when the mother dropped him back home and I asked her how he had been, she said, "He's been just fine. Do you know that he can spell 'sexually transmitted diseases'?"' She giggles at her own story.

'What did you say?' Helen says.

'I wanted to tell her that he can also spell "claustrophobic", "dysfunctional" and "peripatetic". But I didn't.'

'Your six year old has a better vocabulary than I do,' Dooly laughs.

'I hate travelling with children,' Helen says. 'I won't do another overseas trip again until the kids are much older.'

Unless you are partial to having someone drop their dinner in your lap several times over the course of twelve hours, scream because they are hungry, scream because they cannot get past the dinner trolleys to go to the toilets, scream because . . . well, because they can and it is, after all, a confined space filled with people who don't have their own children or who have left theirs at home and are just hoping for some peace and quiet, kids on aeroplanes are no fun. I agree with Helen.

'Last time I travelled with the kids,' I relay, 'when we got to passport control, Aaron just lay on the ground and started howling. I had three bags slung over my shoulders, three passports and customs declarations in my hand and when I bent down to try to placate him, the bags fell and I dropped the passports and forms all over the floor.'

'Crikey!' Fiona says, laughing. 'That could not have been fun.'

'Yeah, and not one person from the hundreds that were queuing was prepared to lose a place in line to offer to help me pick them up. They all just watched with their disapproving eyes.'

'Why should they have helped you?' Liz asks. 'They sensibly left their kids at home. That's why I never travel with kids,' she continues.

'Sometimes you have to,' I say.

'I once delayed a flight because the captain wouldn't allow my pram on the plane—it had to go into the hold—because they were expecting turbulence and you can't have a loose pram knocking around in the cabin,' Ereka says.

'So what happened?' Dooly asks.

'I refused to get on the plane. I said I'd wait until the turbulence had passed and catch a later flight. I just couldn't carry Olivia, I had a slipped disc in my lower back. So they had to delay the flight to find my luggage.'

'I curse people who delay flights like that,' Liz says.

'What happened then?' Tam asks.

'The captain was called from the cockpit and he eventually convinced me, between clenched teeth, to take the flight.'

'And your pram?' Dooly asks.

'Made it into the cabin. And I was upgraded to business class and assigned my own personal flight stewardess, who gave me a tranquiliser. People underestimate the will of a mother whose pram has been sent to the hold,' Ereka finishes.

'A mother's sanity depends on such small concessions, doesn't it?' Dooly sighs. 'It's the little things that get us in the end . . .'

I look at Helen, and she is elbow-deep in artichoke leaves and there is a bit of dressing on her nose. I lean over and wipe her nose with a serviette.

'Thanks,' she says without pausing for a break. I notice she has lined up three little artichoke hearts on the side of her plate—to eat when she has done all the hard work of scraping off the leaves.

'I'm glad you like the artichokes,' I say to her gratefully.

'They're one of my favourites,' she says joyously.

'Talking of favourites, how's Cameron doing?' I ask her.

She gives me a wide-eyed look.

'What?' I say.

'Don't call him my favourite,' she says to me, smacking my arm.

'Okay, I won't,' I say, hushing myself. 'Even though everyone knows he is.'

'Is he?' Tam asks incredulously.

Helen's never actually articulated to me that Cameron is her favourite, but I know he is—maybe it's because he's her baby (for now), or because he's going through a particularly adorable phase, asking the most astonishing questions for a three year old, like 'Mum, do you fold or scrunch your toilet paper?' Maybe it's because Sarah is going through a talking back phase and Nathan is prone to black moods and overeating. Helen lights up when Cameron's around. Surely that's not a sin?

'What's the big deal?' CJ asks. 'Liam is mine. It's no secret. The girls are so bitchy and irritating, and Liam is so loving and affectionate. I just adore him,' she says. 'And I know he stands up for me when TFB starts badmouthing me.'

'Yeah, well, you can have your favourites, if you want, but I don't have favourites,' Helen says.

'I've got a favourite,' Fiona says.

'Easy for you to talk,' Dooly smiles.

'I don't *show* favouritism,' CJ says, building her defence. 'I love all of mine equally—differently. But I like Liam as a person more than the others.'

'Even unconsciously, children sense that and it can cause a lot of sibling rivalry,' Tam says.

'You can't legislate emotions,' CJ says.

'I'm sure every child at some time or another feels like Cinderella, left to sleep in the ashes, while the other one gets to go to the ball,' Dooly suggests. 'That's normal, isn't it?'

'I always affirm my undiscriminating love for all of mine,' CJ adds.

'So as long as they don't know you've got a favourite, it's okay to have one?' Liz asks.

'I can't help how I feel,' CJ says crossly.

'It's a big taboo, having a favourite,' Ereka says. 'But we've all felt it.'

'Not me,' Tam says.

'I think it's a very confronting question,' Dooly says quietly. 'Remember *Sophie's Choice*? Imagine having to choose which child to save and which to sacrifice.'

We all visibly cringe.

'Yeah, whom do you choose?' Fiona asks softly. 'The one you get on with the best? Or do you feel so guilty that you do the opposite and choose the other one?'

'Or do you choose the one who needs you the most?' Ereka asks.

We all silently ponder the profundity of this riddle.

'Thankfully we don't have to choose,' Helen says. 'As long as we treat them fairly, the rest is irrelevant.'

We can all live with that summary, and nod approvingly.

But despite the bubble-wrap of Helen's assertion, the irony, like a fragile Ming vase, remains at the heart of this parcel of thought—though discriminating tastes and discerning opinions on food, books and people are taken as evidence of an examined and meaningful life, when it comes to our children, preferences are unthinkable. In the governance of our offspring, we must judiciously treat all children equally, even though we all know, in true *Animal Farm* terms, 'some children are more equal than others'. And it's not always because some children are lovingly genteel and others are loathsome little wretches. Sometimes for no explicable reason

one, more so than the others, touches our heart in a way that takes our breath away. And the joy of it is only marginally overshadowed by the shame and guilt we feel. Truth has no place in the communist allocation of our affection. In love, as in law, fairness does count for something. But despite the scrutiny to which our actions are subject, thankfully the inner cities of our feelings cannot be policed.

In generations past, when notions of children's wellbeing excluded their psychological health, favouritism was a fact of life. Reviled children (often illegitimate) were excluded from wills and excommunicated from families. Parental love has only recently become a currency traceable to psychological health. These days, a serial murderer could happily rely on a defence of maternal preference for a sibling in mitigation of sentence. Favouritism these days is theoretically child abuse.

All of this subtext is packed into Helen's smack on my arm. She is cross with me, I can tell.

'I'm sorry,' I say to Helen quietly.

'And so you should be,' she says.

'Next week Cameron will have a tantrum and then one of the others will be your favourite,' I say.

'E. Nuff,' she says to me, dipping one of her three precious artichoke hearts into the sauce and offering it to me, despite her barely concealed annoyance.

I open my mouth and gratefully accept her offering. I don't care who knows—right now she is my favourite person in the world.

let them eat pancakes

In the world of food, there are some heavenly combinations. Culinary soulmates. Lamb and mint. Figs and cheese. Then there are those singularly fussy types, insisting, like swans in mating season, on a perfect match. Saffron, for example, is a hard-to-please customer in kitchen matchmaking. Fennel is another. Uncooperative, moody, picking fights with the most inoffensive of staples—like cucumbers and potatoes, which are mild-tempered and just want to make everyone happy. Some unions are easygoing, like even-tempered children, not minding if its appointed playmate can't make the date. A lemon will just as cheerfully drench a chicken as a leg of lamb. Or even a whole snapper. Some, like garlic, are promiscuous, loose in their affection, but generally pleasing all round. Even dependable. Then there are introverted ingredients nestling shyly away, like the G-spot, from everyday use. Requiring initiative, courage and a sense of quest, nutmeg is one of those. It is a glorious spice. And I know how to use it.

One of its finest associates is butternut pumpkin. Ricotta cheese, dull on all other occasions, comes to life in this medley, aided and abetted by orange zest and the slightest dribble of dry sherry. For this night I have made butternut-ricotta pancakes. And my friends (other than Tam—yes, I did use flour for the pancakes, sorry) are swooning.

'Cinnamon?' Helen asks.

I nod. 'But that's not all.'

'Ginger?' CJ offers.

I shake my head.

'Vanilla essence?' Dooly suggests.

Crikey Dooley, therein lies the key to your culinary downfall. I stifle my derision. Tackiness has no place in this recipe.

'Nutmeg,' I say.

To those of my friends for whom cooking is no more than a labour of necessity, this revelation is meaningless. Helen and Ereka, though, both nod, impressed, wise to the finer-tuned insight that nutmeg is not a forgiving spice. An excess—no matter how infinitesimal the surplus—embitters food irretrievably. Too little and you might have spared yourself the exertion—your nutmeg efforts will be overlooked. Most people are too intimidated to use it at all. It requires an adult approach. A willingness to take charge but, like parenting, it is a subtle, undulating art. The nutmeg has done something sublime to these pancakes. I can tell, because even Liz is nodding in approval. Beautiful food commands just this power—easing us into an ecstatic bodily surrender arguably more enduring than any anecdotally inflated orgasm any of us claims to have enjoyed. Knowing this, I once seduced a man with lychees. Eating fruit the right way can be as satisfying as a deep kiss. He watched as I bit into the chitinous exterior, peeled back the shell to reveal the softest curve of flesh and sucked on it like ... let's just say, he had an erection before I spat the pip out.

The pancakes have brought some redemption in the wake of the artichokes. Only Helen, Ereka and CJ braved those toilsome vegetables. The remaining petalled proteas sit like abandoned posies on the platter. 'Oh well,' I grumbled to Helen in the kitchen, as I prepared the pancakes, 'it's *their* loss'; but the effects of being under-appreciated have left their bruises. I am adept at Managing Resentment about Ingratitude. My children, dedicated teachers in this course, generously offer me ongoing opportunities to hone my skills.

Gratitude. It's the expectation that ruins us. I used to visibly cringe hearing Jewish mothers, stereotypically slathering on the guilt, 'After all I've done for you . . .' Now, it is only my hubristic inhibitions that keep me from actually verbalising this genetically encoded phrase to my own biological ingrates to whom the months (which have now become years) of pregnancy, breastfeeding, sleepless nights and personal sacrifices are invisible. Why *should* they be grateful for reaping the benefits of all I do for them, when I doled them out uncomplainingly before they could articulate a thanks? Why indeed? Precocious little smart alecs. 'A thank you never hurt anyone,' I quip back, feebly.

In the eyes of my children, blinded by righteous entitlement, I am invisible. And I try, or I will die in the endeavour, to restore their vision. Frank's philosophy—to give them nothing so they will be grateful for whatever they do get—has been harder to implement than I imagined. I love to shower my kids with treats but I exact thanks, with actuarial precision, for every lolly, treat or chore I undertake on their behalf. Sometimes, though, the books don't balance. I recall one particular afternoon well into those long December holidays, when all the conversations I had had for weeks on end invariably involved Sponge Bob and Blue Eyes Metal Dragon. The heat had driven us to spend the entire day at an indoor swimming pool, with seven thousand other children and their mothers, where Jamie and Aaron had each chosen a new set of goggles, flippers and blow-up aqua toy, and eaten nothing but fried chips and ice cream in hourly relays. On the way home, we stopped for DVDs (my only hope for a few hours of quiet to abate the pounding in my head). As we stepped through the front door Jamie told Aaron, 'We're watching mine first.' 'No, we're watching mine first,' he shot back, slap, hit, kick, thump. 'MUUUUUUUUUUUUUUUUUUM . . . Aaron's hitting me!!!'

Quietly, I warned, 'If you two don't stop fighting THIS INSTANT, there will be no TV at all, no more treats this holiday, no more fun!' I said all this without thinking through that what I really meant to say was, 'I'll make you watch TV for the rest of your lives . . .' *I'm* the one who needed the peace. 'You're a mean, horrible mother,' Aaron yelled at me, his new goggles still on his head, his new flippers still on his feet and his hands sticky with lollies. Yes he was tired, yes he was high on sugar, but that, as they say, was the final straw.

My rage at the injustice of infantile entitlement throbbed me scarlet. If it were at all biologically possible, smoke would have wafted from my nose. Through gritted teeth I listed all the treats they had had that day. That week. In the past five weeks. As they tapped their feet impatiently, I bellowed that they had probably used up three lifetimes' of treats in one morning. And that they were just lucky to have a mother like me. A KIND! GENEROUS!! GIVING!!! SELFLESS!!!! WONDERFUL!!!!! mother like me!!!!!!

'I want to watch my DVD *first*,' Jamie said, with not even a tentative quaver in her voice. Courage she has plenty of. Aaron took off one of his flippers and hit her on the head with it. She started shrieking, grabbed his goggles and snapped them back so they whacked him on his head. He started shrieking.

'That's it,' I said in a voice thin and crisp. 'Goodbye. I am going away now. There is food in the fridge and Jamie can dial 000 in the case of an emergency, but I'm *outtahere*.' As I snatched provisions, the taramasalata dip and baguette crisps, and a bottle of whisky from the cupboard, I told them to feel free to put up posters for a new mother—clearly I am no good. And I headed for the door.

They panicked.

'Oh please don't go,' Aaron begged.

'What if someone steals us?' Jamie said. 'Then you'll be sorry you've been so mean.'

'*Who* should be sorry?' I asked.

'Us, us,' they both nodded. 'We're sorry, we're very sorry . . .'

I looked from one to the other, and back again. A perverse flicker of victory coursed through my veins.

'Very well,' I said, 'but if I hear so much as a peep out of either of you for the rest of the afternoon . . .' I threatened vaguely.

And with that, united in their odium against their nasty mother, they scampered into electromagnetic oblivion to watch DVDs all afternoon, scoff biscuits and trash the playroom. And I slugged down two—oh what the hell, three if I'm honest—Panadol with a glug of whisky, phoned Frank and told him he better come home early, put on my headphones with Robbie Williams playing and sang at the top of my lungs that *I just want to feel real love* from behind my closed bedroom door.

I have made a provisional peace with the likelihood that my children will need therapy later in life, suffering from a condition for which no doubt there will be a name as well as a drug, wrought by the torment of threatened maternal abandonment. But as Frank says, 'By that stage, whose problem will that be?' We all have early childhood traumas to overcome. Why not let this be theirs? When I have laboured with good-natured effort, suppressed my own needs, indulged the whims and requests of those who have no clue about what things cost or how much mess certain activities induce, only to be met with knee-high disgruntlement, I confess I do not, as I so often remind my children, consider the consequences of my actions. No, I also don't think three times before I speak so out burbles my secret desire—to be free from them, if only for a while. Right now I am surviving, by whatever means necessary. And that includes threats, violence, deceit and withdrawals of affection. If my survival comes at my children's psychological expense, I will atone for that at the Pearly Gates.

Unlike our parents' generation, who fucked us up without knowing why and without knowing any better, as long as we're literate and old enough to join a library, we on the other hand have no excuse. The shelves of literature devoted to childhood psychology groan under the burden of information detailing the impact of demand-feeding versus routine-feeding parenting; how to manage sibling rivalry; how to teach considerate behaviour; how to listen to, communicate with and love your children all at once without losing the plot or your mind in the process. Every nuance of parenting is backed up by theory, including one's choice of grammar. Apparently there is a psychological world of difference between 'That was stupid of you' (which leaves a lasting emotional scar) and 'That was a stupid thing to do' (perfectly acceptable). As far as I'm concerned, if a child feels like an idiot after she's taken scissors to her hair 'because I want to look like Barbie as Rapunzel', then that's a great parenting victory.

A little knowledge (about middle-child syndrome, ADHD, autism and Dabrowski's theory of over-excitabilities) is dangerous because it makes our transgressions seem less forgivable than those of our parents, who were just boorishly negligent. Unhappily, all this child-rearing information has been unsuccessful in modifying my parenting (I still shout, smack and threaten). It is knowledge which has failed, in my case, as the poet Coleridge claims to 'return as power'. No, in my case, it has manifested as guilt. Advances in psychology have effectively cornered us into becoming a generation of more attentive, learned, neurotically self-critical parents, who spare the rod on the kids and use it to self-flagellate. And we are stripped of our only refuge: ignorance.

Ignorance, I believe, is significantly underrated. Flipped on its belly, it is romance bleached of cynicism. This whole parenting cycle rests on its murky seabed. The decision to have kids is always an imperfectly informed choice. Nothing else sheds light on the reckless consent to a lifetime with someone you have yet to meet. Find me the fool who would agree to marry a blind date before the date. Or invite a stranger to move into the guestroom, and stay as long he likes. Yet that's precisely what we're doing when we have kids. Are we so self-deluded as to think we've done the maths: take one mummy plus one daddy and baby makes three? Having kids is as much a recipe or simple equation as Butternut + Ricotta = Butternut Ricotta Pancakes. Alchemy is intrinsic to all acts of creation whether womb or skillet-based. Everything and everyone is changed in the process, and you can't tell where the butternut ends and the ricotta begins nor the part the nutmeg's played in pulling it all together. When it comes to surveying the results of your genetic as well as your culinary efforts, as Helen always says, 'hope for the best, but prepare for the worst'.

Liz leans forward, in search of something. Could she actually be after seconds? She hesitates, succumbs. I can barely conceal the grin on my face. I've finally seduced Liz's frigid appetite.

'Know what I hate?' CJ asks, literally licking the plate.

'People who don't pick up their dog's crap in the park?' Fiona offers. I can only imagine how that must rile her.

'No, actually, yes I hate that too, but what I hate even more . . .'

'Men who can't commit?' Tam suggests, attributing preoccupations she'd be better off admitting to herself.

'Men, in general?' Ereka suggests. She has unrolled her second pancake, and is raking her fork through its contents, panning for gold. If she asks I'll just tell her: it's the orange zest.

'Lunchboxes,' CJ says.

We all nod. Say no more, sister. We're with you. Ranking alongside misogynist men (and racist jokes, CJ). Yep. Those little plastic rectangular Tupperwares with our children's names on them that pitch up every single morning with an unrecognisable smoosh of eggshell chippings, squashed banana, half-eaten strawberry jam sandwiches and an apple with a single browning bite in it, all of which has to be thrown out. Lunchboxes confirm that each day as a mother is Ground Hog Day and it all starts with the opening of the fridge and the surveying of the slim pickings on offer. We all feel mortally oppressed by the daily injunction of the lunchbox that sneers: Fill Me. With low-fat low-sugar high-energy high-fibre vitamin-enriched foods. So that your children may be healthy, happy, well adjusted, normal functional members of society.

Again, crucify me if you must: I have not mastered the art of Feeding My Children. Unlike Helen (and Tam, of course), who daily feed their children nutritionally balanced meals consisting of protein, starch, steamed broccoli and mushrooms followed by fruit, I have failed pitifully in the task. Apart from sausages (which arguably fall into the category of fat, rather than protein) Aaron's only other protein intake is from McDonald's burgers and peanut butter. Then, of course, to turn the screws, the schools all went peanut-free. I concede that preventing a child with a peanut allergy from collapsing into anaphylactic shock is a reasonable basis for this policy, but it still buggers up my morning.

'What do you put in Aaron's lunchbox?' CJ asks me.

'On an average day—a chocolate milk, a bagel (plain), a container of cold pasta (plain and only the curly kind), two rice crackers and popcorn. And a green apple.' And before anyone else can get it in I say, 'Yes, I know. It's a starch overload.'

I look at Tam. She just shrugs.

Tam is convinced that Aaron's starch intake accounts for his irritability, bad moods, tantrums, bullying at school, proclivity for torturing our cat and his various other adorable personality traits. A while ago, she earnestly presented me with a list:

Take him to a homeopath (name and telephone number supplied).

Feed him fish oil.

Put protein powder in a milkshake—only lactose-free milk (brand and health shop details supplied).

Take him off dairy. Maybe he is lactose-intolerant.

See a kinesiologist (name and telephone number supplied).

No more preservatives—check all products you buy.

No more sugar.

Definitely no more gluten.

I have, in moments of focused devotion, given each one of these suggestions a fair go. It has cost me a small fortune and my cupboard is full of health supplements that have had a very short workout and a long shelf life. They sit there, a collection of jars and bottles, their contents hardening, nodding to one another, 'Yeah, we've lost her', in hopeful anticipation that someday I might return to the arduous task of administering them. Over the years I have had fish oil spat onto my blouse, carob-covered rice cakes spewed onto the floor, and been called 'a disgusting mean mother' at various intervals. I am not a sucker for punishment. Some things are just too hard.

Sometimes, in a spurt of postmenstrual energy, I renew my efforts to advance Aaron's protein intake. I buy two kilos of fat-free mince, and spend an afternoon rolling and frying (in a smidgin of olive oil) my own homemade meatballs and hamburger patties. I add secretly disguised ingredients. If Aaron sees—or thinks he sees—so much as a spot of orange (grated carrots) or green (parsley or celery) I have tried to sneak in, he will stand before me, eyes blazing with fury, and declare, 'This is Dis. Gusting.' My son is merciless. He will eat green grapes. But not red ones. Seedless only. He will eat bread. Plain. With no 'bits' (white bread). And a piece of cheese. Plain. But if I suggest a cheese sandwich, 'which is plain bread and plain cheese, just holding hands, darling', he tells me 'Eat my shorts.' I bite my lip, but I silently vow he'll never watch another Simpsons episode again in his finicky life.

'I don't think that's so bad,' CJ says. 'Jorja will only eat the "whites of things"—egg whites, the whites of cucumbers, peeled apples and mashed potatoes.'

'See, she's inherited your racist world-view,' I comment.

'Aw, get lost,' CJ sneers at me.

'The only protein Kylie will eat is smoked salmon,' Ereka says. 'Princess that she is. Is there citrus in here?' she asks me.

I smile. 'Orange zest.'

'Not to mention your breastmilk,' Tam reminds her.

'Just to wash it down,' Ereka says. 'I knew it,' she says. 'Divine . . .'

'Tyler doesn't eat a single fruit or vegetable,' Dooly says. 'Unless chips and tomato sauce count as vegetables,' she adds.

'Have you made any progress with Aaron's food repertoire?' Tam asks me, like she's got to rub it in each time she sees me. If we'd made any progress, she'd have read about it in the *Eastern Suburbs Courier*.

I shake my head.

'And how is his behaviour lately?' Fiona asks. I take a deep breath.

My son's tantrums are legendary. My friends have all witnessed Aaron's metamorphosis into a Tasmanian devil, and my reduction (not in the cooking sense) to tears. Despair has driven me to reading: *Toddler Taming, The Indigo Children, Children are People Too, Men are From Mars, Women are From Venus* and *Children are From Heaven, How to Raise Happy Children, You are Your Child's First Teacher,* searching for the life jacket of some method or technique I can grasp. I have tried, God-is-my-witness, to implement all their very useful suggestions. Time out. No time out. Deprivation. No deprivation. Consistency. Following through with threats. Eventually, with an unblemished track record of ruinous efforts, I convinced Frank that we needed to go and 'see someone' about Aaron.

I had been walking around for months with the names and phone numbers of several child therapists in my diary. Now Frank does not lightly involve third parties in his private life. He was brought up with a firm hand and very little indulgence. He openly admits to believing that people who need therapy just need to 'pull themselves together' and get on with it. Nothing a cold beer and a footy match on TV can't cure. His singular childrearing philosophy is: 'I speak, they listen.' He only speaks once. And when they don't listen, he gives up. He defers to me. After all, I am the one who wanted kids.

I love Frank for many reasons, not least of which is that he has never raised a hand to our kids. I grew up with a father who smacked me. And there are few childhood injustices I remember with as much pain as that of being hit by an adult, without being able to defend myself or retaliate. I also worked for six years with battered women. I have little patience for people who inflict physical pain on those weaker than themselves.

Please don't ask me. Let me rather ask you. Do you hit your kids?

Fiona doesn't. At our last gathering she said simply, 'I would never hit Gabriel.'

'Do you shout at least?' I had asked hopefully.

'Every mother shouts,' she had said. 'It's not my preferred mode of communication, but I do shout. Sometimes.'

Yeah right. Fiona never raises her voice. She just said it to bind our unity, isolation insurance. No one wants to be branded The Only One Who Doesn't Smack. Except for Tam. Maybe it was said compassionately, to make the rest of us feel better. I might as well confess my envy at Fiona's self-righteous contention. I wish I had the history to justify an assertion without any trace of hypocrisy of, 'It is wrong to hit your kids'. She's right. In theory. Unfortunately, I got stuck in the turnstile to the practical. Unlike Fiona, I *have* raised my hand in anger to my children. Unlike Fiona, I *have* caused my children to cry with shock and horror. Unlike Fiona, I *have* witnessed my own reddening handprint come up on their soft skin like hidden codes on a treasure map. And unlike Fiona I have been consumed with the self-loathing and shame that follows in the wake of that glorious primitive Biblical sense of justice, an eye for an eye. Or a smack on the bum for putting chewing gum in your sister's hair.

But I, unlike Fiona, do not have a kid like Gabriel—soft-spoken, calm and utterly inoffensive, apart from his quirky eccentricities which do not impinge on his mother's sanity. But perhaps that is because Fiona, unlike me, is herself soft-spoken, calm and utterly inoffensive. And let's face it, she's only got one child, which is like having none compared to two. Even among us, there is a hierarchy of motherhood, depending on how many and how old your children are.

'Aaron *is* a challenging child,' Fiona had said to me.

She was just reaching out, trying to be generous. But I bristle at kindness underscored by psychoanalysis and pity. My guilt and shame, like two lumbering wall-facing zoo-caged bears, don't need sympathetic onlookers. In the toss up between what pisses me off more, it's a difficult choice between my own wretched striking out at my kids or other's condemnation of me when I do. For this reason I have developed an exaggerated empathy for other mothers, often in supermarkets, a tiny newt of a newborn in a stroller or strapped to her in a sling, struggling with an impossible toddler throwing a tantrum. Public scrutiny is all it takes for her cheeks to become flushed, and for her newborn to start howling. Between the tinned soup and the dairy aisle, she is pinned by reproving stares. If she raises her voice or her hand, the onlookers' verdict is 'nasty mother, poor kid'. If she tries calm reasoning, but the tantrum escalates and her control of the situation slackens, people still tut-tut, 'weak mother, bratty kid'. No one ever looks at her and thinks 'nasty kid, poor mother'. Except maybe other mothers with equally deranged toddlers.

'I don't *like* to hit mine,' CJ had said as if enjoyment had anything to do with it. 'But I have, when the situation just gets so out of hand that you have no option. But you shouldn't do it in

anger. Just in a calm and controlled way.' Yeah, like those death-row orderlies who calmly flick the switch.

Fiona had shaken her head. 'I just don't think it achieves the message you are trying to get across—that resolving your difficulties with aggression is the way to behave. You are not modelling the behaviour you want your children to learn,' she had said.

This was the very argument that persuaded me about the ethical absurdity of the death penalty when I was at law school. You can't teach people that killing is wrong by killing them. Not with a straight face, anyway. Restraint in the face of brutality is strength's trump card. But with Fiona and Tam, I do wonder where the fury goes, and ultimately whether a shouting, hitting mother like me is not somehow less damaging to a child in the long term than one who always swallows her gall and resists the impulse to lash out. Isn't there something more sincere about an honest response, which may be 'I'd like to break your neck', rather than, 'How about some time out for you to think about those hurtful things you've said'? While I envy the adult self-discipline of converting the raw energy of brutal anger into placatory murmurs, there is something stifled and insincere about them. Perhaps it's my Jewish background—we're a shouting, wailing, moaning tribe. I'm at ease with uproarious emotions. And let's face it, I don't need kickboxing or Prozac.

But on that day, sitting talking about it with my girlfriends, I vowed 'no more spanking'. Despite the delicious momentary release of anger, like a sneeze that's been building up, the suffocating regret in hurting someone you love is what lingers. On that day they all convinced me to go and see a child psychologist.

I braved the resistances Frank put up. I told him he *had* to come with me. He owed it to Aaron. He owed it to me. I cried. I begged. Eventually I refused him sex. So he agreed to come along.

She was very nice, the child therapist. An elderly woman living in a fancy house in Dover Heights. She was friendly and warm, and offered us something cold to drink. I accepted. Frank refused.

I began the story of our son's wild antics.

She nodded and took notes.

Frank said nothing for a long time and then he began to speak. He spoke about his upbringing, his frustrations with the constraining trivia of fatherhood, our financial and emotional challenges as new immigrants, the irreplaceable support of family, and his own petty angers, magnified in the microcosm of our nuclear family. As I listened, I understood for the first time how profoundly difficult fatherhood has been for him. And the depth of his love for me when he agreed to become a father so I could become a mother. I grew even fonder of him.

Our therapist was compassionate. She gave us rules for the week.

Rule No. 1:   No shouting (in fact, talk in almost a whisper so he has to strain to hear what we are saying—when we shout, people do not listen).

Rule No. 2:   Remove Aaron to a safe place when he has a tantrum or alternatively tell him 'I have to go into my room and shut the door because your shouting is hurting my ears'.

Rule No. 3:   No smacking.

Rule No. 4:   Keep notes of when he fusses—does it coincide with hunger? Tiredness? Some other factor?

Rule No. 5:   When in doubt, refer to Rule No 1.

We left armed with a plan. We were not going to shout. I could not have been more committed to this plan of action. I was going to fix this problem once and for all.

Day One after the Therapist: I do not shout. When Aaron has a tantrum at 4.23 p.m. because I do not have sausages for dinner, I calmly tell him that I have to leave the room because his shouting is hurting my ears. I go into my room and close the door. Aaron flings himself at the door and opens it in a rage. I remove him from my room, close the door and hold the handle up. He pounds at the door, trying with all his might to open the handle. He is a strong little bugger. But I succeed. For now, I am stronger. I calmly repeat over and over that as soon as he stops fussing, I will come out. I suggest to him that it would be best if he stops fussing. He continues to cry and scream for eighteen minutes. But the crying stops. I come out from my room, my hand numb from holding the door handle up. I hug him, feed him, bathe him, read him *Where the Wild Things Are* and *Chicka Chicka Boom Boom*. He goes to sleep telling me 'You're the best mum in the world'. I have a lump in my throat. Maybe I could be.

Day Two after the Therapist: A repeat of Day One.

Day Three after the Therapist: A repeat of Day One up until about fifteen minutes into the tantrum. Eventually, Aaron screams at me, 'You stupid fucking idiot!' I wish I could say that I continue to sit happily on my side of the door and wait for the tantrum to subside. But unfortunately, that's not how things go at all. No, instead, I fling open the door and yell at Aaron while spanking him on his bottom, 'How DARE you speak to me like that? Don't you EVER *(smack)*, EVER *(smack)* talk to me like that again *(smack)*!!!!!'

I hated myself for days after that. But the sun went down with him being hugged, fed, bathed and read to. He went to sleep telling me 'You're the best mum in the world'. Children are so forgiving. Psychopathically so.

Fiona is looking at me now, waiting to hear.

'He's doing so much better,' I say.

the kitten bribe

The dish has been scraped as clean as a chocolate cake mixing bowl once my kids are through with it. The pancakes have been a resounding triumph. All those valiant enough to brave the brutalities of gluten concur. Tam sits apart sipping her water, miffed to have missed out but shored, at least in her own mind, by her moral high ground. Liz has even said that I *must* email her the recipe, she's 'sure Lily could whip them up'. I have promised, the way we blithely pledge to 'keep in touch' with people we meet at holiday resorts. I am privately satisfied that without the nutmeg instinct of a true cook's heart where love not measurement matters, even dear old Lily (there for the money, not the love) won't be able to crack these pancakes.

But I can't explain to Liz that cooking is an art, not a science—she is too immersed in that masculine left-brain mode. But, given how she's reacted to the pancakes, I know indisputably that somewhere inside her there's a girl dancing in a glade of moonlight.

Ereka, pancaked up to the gills, has taken to the balcony for her second joint. The rest of us are all sprawled out or lying curled up on the couches, like a family of fat warm cats, hoping for some digestive relief and making way for what follows. I am sitting cross-legged on the floor in my socks beside Fiona, who has her fingers in my hair massaging my scalp. If I could purr, I would. Dear Lord, if only men knew that the secrets to a woman's pleasure nestle in such unassuming places as her hair follicles.

Tam bothers the stillness. 'What's the time, anyone?'

'Oh who cares?' Helen says. 'It's not time to go yet, just relax.'

'I have to be there at the crack of dawn,' Tam says, knocked back. 'You know how these private schools are . . .'

No one suggests differently.

Then CJ asks, 'How is Jamie doing at her new school?'

My voice comes out slow and easy. 'Much better,' I say. 'Public schools are very underrated . . .' Dooly nods, not that she and I have much choice in the matter. In the end, for us it was a toss up between private school fees and groceries. Three months ago, Frank and I were forced to take Jamie out of a private school and move her sideways, we trust (downwards I fear), into a public school.

'They all learn to read and write no matter where they go,' Tam says reassuringly. The hollow frivolity of an opinion of one whose boys are at the most expensive private boys' school in Sydney is lost on her.

'Yeah, kids can do without all that pressure,' CJ says. Her kids are also blissfully ensconced in private school education, even though it is courtesy of TFB.

While I'd welcome all research that corroborates that there is in fact no difference between private and public schools, especially in the primary years, I myself am the product of that pernicious exclusive enclave of private school education. My parents battled it out in true Jewish parent martyr-style to afford private school fees, and I emerged from the private school system, pampered and puffed up, with six distinctions and a scholarship. The world, I was led to believe, was my oyster. And wanting more, not less for my children, my hope is that they too should sup at the mollusc of the universe with enfranchised equality.

'I just hope we're doing right by her,' I say meekly. 'I don't want her to miss out on opportunities because of it.'

'Sending them to a private school doesn't guarantee anything,' Liz says. No comfort there either, her kids are also privately bespoken for.

'Private schools are just an elaborate and expensive form of insurance against parental guilt,' Helen says. She has lifted up her shirt and is rubbing some of Fiona's chamomile oil onto her belly, flap and all.

'Maybe,' I concede, 'but you get the martyr licence if you go the private route—if your kids become delinquents, you can blame the school and claim, "we gave them the best shot at life". But when you go the public route, if your kids flunk out, well, you just have to take some of the blame for not depriving yourself enough, and for scrimping on their education. And I can just hear the fights now about who gets to bail Aaron out of jail and who's going to look after the baby while Jamie does her HSC exams. Given the options, I'd rather get my martyr-licence.'

The girls are laughing at me. But actually it's no laughing matter—only those who have the opulence of options can laugh.

'Has Jamie made any new friends?' Dooly asks.

'I think so,' I answer. But there is a cramp in my heart, the body won't let you scuttle past with nonchalant assurances about your child's adaptation skills.

'How did Jamie take it when you broke the news to her?' Liz asks.

Now I grasp Fiona's hands and turn to look straight at Liz. Jamie, in the litheness of her innocence, had by the age of four just rearranged her world to accommodate a series of unrelenting losses—grandparents, cousins, aunts, her two cats, Rain and Shadow, her mountain (as she used to call Table Mountain, which we could spy above the avocado tree from the verandah of our home in Cape Town), her nanny, Thandi, and her school built along a stream, and through whose grounds goats, turtles and rabbits would frolic. Then came three house moves in the three years we have been in Sydney. Each time we packed up, she would sigh and say, 'Will this be our home forever?' She had been in her private school for two whole years—the only constant factor in her life. It would have been kinder to rip her fingernails off one by one, I suspect, than to tell her 'It's time to move again'. The look in her wide brown eyes kept me awake for a week of midnights as I lay in bed staring up at the cracking plaster on the ceiling.

'Let's put it this way, I haven't been nominated for the Mother of the Year award,' I say.

'Guilt works much better than caffeine in keeping you awake at ungodly hours in the middle of the night,' CJ says. 'Trust me, I know.'

'But I made it up to her—she got a new kitten. I told Jamie she could have a new kitten if she changed schools.'

I suppose, technically, you could call it a bribe. At the very least, it was a low move, I confess. She loves animals and I was desperate. The dreamy contemplation of her very own kitten short-circuited her disquiet about changing schools. At least initially.

'Did it work?' Tam asks, knowing the answer to her question, but prompting me to my admission nonetheless.

'Hardly. A kitten and a new school have no correlation to one another. She seemed in high spirits for the first few weeks, but one day in the car home she just burst into tears.'

'Tired,' Helen says. 'They're just little, school is a long day for a kid.'

'No, I recognise tired,' I say. 'When I asked her why she was crying, it all came out: that the girls were horrible and she had no one to play with, that she was trying to be happy, that she wanted to be happy; that she was pretending to be happy. Why are you pretending, I'd asked. And she said, "Because you want me to be happy".'

'Poor poppet,' Fiona says, returning to my head with renewed consolation.

'There is nothing worse than the pain of watching your child suffer,' I say.

I cast my gaze at Ereka, who is still on the balcony, relieved that my trifling pain is not up for scrutiny against the weight of hers.

'It's clear that it's important to her to keep you happy,' Tam says, and whatever insinuation nestles in her remark, I accelerate past it like I pass teenage hitchhikers. Without so much as a backwards glance.

'I told her that she never has to pretend to be something she is not. Especially to make me happy,' I say.

'But the truth is, we know that our children want to make us happy,' Tam says. 'That is their most abiding need—for our approval.'

I gulp. I suppose I knew that. I had taken Jamie at her most vulnerable, added in a kitten bribe and manipulated her into doing precisely what I wanted. I suddenly feel positively queasy as the memory of her sitting in the corner of the kitchen with her kitten on her lap surges into my mind, clogging it like an overflowing cistern. Is my self-deceit so accomplished that I convinced myself that a $150 scrap of black fur (fully vaccinated but not house-trained as it turned out) would brace a six year old for vicious playground exclusions, and for being the only girl in her class not invited to Clementine's birthday party? Bad mother. Bad bad bad bad mother.

'I'm a bad mother,' I say, trawling for contradiction.

'No, you're not,' Helen says, obliging, smacking my head and accidently hitting Fiona on the wrist. 'You didn't have a choice— most mothers wouldn't have bothered giving their child something in return. They would have just said, "You're changing schools. End of story".'

'Maybe I thought she might not notice her unhappiness so much if she was distracted with her new kitten. Perhaps I tried to buy her resilience with something she could love, so that even if she had no friends at school, at least she'd have a friend in her cat,' I say, parsing out my thoughts, unpacking my twisted logic for public scrutiny.

'Manipulation is a survival tactic,' CJ says. 'Don't knock it.'

'And then another cat in the neighbourhood bit her kitten and it got a suppurating pus-infested lesion, and the vet told us it would cost $500 to drain, unless I could do it myself. So I did the calculations: it would be cheaper to buy a new kitten than to have this one fixed.'

'What did you do?' Dooly asks, opening a chocolate and scrunching the wrapper into a small ball, which she leaves on the side table next to five others just like it. The box of Favourites sits open on her lap.

'I was in a quandary,' I say. 'She loved that new kitten so much, and we had forced her to change schools. So I put on a pair of rubber gloves and braved the suppurating territory.'

'I did offer to squeeze it for you,' Helen says, leaning over to Dooly and foraging in the box of Favourites. She loves a good pimple, abscess or oozing wound. Mad bitch.

'Yeah, well, I did it all by myself. I gagged and retched, but managed not to vomit when I removed a piece of pus, the size of which makes my whole body shudder when I think of it. The wound healed. And everyone is happy now.'

'It's funny how mercenary we become to pets after we've had kids,' CJ says. 'On the hierarchy of survival, they are the lowest on the list.'

'Financial stress has made me ruthless,' I agree. 'You know, I would rather get a cleaner in and have my house tidy for an hour than get the cat vaccinated when it comes to my last sixty dollars. And I would certainly rather spend five dollars on sushi than on a flea collar.' I hear Fiona's soft chuckle from behind me.

'We know you don't agree, Dooly,' CJ says. 'You're a much nicer person than the rest of us.'

'Hardly,' Dooly says modestly. But she is. I mean, she's nicknamed after Doctor Doolittle, and though she can't talk to the animals, she can do just about everything else. She's got that horse-whispering talent. Her concern for her boys' menagerie of pets is legendary. They have mice, two cats, a dog that needs walking daily and a budgie. Unlike me, she ensures the welfare of her children's animals with allegiant dedication and I am certain she is silently horrified at my negligence. I don't think she has spoiled herself with a new pair of shoes or underwear in the past five years. And—can I be making this up?—she cleans the mice once a week with cotton buds.

Two months ago, Luke's budgie was out of its cage, having its daily fly around the kitchen, when it flew into the large pot of chicken soup she was making. Carry on stirring, pluck the feathers out later, and plead ignorance, I say. It flew away, we'll get another one. No, not Dooly. She rushed the budgie to the vet. It cost her $353 to have it seen to (that's the cost of about twenty new budgies). And she had to administer antibiotic ointment to it for weeks thereafter. The budgie has never been the same. It now suffers from post-traumatic chicken-soup syndrome. It has become a complete nuisance and makes a huge racket, squawking for no good reason as twilight approaches. Poor Dooly. She seems to collect things that suffer from mental disorders and require vigilant maintenance. She's comfortable with feebleness and has a patience for ailing creatures that I simply lack. I so jealously guard my resources of time, energy and money; they get doled out in this order—kids first, Frank if he's lucky, me last.

'Talking of which,' Fiona says, 'how is Luke's budgie doing?'

'He's still a bit fucked-up actually,' Dooly says. 'I don't think he'll come right.'

Helen and I look at each other and she starts to giggle.

'You two are just horrible,' Dooly says. 'You have no pity for that poor budgie.'

Helen and I try to stifle the giggling, but we can't. Soon Fiona and Liz have joined in, and before long we are all laughing so hysterically that Tam, before her operation, would have wet her pants.

'I'm not that horrible,' I say. 'I just can't cope with that level of dependency. Frank sometimes jokes that if he ever became a quadriplegic like Christopher Reeve, I would drop him like a hot rock and pay someone to wipe his bottom and his dribble.'

'And rightly so,' Liz says.

But I'm not that callous. Frank is teasing me when he says this. He and I both agreed years ago that we would stay together as long as the good times outweighed the bad. Cleaning bedpans wasn't part of the picture. Neither of us could bear the thought of saddling the other with those excruciating acts of noble indebtedness to the one we have loved. It probably belongs in the basket of reasons why we did not marry for so many years. Both we lawyers squinted cynically into the eye of the sweeping promise to love one another forever. We agreed to take our relationship day by day.

But then my girlfriends got hold of me a year ago.

'You're a commitment-phobe,' Liz had said.

'You're scared,' Tam had piped up.

'You're hoping somebody better will come along,' Helen had quipped.

'Robbie Williams?' CJ had suggested.

'I don't believe in marriage,' I used to say. 'I don't see how it makes any difference at all.' They all assured me that it *did* make a difference. God. Witnesses. More difficult to walk away. Really. Like eight years together, two kids, and an immigration under the belt would wither into inconsequentiality without that piece of paper.

CJ, I suspect, quietly admired my resilience in the face of pressures to marry. She was hitched, white wedding gown and all, to TFB for five dismal years, and you should hear her on the wedding industry and the false promises of romantic love. In the end, all her inner girlchild who wanted to be a princess for a day ended up with was the best private schools for her children—TFB's guilt-balm for his absentee parenting and for not really giving a shit about his kids. I think CJ would just fold over with gratitude if he'd fly them out to Melbourne once in a while so he could see what they look like these days.

My girlfriends' assault on my attitude to marriage riled me. As if their marriages are all so perky. As if they're more grown up because they've got wedding albums and threw a bouquet. For days afterwards I muttered private retorts that took me that long to formulate. But when the muttering settled, I knew that within the fronds of my coiled ire nestled a truth furled away somewhere in a blind spot. What was that truth?

Am I scared of commitment? Yeah, of the kind of commitment the pig has to the bacon industry. But not in the forsaking all others sense. I have been (technically) monogamous for eight years (if you discount a couple of fantasies along the way). I've got two small kids and have no designs on seducing strangers, despite the fact that my flamboyant desires are easily aroused by teenage boys rugged with testosterone (did I mention Robbie Williams?) not to mention a dish of seared carpaccio of beef with chilli, ginger, radish and soy dressing. I am not planning on going anywhere.

Was I scared? Maybe, a little. I feared that with marriage, something would happen to me. That the untouchable inner flame of my identity—the uncompromising, mysterious, secretive gypsy flare, precious and hard won—would get, even inadvertently, snuffed out. I had no interest whatsoever in becoming some man's wife (even a man as lovely as Frank), and was overtly hostile to the idea of being seen by others as some man's 'wife'. I didn't want to give all of the treasured delicacies of myself away. I wanted to keep some for a rainy day. What day was that? The day Frank and I parted ways (thanks it was fun, but it's over now)? The day my perfect soul mate came blundering through the front door with a 'pack your bags our cruise is leaving'? The day I woke up to the simmering realisation that actually I wanted to be a Buddhist nun? Maybe the day the kids no longer needed me, and I could become my own self again. Demothered. Demoted back to me.

I began to scrutinise Frank, from the corner of my eye. I monitored closely as he played yet another round of poker with the kids, repeated the rules of chess for the twenty-seventh time, drummed the four and six times tables into Jamie's head and offered to take the kids to the Wiggles' concert ('You'll only start hurling abuse at Dorothy the Dinosaur before interval,' he chided). Each time he brought me coffee in bed in my preferred mug, the one with the painted eggplants and sweetpeas, or nudged me to 'spend the day writing' while he spent the day with the kids at the beach and brought home Thai takeaways ('choo chee prawns, your favourite'), I softened. I surveyed the grind of his life, his commitment to a job that does not intellectually challenge him, but that pays rent and bills.

And there it was. The truth of it all—*he* is my soul mate. Who else qualifies but that person you opt to father your children? He, to whom you can still make passionate-enough love, after eight years together? The only living soul who knows and gives a damn when you need a foot rub, a bar of chocolate *right now* or to be left alone, without needing it spelled out?

And so, several weeks later, he was on his way out with the garbage when I blocked his path and stated, for the record and for eternity, 'I love you enough to marry you'.

He dropped the garbage and, with uncharacteristic tears in his eyes, he murmured, 'I never thought I would ever hear you say those words'. Not that he was waiting to hear them, he assured me, lest I thought he'd gone soft.

As the idea of marrying Frank did the roundabout in my heart I befriended it, tentatively at first, soon allowing its robust pull to an ancient bond in which people ritualise their connections. Despite our commitment in having parented children together, marrying would be a personal assertion of how love abides—through nappies,

sleepless nights and the desolations of early parenting. Our marriage was in honour of the history of our stamina, loyalty and the resilience of our partnership, not a wishful white weddinged grope into the future.

I am pretty certain that my mother-in-law's furtive plea to me, 'think of the children', whispered in the early days of my pregnancy with Jamie, had no bearing on our decision. 'What will people say?' she'd tried. Clutching my arm with her left hand, wrinkly and tough with her wedding band almost moulded to her finger, she implored, 'It would be nice . . . before I die . . . to see you married . . .' After eight years, I believe our parents had resigned themselves to our unconventional coupling and had made some kind of peace with it.

But all children secretly want to make their parents happy. And our parents manipulate us with kittens* and their own fragile mortality to get what they want. Eventually.

---

* Sadly, Jamie's kitten, Midnight, became ill and had to be 'put down' some months before the publication of this book. This chapter is dedicated to his memory.

CHAPTER 9

other people's business

'Close the bloody door!' CJ barks, not unkindly, but with more indignation than a prickly breeze justifies. Ereka, on her return from the balcony for the second time, did not secure the door properly on her way back in. The cool night air has slunk in with her. Alcohol does not enhance CJ's most winning qualities and, before long, it will slacken the taut helix of her bitterness and cause an erratic unravelling. I feel mildly panicked at the thought.

'Oops, sorry,' Ereka mutters, turning back to shut it. She has that goofy drug-induced expression. There is freedom in her eyes, something lovely and silly. Maybe she should think more about Prozac, I find myself thinking. Fiona's fingers have not tired from massaging my scalp, and I'm about to tell her she can stop, I'm sure she's had enough.

'What were you all laughing about?' Ereka asks.

'Luke's budgie, who flew into the chicken soup,' Liz says.

'You wouldn't consider putting him down?' Ereka asks Dooly, heading for the table. She surveys the leftovers with renewed enthusiasm and then rummages among the dirty plates for hers, can't be sure, takes one anyway and starts to dish food onto her plate.

'No,' Dooly says. 'I mean, he doesn't have much quality of life, but I don't think he's in pain. He is a pain, but he's not in pain ...'

'Just don't make chicken soup again while he's flying around,' Fiona says to Dooly, as her fingers press my cranium from all sides. There is such intimacy in touch, and yet Fiona's touch feels remote. Like her heart is not quite in it. Maybe that's how one can do the touch-thing all day, being there in body, elsewhere in spirit. Prostitutes claim that much.

'Yeah, that was my fault,' Dooly says mournfully. She unties the scarf from her waist and rolls it into a ball on her lap. Why she can't just pack it in her bag and tell Luke a lie is beyond me.

'That's nothing, compared to what I did last week,' Ereka says, talking through a pulp of half-masticated food. 'I fucked up biiiiiig time,' residues of broccoli from the Thai curry—which must be cold by now—evident when she speaks.

'Don't you want me to warm that up for you?' I ask. 'It can't be nice.'

'It's perfect,' Ereka says, shuffling back to the lounge and looking for a space to comfortably sit and eat. She opts for the floor, placing her dish on the coffee table.

Helen has stretched out on the only sofa and CJ has oiled her up and is massaging her neck and back—though 'massaging' is probably a generous term for CJ's clumsy kneading, which from the way Helen's face is scrunched up feels as horrible as it looks.

We all love a big fuck up—whether it's overlooking to pack a lunchbox and having the school phone to remind you that feeding your children is your responsibility, not theirs (Dooly last month);

forgetting to take someone else's child home with you from school and receiving a rushed 'no thanks', when you invite the kid over again (CJ two months ago); or driving over the kindergarten rabbit you have been minding in the school holidays (Helen in the last school break).

'Tell us,' Dooly implores Ereka. 'What did you do?'

In between mouthfuls Ereka relays: 'Last weekend we were invited to Ethan's, an old school friend of Jake's, for a lunch. Jake was Ethan's best man when he got married to his Swedish wife Uma who, by the way, looks like an Aryan model. Tall, blonde, green eyes, perfect skin. It's pretty depressing.'

We all curse her good looks. Even Liz, who is by all standards gorgeous.

Helen has told CJ, 'It's enough, thanks that was great,' and has now sat up. CJ is rubbing the oil into her own hands and over her face.

'Anyway, they have this four-year-old kid, Christopher, and he's quite the spoiled only child. Olivia managed to get herself onto Christopher's tricycle. She was sitting there, holding onto the handle bars, when he came up to her and said "get off, it's mine". You know Olivia—she just smiled at him. So Christopher took hold of the handlebars and pushed Olivia off the bike.' Ereka stops chewing her mouthful of lasagna and looks at us. We all wait for her to continue, but she only continues chewing.

'Did he know that Olivia was ...' Tam pauses, '...um... couldn't really understand him?'

Ereka swallows and clears her mouth. 'Apparently they had explained before our visit that a little girl with "a brain-problem was coming over so be nice".'

'Sometimes kids don't understand what that means,' Tam says.

'Yeah, but that's just mean behaviour, whether or not it was Olivia on the bike,' Helen says, seemingly relieved to be out of CJ's clutches.

'Another kid might have put up a fight,' Dooly suggests.

'But that's not all,' Ereka says, chewing another mouthful of Lily's lasagna, also cold by now, the cheese hard and brittle. She pauses, chews slowly, swallows. We're all waiting to hear.

'What?' I nudge.

'Well, I'm not normally judgmental of other kids' bad behaviour, or other parents for that matter,' Ereka says. 'I mean, we all make mistakes, right?'

We all nod.

'But Olivia was inconsolable. She had landed on her bum and hit her arm on the concrete, but I think the shock was what got to her. Jake picked her up and was comforting her and I stood there—I must have been in shock myself—waiting for Ethan and Uma to do something. I mean, isn't that what you'd expect?'

'Sure,' Helen says.

'Well the two of them, without even getting up or putting their drinks down, said in this sort of bored voice, "That wasn't very nice, Chrissy". I mean, that was it. The full extent of the reprimand.' Ereka's face and neck are speckled pink with the embers of an anger fanned in the retelling.

'Are you serious?' I ask.

'Well that's why he's the brat he is,' Liz says. 'It's not his fault, his parents are to blame.'

'It must have been hard to stay after that,' Helen says.

'Well, we didn't stay long,' Ereka says, chewing on a baby beetroot. Her teeth are stained mahogany as she speaks. 'Not after what I did.'

'What did you do?' we all say almost in unison.

'Yeah, what the fuck did you do?' CJ asks, standing up to refill her glass. One of us should tell her she's had enough.

'I didn't even think. I just walked over to Christopher on his bike, pulled him off by his collar and gave him such a hiding that he was screaming louder than Olivia.' Ereka looks at us anxiously.

'You didn't!' Liz says. She chuckles.

Ereka nods. 'I smacked him twice on his bottom,' she coughs as a swallow of food goes down the wrong way.

'Good on you!' CJ laughs wildly, gesturing a toast with her newly refilled glass.

'That was bloody brave,' I chime in.

'How did Ethan and Uma respond?' Fiona asks, guarding her response for now.

Ereka is watching all of our faces very closely. She keeps quiet for a few moments. 'They were shocked. Naturally. I think this was their Little Prince's first encounter with the hand on the bottom. I'm pretty sure of that. Uma took Christopher inside and they never came out again. Ethan excused himself too, at some point, to go inside to check on them, and then Jake went in and said goodbye and we left.'

'You deserve a medal,' CJ says, coming over and kissing Ereka on the top of her head. Ereka doesn't look convinced. Her gaze falls on Tam, who is fiddling in her bag with her mobile phone. We all turn to look at Tam too. Tam looks up to see us all eyeing her, awaiting her verdict. She senses our anticipation.

She clears her throat, puts her bag down on the seat next to her. 'I would probably have wanted to do what you did,' she says. 'I might not have been brave enough, though. I might have said something to the parents, like "I wonder if Christopher understands how much Olivia is hurt", or something along those lines.'

'Yeah, you're right, that would have been the right thing to do,' Ereka says miserably. She puts another fork of food into her mouth and chews feebly. 'I feel very guilty.' She carries on chewing. 'I had no right to do it, and if I had thought about it for even a second, I would have stopped myself. I would hate it if someone else hit either of my kids, whatever the provocation.'

'Your kids wouldn't behave like that,' Dooly says. 'I can't imagine Olivia or Kylie being that mean.'

'Mine would,' I say wryly.

'I just could not bear that this child had not been shown how wrong his actions were,' Ereka says imploringly, spiking a prawn with her fork and raising it to her mouth.

'You're like Mr Pinkwhistle,' Fiona says softly.

'Who?' CJ asks.

'You remember that Enid Blyton character, Mr Pinkwhistle, who goes around righting wrongs. He teaches bullies a lesson, fixes broken things . . . that sort of thing . . . ' Fiona says.

'Oh yeah, I remember those stories from when I was a little girl,' she smiles. 'Mr Pinkwhistle . . . he had a cat, didn't he?'

But even as we loyally take Ereka's side in the invisible parenting ring between smackers and non-smackers and applaud her, this is a tricky one and she knows it. As mothers, within the kingdom of our homes we reign freely, disciplining our kids consistent with our esoteric value systems however obscure and cryptic they may seem to the outside world. But few of us have crossed the borders and ventured into the unknown territory of disciplining other people's children. Especially with the palm of our hands. Usurping that responsibility—even if it seems to have been abandoned by its rightful rulers—is borderline imperialist. But then again, the rules are different for Ereka. Uncertain, I pat her on her back anyway.

'In Africa they say it takes a village to raise a child,' I say, thinking about my childhood in Africa where I was soundly disciplined by my nanny, who used to smack my bottom with a wooden spoon from the kitchen drawer. 'Kids are a communal responsibility.'

'That's in Africa,' Tam says. I try not to take this as an insinuation that I don't fully belong to a first-world culture.

'I don't think you have to be in Africa to accept that it is completely reasonable for another adult to reprimand your child when he tortures insects or decants mud into the swimming pool,' I say, without even turning to look at her. 'Or breaks another child's butterfly net,' I add.

My allusion remains elusively esoteric. I'll bet Kieran never thought to mention it. Had he done so, I envisage her rejoinder, 'That's so creative of you to investigate what happens when you twist plastic in half. Here, why don't you try it on the feather duster?'

'Yeah, I think I'm with you, Jo,' Helen says. 'I get exhausted knowing that it is up to me alone to teach my kids not to pick their noses in public, or to remain calm in an emergency, or to cross the road safely. I like it when other adults chip in. I get sick of the sound of my own voice, sometimes. Don't you?' she says to Tam.

Tam shrugs. 'I think actually that disciplining my kids is my job. Some things you can't delegate.'

'Trust me, honey, you can delegate it all,' Liz says. 'Lily is living proof of that.'

'That's your choice, Liz,' Tam says. 'But I'll bet even you'd get cross if a stranger shouted at Chloe and Brandon. Or hit them, for that matter.'

Liz contemplates for a moment. 'You're probably right, but I wouldn't blink if one of you filled in for me when I'm not around. That's what friends are for, isn't it?'

And almost in unison, Helen and I start to sing the chorus of Dionne Warwick's 'That's What Friends are For' madly off-key. CJ joins in.

I put my arm around Helen and we sway from side to side on the sofa. Helen is my children's surrogate mother and has to ask no permission for taking matters into her own hands. Likewise, I feel the same freedom to tell her son Nathan that encouraging Aaron to squash bugs is an evil sin, and those who encourage it will make God just as angry as those who do the actual squashing.

'Remember when we were on holiday last year and I left you alone with the kids for a few hours,' I say to Helen.

'I remember,' she says.

'What happened?' Tam asks, like she's got to know every detail.

'I think it was Helen standing at the door waiting for my return with her car keys in her hand, ready to escape the minute I walked through the door that gave her away. She was in the foulest mood I've ever seen her in. She only said three words to me: "your fucking son".'

'It was pretty ugly,' Helen says.

'And he didn't respond to your disciplining him?' Tam asks.

Helen laughs. 'Yeah, like a bull responds to a red rag.'

'You'll see, he'll grow out of it. He'll be an interesting man,' Tam says kindly. And that's one of the nicest things anyone's ever said to me about Aaron. I smile back at her, overly appreciative.

'At least you recognise when he's been mean, and you discipline him,' Ereka says.

'In Aaron's case, it's not like you can miss the meanness,' Helen says. I frown at her. Only mothers are allowed to say things like that about their kids. But I know her remarks are unintentionally stinging. She'd never be critical of me.

'Ethan and Uma did,' Ereka says.

'Maybe they're stupid,' Helen suggests.

'Lazy,' I say. 'It's just sheer laziness not to discipline your kids when they've done wrong.'

'They weren't lazy. They just have a totally different approach to parenting than Jake and I do,' Ereka says.

'And they don't have a child like Olivia,' Fiona says.

'I suppose if I felt Olivia could fight her own battles, I wouldn't intervene as much. But ...' Ereka's voice trails off, her thoughts trying to assemble the shards of shame, guilt and sadness into coherence. She contemplates her empty plate. ' ... She was helpless, so bewildered by what had happened and all I could do was to lash out, to make that child feel for one second what Olivia had felt.'

'I think it's perfectly understandable,' Fiona says consolingly. 'No one judges you.'

'Do you feel more protective towards Olivia than to Kylie?' Dooly asks softly.

'Of course I do. She doesn't have the tools to mediate a scary and unpredictable world, the way normal kids do. I think if it happened to Kylie, I would use it as an opportunity for her to stand up for herself, and I would teach her how to say no, the way all girls should be taught. But with Olivia, I feel she's been so short-changed, I just want her not to be hurt, because she has no way of making sense of it, and learning from it.'

'I also stepped in the other day,' CJ says, loudly. Ereka's story is barely out of bed, the sheets are still warm, and CJ's now rushing in with her 'Me Too' story. I can scarcely conceal my annoyance.

'What did you do?' Ereka asks, maybe relieved, transgressions of the mothering code apparently rife elsewhere.

The vodka in combination with the headache tablets have done their damage. She's working up to a big cry, I can feel it. 'Jorja's been going through a rough patch at school. She just can't seem to find a little friend. Girls can be such bitches. Last week she was caught stealing money from another kid's bag.'

'All kids go through that stage,' Tam says. 'It's age-appropriate.'

CJ ignores her, continues. 'So I confronted her, ready to come down on her like a ton of bricks, pull out the most heinous punishments ... and get this,' CJ pauses, and I am aware of the tremor in her voice, 'she told me that this boy in her class she's got a crush on, promised he'd play with her at lunch if she gave him two dollars. So she stole the money.'

'Oh, how heartbreaking,' Fiona says.

'Yeah, and that little shit of a boy didn't play with her. He took the money and bought himself and his friends ice cream from the canteen. Jorja sat alone at lunch.' CJ sniffs. 'Kids are sometimes more devious than some of my worst clients,' she says.

'So what did you do?' Helen asks. She tosses the box of Favourites back to Dooly, though she hasn't asked for it.

'I told her that she'd just had lesson number one in "Men are Shits",' CJ snorts, laughing.

'You didn't!' Fiona gasps. 'Don't fill her head with all that stuff—she's so little.'

'Relax, I'm only kidding,' CJ says. 'But that's what I should have said, hey? I mean, that's the truth of it, isn't it?'

None of us dares contradict her. We all commiserate. Poor little Jorja.

'What hurts so much is that this happened days earlier, and Jorja had been holding all this inside her, hoping somehow the shame would go away without me finding out,' CJ says.

Fiona pulls her fingers from my hair to put a hand on CJ's shoulder.

'Our children's withheld confessions allow them to grow away from us,' Tam says. 'It's okay for her to have secrets from you.'

Sometimes Tam really is wholly profound. I try to memorise what she's just said, I'm sure I'm going to need it someday.

'It's moments like that when I really feel how short-changed my kids are. With the divorce. And Tom such a fucking non-father. And me so busy and distracted with my clients' shit.'

'You're doing your best,' Dooly says. 'What more could you do?'

'I told her that she is never to buy someone's friendship. It's better to be alone with dignity than to buy friends. And then I went straight to the school directory and called the boy's mother.'

'Did you really?' I ask.

'Yeah, and I wish I hadn't. She said, "I think you should worry more about your daughter being so easily influenced than by my son's entrepreneurial ventures." Then she said, "If Craig told Jorja to jump off a cliff, would she do it?" It was like she was criticising me as a mother and what a failure I am, because my kid is so needy. I was almost in tears myself. I felt so aggrieved, I wanted to say to her, "Do you know what it's like being a single mother? Do you have any idea how hard it is for my children day to day?" But I didn't. I shouldn't have called her. But I have no one to bounce these things off, you know. No adult around to help me process all this stuff.'

CJ is tearful as she speaks. Helen puts her arm around CJ's shoulders and CJ leans her head against Helen's.

'When I put the phone down, I just sobbed and sobbed. Like there was this huge well of grief and rage, not just directed at this smug bitch, but just at how it's all turned out for me. For the kids, you know.'

'It can't be easy, being a single mum,' Ereka says.

'You're doing the best you can,' Dooly says.

'You're doing a great job,' Fiona says.

CJ smiles. 'You're all crap liars.'

'We're not lying,' I say. 'We haven't walked a day in your shoes, and none of us would cope the way you do. You just get on with things. Your kids are lucky to have you.'

'Liam saw me sobbing like that,' CJ says. 'And he came and put his arm around me and said, "Don't cry, Mum. No one in this world is worth one of your tears".'

'That Liam of yours . . .' Fiona says.

'Can I reserve him for Jamie?' I ask. 'I'm sure arranged marriages will come back in fashion one of these days.'

CJ smiles. 'He and the girls deserve so much more—from their dad, from me. How could I have fucked it all up so completely? Choosing such an arsehole for a husband? My kids are effectively fatherless.'

'But they're not motherless,' Helen says.

'And you're bringing them up in a very real way,' Liz says.

'And you stand up for them, and fight for them,' Ereka says.

CJ sniffs. Smiles through her misery. 'So do you,' CJ says to Ereka. 'Christ, I need a cigarette.'

'Have another drink,' Helen suggests. I look at her with wide eyes. Is she mad? The last thing CJ needs is another drink. Some black coffee, maybe.

'I think both of you are very brave,' Dooly says, nodding at Ereka and CJ. 'I can't imagine doing what either of you did . . . And it's not like I've never thought about it. There was this ghastly father at one of the kid's soccer matches a few weeks ago, who was shouting out "You pussy" to his son when he missed a goal. I just wanted to go up to him and tell him what a jerk he was, these kids are just six years old, but of course I didn't.'

'Sometimes we have to bite our tongues and just stay out of other people's business,' Tam says.

'And sometimes we have to take a stand and do what's right, even if it is construed as sticking your nose in someone else's business,' I come back.

'It's knowing where that line is . . .' Fiona says gently.

'And having the guts to cross it sometimes,' Dooly says, looking at Ereka with kindly eyes.

'Thanks, Dooly,' Ereka says. 'But I feel bad because I've put the nail in the coffin of Jake and Ethan's relationship. And even though Jake says he understands exactly why I did what I did, I know he wouldn't have done the same—Olivia brings up issues for me that she doesn't for him, and Jake is just not a smacker. I don't think he has a violent bone in his body.'

'Even when he's stressed?' Helen asks.

Ereka nods.

'That's amazing,' Helen says. 'David is so stressed at the moment, I feel like he is about to explode at any time. In the past month, all he does is shout at the kids all the time.'

'Why's he so stressed?' Fiona asks.

'I think it's that he's trying to bring out a new range for next year, and expand the business, and we've had to remortgage the house. Maybe it's the pregnancy as well,' Helen says. 'I think he's anxious about the financial stress of another kid, and he's been saying he doesn't get to spend enough time with the three we've already got.'

'Those are all valid points,' Liz says.

'He intimated—more than once—that maybe we should consider a "termination". Fuck, what a word, termination,' Helen huffs.

'Would you . . . ever consider an abortion?' Tam asks.

'No, not with a healthy pregnancy,' Helen says. 'I just can't bring myself to do it. It seems so . . . barbaric, now that I've got three kids and I know what a healthy foetus turns into.'

'It is barbaric,' Tam says. 'Very barbaric.'

'Oh please,' Liz says. 'If I fell pregnant again now, I'd have an abortion and thank God I live in a first-world democracy where my life and my wishes count for something against the rights of a tadpole. I am so finished with small kids.'

'I just can't get my head around it,' Helen says. 'And that tadpole is a fully formed baby by twelve weeks.'

'In that case, I've murdered two fully formed babies,' CJ says. 'I've had two abortions . . . and you're right, Hel, it is horrible.'

'Why did you have two abortions?' Tam asks CJ.

'Poor contraception when I was in my late teens and early twenties,' CJ says.

Tam looks visibly ruffled.

'At least David's had the grace to leave the choice up to you,' Ereka says.

'Yeah, but as much as it is my body, it's also his business.'

'If he'd left his penis out of your business, you wouldn't be having to deal with this business,' I say.

Hel laughs. 'Yeah, but every so often, I like him to poke around in my business . . .'

'The only one who suffers is the woman,' CJ continues. 'The men just walk away, while we're the one's left bleeding.'

'Come, CJ,' Dooly says, getting to her feet. 'Let's check out the lights on the water.'

And with that Dooly, with the instinct of a sheep dog, herds CJ out onto the balcony where the openness of the ancient sky awaits to swallow all losses into infinite space.

where you draw the line

Dooly, first winding the scarf around her neck again, has taken CJ out onto the balcony, the social worker in her alert to the early signs of dignity's deterioration. Stepping in, she provides the trapdoor to self-respect, 'let's go for some fresh air'. Such small gestures can save us, a friend's timely intervention; a deflection; the distraction of walking out into the night's sheltering darkness. Kindness is underrated alongside the grandiose traits to which we aspire—intelligence, integrity, self-awareness ...

Helen gets up noiselessly and walks over to the CD player, into which she inserts a disc.

'Is this *the* CD?' I ask her. She doesn't answer me. Helen hoards a stash of 'surprises' for me. 'You're gonna love this ...' 'Just wait till I show you that ...' 'I've got the best present for your birthday ...' Invariably, the saved up treat, a tidbit of gossip in which I have no interest, some chick-lit book I would never read, a movie on DVD I have already seen, will fall short of ringing my bells, but I never grow tired of the way she cherishes the little nothings in life. Our days are flaccid with domestic trivia, rank with nothing special, and the best defence is Helen's skill—a full-blown attack with that ridiculous laugh of hers, of mad celebration.

The music starts and the message of the song is that you should marry an ugly girl if you want to be happy for the rest of your life, because pretty girls are just trouble. Such misogynist crap, but a good get-up-and-dance beat, nonetheless. Helen turns up the dial on the volume and grabs my hand, pulling me to my feet. She starts to boogie in the way that only a short plump curly-haired woman in Ugg boots like her can, ramming me with her well-padded buttom and making absurd pelvic undulations. I copy her, as we both laugh outrageously. In only a matter of minutes, I am out of breath.

'I need more to drink,' I say.

'Me too,' she says, following me to the dining room table.

The tub of strawberry daiquiris is empty. It is a horrible sight. Helen morosely scoops out the last of the mixture with a dessert spoon, taking the first, offering me the second.

'It seemed like so much when I bought it,' she whines. 'How can we be out of it so soon?'

CJ and Dooly return from outside, arms hugging their bodies, Luke's orange scarf around CJ's neck. The bite of the cool night's air has slapped CJ's cheeks pink; she seems chastened, for now. She wanders over to the table to survey what's left in the eating department. Dooly gives me a flicker of a smile. I've never really given much thought to how good she must be at her job, unwearyingly agreeing with Mrs Buchanoltic that the price of eggs has really gone sky-high, while fastening her geriatric nappy before she goes out in public. That takes a special kind of person. The kind I am not.

'What about my bottle of wine?' Liz suggests from the sofa, where she has organised herself with a couple of scatter cushions under her neck and lower back.

'I think if I mix drinks, it will make me giddy,' Helen says.

'Oh go on,' says Ereka, 'you can get as drunk as you like tonight. You're off-duty.'

'She shouldn't get too drunk,' Tam says. 'She *is* pregnant.'

'Didn't you drink when you were pregnant?' Fiona asks Tam.

Tam shakes her head. 'I also didn't eat sushi or oysters, because of toxoplasma that can affect the baby. And unwashed vegetables are also dangerous. They could have listeria, salmonella or campylobacter bacteria. All of which you want to avoid while the baby is growing.' Tam must surely be eligible for an honorary degree in Knowing Better Than Everyone Else.

CJ snorts. 'Well, I drank, smoked and ate whatever I liked during my pregnancies, and my kids are fit and healthy. It's really a bit overboard all this deprivation in the name of the unborn, don't you think?' She grabs a sushi roll, and looks for the soy sauce.

'In that little dish,' I say, pointing to the little green leaf dish.

'No, I don't think,' Tam says. 'It's not a big deal to lay off the alcohol and cigarettes for a few months to give the baby the best chance possible.'

'No need to get so worked up all of you,' Helen says. 'Everyone draws the line somewhere, and I am drawing the line here,' and she puts as much of her head into the empty strawberry daiquiri tub as will fit.

'You're a bloody lunatic,' Liz says.

Helen's head emerges. She is grinning like a Cheshire cat and has bits of strawberry all over her face.

'Go and wash yourself, woman,' CJ says, now unwinding the scarf from her neck and draping it absent-mindedly over the back of a chair. 'Thanks Dooly, I'm warm now . . .' she says. Dooly nods and smiles from the sofa.

'Don't drink any more,' Tam says imploringly to Helen.

'Don't you all get your knickers in a knot,' Helen says. 'But I am going to do a wee, if you'll all excuse me,' and off she toddles to the bathroom.

'Don't forget to flush and wash,' CJ calls after her.

'It's not a number two,' Helen calls back.

'Be sure to take notes so we can have a blow-by-blow account of your adventures on the loo on your return,' Liz says chidingly.

'Have you got something more interesting to talk about than Hel's ablutions?' I ask.

If I don't, please shoot me,' Liz says.

Just like animals should be free to roam, mothers should be free to discuss certain ordinarily taboo subjects. Bowel movements, for instance. Menstruation. Constipation. Urinary tract infections. Sexually transmitted diseases. Without these as available topics, our dinner conversations would be immeasurably impoverished.

Poo is a big conversation piece. We generally steer clear of discussing our own, unless someone's going for a colonoscopy or has had a particularly bad week with haemorrhoids. We *do* draw the line somewhere. But mothers are in the business of bowel movements. We are responsible for both the frequency and consistency of our children's wees and poos. The tarot of our mothering skills is read in the porcelain bowl of the lavatory, like tea leaves in a cup. Constipation signifies that our children's diets clearly lack sufficient fruit and roughage. Last year, Liz cursed about having to rush Chloe to the Emergency ward one night before a huge presentation, because her 'sore tummy' was really two weeks of backed up faeces. Since then, Lily's under strict instructions to write down every time Brandon or Chloe go to the toilet and

must question, 'A number One or Two?' On their fridge is one of those lists that will haunt those two poor kids in years to come (Monday Chloe 111211; Brandon 121121) but which gives Liz peace of mind.

Diarrhoea requires we ply our offspring with fluids because kids get dehydrated with alarming efficiency. And, with a special kind of attention to detail, getting your child to eat corn is revealed as a somewhat hollow victory; those little corncobs come out as yellow and whole from the bottom as they went in at the top. Of course, corn is one of the things Aaron will eat.

But without a doubt, the gold medal for outstanding parenting goes to he or she who, with the least trauma to all concerned parties, oversees the graduation from nappies to the potty to the toilet, to the I-can-wipe-my-own-bum stage. No matter how squeamish, poo-averse or anally retentive we are, the burden of effecting that transfer is ours alone to carry and cannot be auctioned off.

It is an immensely comforting thought that most kids make it into adulthood, nappy-less, with the ability to wipe his or her own bottom, being a relatively important life skill and all. But at which precise point between birth and adulthood we put our foot down and insist on independence is largely a matter of personal preference. Jamie, at the age of two and a half, having observed my toilet habits, simply began to imitate me, and thus ended toilet training. However, by the age of three and a half, Aaron seemed perfectly content to spend the rest of his life in nappies. The preschool he was booked into had a toilet-trained policy. The pre-admission notice asserted with well-meaning condescension (a rabid trait in preschools): 'Please ensure your child is able to handle his or her ablutions independently. We have fifty children to look after, and we'd have no time to teach your children anything, if our staff had to spend all their time wiping little bottoms, would we?'

I had three weeks in which to upgrade Aaron's ablutions. And I took to the task like a woman possessed.

At that time, Aaron was fanatical about dinosaurs. Until then, the vistas of my dinosaur knowledge spanned the following two facts: they lived a very long time ago and they are all dead now. By the age of three, however, Aaron could recite all the Latin names and relay the peculiar eating habits and preferred habitats of each species. Pre-empting a battle, I shrewdly bought a heap of plastic dinosaurs, my currency for the ensuing negotiations. A plastic dinosaur for each poo in the toilet. An uncomplicated transaction. I figured that if a child could know the difference between an Apatosaurus and a Diplodocus, he was old enough to use the loo. I explained the system to Aaron and extracted an up-front willingness to cooperate. It seemed like such a foolproof plan.

But things did not run smoothly. We ran into our first snag when Aaron refused to sit on the toilet, 'just for fun, a chat', as the books had encouraged. 'Get him to make friends with the toilet.' And when he really needed to poo, his screams for me to put a nappy on him drowned out my calm but cunning lures of a new Tyrannosaurus rex. The harder he screamed, the colder my heart hardened. The more he refused the more vividly did I envisage Gretchen Oates, the preschool principal, shaking her head, saying, 'I'm sorry, we just can't take them if they are just not ready to use the toilet.' Ready shmeddy. I'd *make* him ready. In an act of shuddering cruelty, I refused to put a nappy on him. Instead, I grabbed him and plopped him on the toilet. 'No, no, no, no,' he screamed. In the calmest voice it is possible to muster in these circumstances, I told him that the most beautiful Pterodactyl, who kept me awake every night with his cries from my cupboard of 'Let me out, let me out, I want Aaron', was just a poo away.

Aaron stopped yelling momentarily and narrowed his eyes at me. 'I want to hold him,' he ordered.

'Not until you do your poo in the toilet,' I said.

'I want to hold him!!!!' he yelled.

'Will you do a poo in the toilet then?' I asked. He agreed. So off I went to get the new Pterodactyl. Aaron sat on the toilet clutching the new dinosaur.

'Don't need to do a poo,' he said.

So he hopped off the toilet.

'Give me the dinosaur back,' I ordered.

'No, it's mine,' he said.

I snatched that unmerited dinosaur out of his hands and disregarded his wailing and thrashing about with the same calm demeanour one is called upon to muster when a rabid Rottweiler froths at the mouth in your living room. But Aaron got me back. Two minutes later I was cleaning up a poo that he had done between the bathroom and the garden.

Weeks passed in this manner. I, on my hands and knees, buying a three-year-old's poos with plastic dinosaurs. It counts as one of the low points in my life. With sufficient repetition and association, the theory of torture has it that it is possible to get people to do just about anything. It only took another five or six similar incidents before Aaron got the hang of it. By the time preschool started, he had a huge collection of dinosaurs and could poo just beautifully on the toilet.

I have no wish for a psychologist's estimation of the total number of sessions Aaron will need to repair this damage. Some day he will probably be on a couch in a therapist's office, working through the conundrum of why the mere mention of Jurassic Park works like a laxative. Godhelpme if Tam ever finds out about this. She'll shake her head disapprovingly and cite a dozen books that

support a child's need to become independent at his or her own pace. I don't want to know about it. I also don't want to talk about the fact that all of Helen's kids toilet-trained themselves by the age of two—even out of night nappies. Unlike Ereka, who is totally relaxed about when Kylie weans, unlike Dooly, who let Luke drink from a bottle until he started school (and may still do for all I know), unlike Tam, who puts nappies on Michael because he still wets his bed, my patience in certain matters is a little on the parsimonious side. Just as children develop in their own time, so each of us parents at her own velocity. We all draw the line somewhere.

'Shit, I nearly forgot, I've got something for all of you,' Liz says, standing up and heading towards her little maroon suitcase. As she passes me she asks, 'Are you still cooking three different meals every night?'

I nod my head, barely.

'You are your own worst enemy,' Liz snorts. She unzips her suitcase and starts to fish around for something.

I can't argue with her about that. But then again, Liz doesn't care about food. I am aware that in most households one meal a night generally suffices to keep everyone going. In my kitchen, however, there is a menu each night: the adult meal (salmon fillets, Thai curry, lamb stew); Jamie's meal (fish fingers, a lamb chop with mashed potatoes, pasta with homemade bolognaise sauce); and Aaron's (sausages—with the red skin only—or plain pasta—curly only). Even though my callousness extends to forcibly toilet training a child, I cannot imagine the pitilessness of a heart that could force-feed or, even worse, let a child go hungry. While I have zero indulgence when it comes to how it exits, I am prepared to indulge different tastes when it comes to food going in.

Though I do not obsess over nutrition the way Tam does, even I know that bread, pasta and rice don't qualify as a 'balanced' diet. And so, in a spurt of devoted commitment, I once bought one of those cookbooks with 'Meals for Babies and Toddlers', figuring there could be no magic to guilt-free childhood nutrition. I was wrong. With every page, my despondency flared. Each recipe was a malicious jeer. By the dessert section, I had lost all heart. There was a 'Monster Baked Sandwich' with 'strategically placed slices of cucumber, zucchini, carrot, tomato, with bean sprouts for the hair'. Egg Mice. Egg and Strawberry Flowers. I felt particularly oppressed by the Cottage Cheese Clown recipe. On a cheerfully colourful plate lay half an English muffin covered with cottage cheese. The recipe's instructions went as follows:

> make the clown's eyes with the cucumber, cheese and halved
> green beans;
> cut the tomato in half to make a nose;
> make a mouth out of the large slice of tomato and cut the
> remainder of the slice into a triangle for the hat;
> add orange wedges for ears.

The recipe was a dud. It failed to include tips on how to get your child to eat cottage cheese, cucumber, green beans (halved or not), tomatoes and orange wedges in the first place. Moreover, if one were to heed the natural consequences of this recipe and sculpt mincemeat into Bart Simpson and mould vegetables into Sponge Bob Square Pants, would a child ever just be satisfied with a plain piece of toast and cheese? The exponential expectations of little people at mealtimes would destroy me in a week. I tore the book to shreds and poured myself a glass of red wine. It's a calling making sure that one's kids don't overdo sugar or salt in their diets and that there's a balance of carbohydrates, proteins and roughage.

A Life's Work. I can just picture it now on my tombstone, 'Here lies Joanne Fedler. A wonderful mother, who fed her children well'. Problem is, there are other things I have in mind to do with my life.

Some day there will be a Survivor for Mothers show, with an immunity challenge to make the most technically impossible and intricately complicated birthday cake. A street map of Australia. Einstein's theory of relativity. The human body in 3D. Dooly, though an appalling cook, does better with baking and would have a good stab at winning this challenge. I once called her after nine p.m. one evening only to be told, 'I can't speak now, I've got to get to Woolworths because Max has bought the wrong kind of liquorice for Luke's Pokemon cake.' She wasn't joking. Dooly will endure a week of unravelling exhaustion just to have the cake exactly right. Perfectionism is a form of masochism with which mothers are particularly afflicted. Luke, I assure you, would never have noticed the difference but that, of course, is not the point and only someone who has never set herself the task of building a Barbie of Swan Lake out of sponge cake and icing would be so churlish as to point this out.

I'm not saying I'm better than any of my friends. I too have been reduced to food games. Frank and I, on one of the three nights we have gone out together in the past three years, were once attempting to leave our kids with a new babysitter. Aaron didn't like her hair. It was too short. He wanted a babysitter with long hair. In a moment of sheer genius, I sliced his sausage into 'money' pieces and hid them in a hill of mashed potato. I bequeathed him The Magic Spear (a fork), for he had been chosen to seek out the treasure buried in the mountain. But he had to destroy it, or else the forces of darkness would rule the earth. I suggested he just swallow them. Frank and I then bolted for the door.

While Aaron might have been hurried along to the joys of toilet-based ablutions, he exacts his price each evening as dinnertime approaches. Which just goes to show that his favourite toy, despite his huge collection of plastic dinosaurs, is the one he can switch on and off, bend over backwards, snap in half, and stomp all over and which responds to 'Mum' when he needs a bum wipe.

Liz returns to the lounge room with a box. She opens it up—it is full of bottles of nail polish of every colour you can imagine.

'Freebies,' she says. 'We just did their new ad campaign. Take whatever you want.'

We all swarm around the box, despite the fact that none of us—other than Liz—ever wears nail polish.

Without even thinking, I grab the fire-truck red.

'Do you think that colour suits you?' Tam says. 'I'd have thought a more browny colour is more you.'

'Actually,' I say, 'red is very much my colour,' as I open the bottle and begin to paint my nails, uneven and chipped from hours of preparation in the kitchen.

'And I'm sure there's a pale pink somewhere in there,' I say, 'to match your outfit.'

'Oh, I don't use that stuff,' she says idly. 'They're full of toxins ... highly carcinogenic ...'

And with that she leaves me to contemplate, with punctured elation, my deadly red fingernails.

CHAPTER 11

warriors of the witching hour

As I finish painting the nails on my left hand I note that Tam is looking at her watch. I extend my fingers straight out to survey my work. Red's a little wanton for me. I look absurd with red nail polish. A right tart. Mutton dressed as lamb, I can just hear the deluge of snide asides from Frank when I walk through the door tomorrow.

It is that time of the night when, as a rule, I am tucked up in the sanctuary of my own blessed bed, two pillows, one soft, one firm, a glass of water next to me, book in hand, wiping clean the slate of the day, preparing the whiteboard of my brain for the clutter of prattling, bickering and unreasonable demands of tomorrow. 'Beauty sleep', of course, is the exclusive indulgence of the childless. I gave it up years ago.

Helen returns from the loo without a trace of strawberry daiquiri on her face, smelling of lavender handsoap.

It is way past my bedtime—that beautiful oasis to which I hearken all day long, folding me into its hushing embrace, when all demands for this twenty-four hour period have passed and I can finally, selfishly, do something entirely for myself: fall asleep. If I'm not pyjama-ed up and snuggled in by ten p.m., my irritability swells exponentially with passing minutes. I am like a hungry toddler when I am tired—it can get ugly very quickly. A night owl I am not, like Helen and CJ who are both crotchety morning people but can go on all night, nattering away with a glass of wine. But we are all here to sleep over, and though I know I am going to be a ratty cow tomorrow because we'll get to bed later than I can realistically endure and I'll probably battle to fall asleep in a strange house so far away from my kids, there is *no way* we can end this evening early.

The role of party pooper has already been claimed by Tam, so I'll lurch valiantly on towards midnight at least. I have also rented two DVDs for us to watch—*Amy's Orgasm* and *Along Came Polly*—the kind of DVDs from which Frank excuses himself with a smartarse 'I've got some root canal therapy I'd hate to be late for'. It's the perfect mental fluff Hollywood churns out just for nights like tonight. Although any interest I might have been able to muster in Amy's sex life or Polly's antics is rapidly waning. I covet Tam's curfew—soon she'll be tucked up in her own bed, fast asleep. I yawn. Monstrously.

'Don't even think about it,' Ereka says, looking up at Tam from the box of nail polish. In Ereka's lap loll four bottles, a rich purple, a pale gold, a glittery blue-ish one, and a burgundy.

'I've got to get up early tomorrow,' Tam says with that kind of fake regret.

'Got to, got to, got to . . .' Helen says. 'Just say "fuck it, I don't got to".'

Tam smiles wanly. As if we don't understand what it's like to have a gifted child. She looks at us benevolently. 'I really do think I need to make my way home. What about you, Ereka?'

Ereka leans over the side of the couch and stretches her back. The four nail polish bottles clink in her lap. 'No way, I'm having too much fun. I wonder if I could do a whole portrait in nail polish? Do you think there's a market for nail polish art?'

'I doubt it,' Liz says decisively.

'But if it would get you to paint more, I say go for it,' Fiona encourages.

'Yeah, isn't it time for you to have an exhibition or something?' Dooly prods.

Ereka snorts. 'At the rate I'm going, you all can have an exhibition posthumously, and split the proceeds amongst yourselves—I'm sure you'll each at least get a purple tint and blowdry out of it.'

'Such talent, such a waste,' I say mournfully.

'Yeah, next lifetime I'm gonna ask to come back as a gay man and go live on an island somewhere and paint till my fingers bleed,' Ereka sighs.

'I'm sure your art is very relevant,' Tam says to her.

'It's not relevance I lack, it's time,' Ereka says. And then, 'Are you leaving?'

Tam nods.

'C'mon, Tam, don't rush off,' Fiona says benevolently. 'Pretend you're young and single again.' Fiona has finished looking through the nail polish and has chosen two for Kirsty—a nude French manicure colour and a metallic lavender.

'What are those?' Helen asks, eyeing the box a-tinkle with colours.

'Freebies,' Liz says, 'help yourself.'

'No thanks,' Helen says. 'You know me and makeup . . . c'mon, Tam, you can't go yet.'

'Once you go, that's it. Who knows when we'll get to do this again,' CJ says.

'We haven't even had dessert yet, your dessert,' Liz points out. Rich coming from her—the last of the great dessert eaters.

Tam is defeated by all this clamouring. I'm irked at the way she always casts the line of her threat to leave, hoping to hook an attentive affirmation of *stay! stay!* At the rate she's going, she'll leave with a cooler-bag brimming with confirmations that she is wanted. 'Oh all right, I'll stay a bit,' she sighs.

'Good,' I say, successfully mustering a compassionate retort— after all, she did have a nervous breakdown two years ago. 'You put everyone else's needs before yours.'

'Isn't that what mothers are supposed to do?' she asks. And that's Tam to a T. Now my innocent observation is begging for justification.

'To a point,' I say. 'But you are an extreme case. Don't you remember what it was like to be the person you were before you had kids?'

She doesn't even pause before saying, 'I wouldn't want to be that person any more.'

I look at her quizzically. 'Really?'

'I like myself a lot more since I became a mum. Before I had the boys, it was all about me, and that felt pretty empty. Now that I have them, I love having other people to worry about, people whose needs are more important than mine.'

There are two ways of taking what she says. Personally or not. I consider the options. I put my children's needs before my own, don't I? Didn't I give up my career to work from home? Doesn't my life revolve around my kids' activities? Okay, so I haven't taken Aaron off gluten, but I'm just too damn tired to go there.

'It'd be nice to have one or two of my needs met,' CJ says, blowing on her nails which she has slathered with a luscious plum colour. 'Thank God for Harvey.'

Tam wouldn't know, but in the past three years I have waited in vain for a month where I'll have a spare hundred dollars to buy an entirely impractical but devastatingly desirable white fur-lined winter jacket for myself. Or a full-body massage. Or that new technology anti-wrinkle cream that promises overnight results. Instead, I squander whatever remains after groceries each month on impulse purchases for Jamie and Aaron, which neither of them need, but I do so love to see their faces light up when I say 'Have I got something for you!' And as I dole out my last twenty dollars for the Bratz pencil case and Hulk pajamas, I sigh a little internal exhalation of contentment. I am a mother who has children to buy things for. I matter. I put my kids' needs before my own like any other mother. Tam can't lay exclusive claim to that little island of self-sacrifice.

'Before I had kids, I used to be completely self-centred,' CJ says, 'in a good way, I mean. I did yoga, book club, and I even had time to volunteer at the Legal Centre in Redfern. Now I just wish I had time to pay all the bills and catch up on the laundry.'

We nod. I have vague memories of tai chi classes at dawn on the beach, pottery over large glasses of wine, movies and skim macchiatos, meditation weekends in rural retreats, facials and pedicures. I had the luxurious sense that my life was a bottomless pot of golden hours to be dipped into with unrushed languor. I wonder how much of the inclination to parenthood rests on the inability to truly believe, with the mulish conviction of an agnostic, that motherhood, while being a doorway ushering in new experiences, is that same aperture through which all you have ever hitherto held dear will bolt.

'I loved my three month overseas trips,' Helen sighs. 'Venice still calls ...'

'I enjoyed just going to the toilet without being followed,' Ereka says.

'I find you can tell immediately if people have kids or not,' Dooly says. 'You know, it's like, they call at five p.m. to discuss something when kids are going wild and screaming. Or you go into someone's home, and it's filled with ornaments and white lounge suites and you sit there, nervous that your child's going to spill something on it. Or they want a meeting at eight a.m. or three p.m., just at drop-off or pick-up time. Our lives follow a different rhythm as mothers. People without kids think life is a series of adult dinner parties with no mess and no fuss.'

'But that's the reality,' Fiona says. 'Until you have kids.'

'I find it difficult to remain friends with people who don't have kids,' Dooly says, plumping with confidence.

'Now that is the truth of it,' CJ declares. 'In fact, I've recently made a principled decision not to spend time with people who don't have children.'

I halt in mid-brush of my pinkie finger, and look up at CJ. I think of all the amazing, creative, successful, interesting people I would have to expunge from my life if I were to adopt CJ's code.

'That's a bit radical, don't you think?' I ask.

'The time has come for the world to know the truth. That unless you are a mother yourself, you have no clue about how hard motherhood really is,' CJ asserts. CJ's just nabbed Dooly's point by taking it up a notch, but Dooly seems unfazed.

'We all know that it's hard,' Liz says, 'but why write people off because they don't have kids?'

'I'm tired of trying to communicate across a language divide with an alien species. It's why I can't find a man—because men who don't have kids just don't get what I've been through and what it's like to be a parent. When I cancel a date because a child's got a temperature, that's the reason. I'm not looking for an excuse. Get a babysitter, they say. Only someone who doesn't have kids would say that.'

Liz raises her finely shaped eyebrows, thinking what we are all thinking, that she herself would say just that. I look around at this motley gathering of women. At this moment in time they are my closest friends, and yet we are only held together by the gossamer thread of motherhood. We are all warriors of the witching hour. Without kids to discuss, stripped of our rights to grumble and whine to one another, without providing mutual opportunities for intermittent escape, would these connections endure with woody density, or could the hollow husks of these friendships be easily discarded?

CJ's comments pirouette around in my head, snagging a memory from years back. My sister, childless at the time, used to insist on calling me every day at 5.30 p.m. Through shrieks and squawks from my side of the phone, she would blithely chatter away about the crush she had on some guy at her work, while I balanced one kid on my hip, wiped mucus from the face of another, ran a bath, switched off the spaghetti and changed a nappy with the phone crooked under my chin.

Eventually I forbade her to call me after Aaron nearly drowned in the bath one night while I was multi-tasking myself into a frenzy and did not respond immediately to Jamie's nonchalant calling, 'Muuuum, Aaron's wriggling ... and splashing me.' 'Wriggling' was perhaps less accurate a description of what Aaron was doing than 'thrashing for air'. But then again, Jamie was only three and her vocabulary was limited. Actually, while I had paused for that glass of water I'd been trying to have all day, straining to muster enthusiasm for the excruciating details of my sister's libidinal excesses, Aaron had managed to slip down through his bath ring and submerge his head under water. He had been convulsing for air while I was listening to: 'He said, "You're really on my mind", and so I said, "Is that the only place you want me on?"'

As I, sobbing with terror, held my spluttering frightened little person to my chest, the clarity of what it would take for a child to drown dawned. Nothing. A moment's distraction. A phone call ill-timed. A turned back to switch off a bubbling pot. What net of cosmic kindness held that nothingness at bay? Luck? Karma? The angels and fairies? A physiotherapist had once told me, while easing the pain of my sciatica, 'My three year old drowned in our pool'. The swing the child had hopped off was still rocking when the irrevocable was confirmed. In my worst nightmares, that haunting image chills me awake. I never went back to that physiotherapist. I couldn't bear to be near the chasm of her confessed loss.

Thereafter, I became incensed at the callous idiocy of those who call mothers between five p.m. and eight p.m. I carried my self-righteous indignation like a flag. And woe behold the unsuspecting new recruit from market research companies who rang or knocked at the door during that time. 'Tell your boss that people are *busy with kids* at this time', I'd yell into the phone. The more courageous would venture, 'Can I call again at a more appropriate time?' 'Yes,' I'd laugh hysterically. 'In about ten years.' I staggered through the witching hour with trepidation, plugging the hunger and exhaustion-induced mayhem of my crazed, inconsolable offspring, as new leaks and spurts popped in their wake.

'I ended a friendship a few years ago,' Helen says. 'She was a friend from school, childless, still is, and invited me and David and the kids to join her for a holiday on—get this—a houseboat. Not one of my kids was water-safe at the time.'

'Crikey, so what did you say?' Tam asks.

'I told her, "Okay, I'll run around after the kids to make sure they don't fall into the water, and you feel free to just relax". She was mortified. She said, "Oh, I'm so sorry, I just didn't think..."' Helen recalls.

'It's not that she didn't think,' Ereka says. 'It's that she didn't think like a mother.'

We all murmur with approval. It is impossible for a mother to illuminate the neurotic convolutions of her mind to a non-mother. Mothers will extrapolate every scenario's innumerable possibilities, seeking out jeopardy, imagining the worst, assessing the risks, calculating the infinite logarithmic outcomes of any otherwise seemingly benign circumstance. Blake may have 'seen a world in a grain of sand and heaven in a wildflower', but mothers see 'a lost eye in a sharpened pencil; a broken skull in a skateboard...'. Headaches might indicate a brain tumour or meningitis as we check for stiff necks. You never leave a child alone in front of a bowl of soup because—didn't you know?—'a child can drown in a teaspoon of fluid'. The streets of our minds are crowded with a carnival of horrible terrible 'coulds' and we say no a lot, because of this wearying enduring parade. 'The problem with grown-ups,' Jamie once said to me, 'is that they always say no.' I had to concede that 'no' was probably the most overworked word in my parenting vocabulary; but how could I explain to her that she should see 'a world of love in every no'?

'Take someone like my sister, though,' Liz says, 'who has been trying to fall pregnant for nine years now, and just cannot. She is dying to have kids ... and she's very kid-friendly. Probably more so than I am.'

'Dale?' Dooly asks.

Liz nods.

'She's an exception,' CJ says. And then, more kindly, 'How is she doing?'

'They've been told now finally to give up, after spending I don't know how many tens of thousands of dollars on IVF,' Liz says matter-of-factly.

'Poor thing,' Tam says. And for a moment, we all stop. Pause to imagine the unimaginable—that we too might never have been initiated as warriors of the witching hour.

'The two hardest phone calls I have ever had to make were to tell my sister I was pregnant, with Chloe and then with Brandon. And even harder because I was the sister who didn't really care one way or the other about having kids, and she of course has always been maternal, always wanted them,' Liz continues.

'Isn't that a cruel irony?' I say.

'It is one of the saddest things I have ever had to witness. My sister's pain at not being able to have kids,' Liz says, compassion strangely becoming for her.

'Why don't they adopt?' I ask.

'They don't want to,' Liz says.

'Why not?' I ask.

'They want to have their own biological children, not just any kids,' Liz says.

'But surely part of the desire to have kids, is to love a child. Does it really matter what genes it carries or what it looks like. I mean, none of us knows when we are pregnant what our children will look like or who they will turn out to be. And we love them whatever they are,' I say.

'People want to have their own children,' Liz repeats, like I'm a new recruit at her agency being taught that when she speaks, just take her word for it.

'But we don't "own" our children, anyway,' Fiona says. 'Aren't they just on hire-purchase for a while?'

'They are the sons and the daughters of life's longing for itself,' I say.

'What?' Helen asks.

'Kahlil Gibran, *The Prophet*. "They come through you, but they are not from you, and though they are with you, they belong not to you …"' I continue.

'Yeah, they come through you,' Liz points out to me. 'Through *you* being the operative word, not "through an adoption agency".'

'Why don't you donate some of your eggs to her?' Helen asks.

'The problem isn't with her, it's with Frederik—low sperm count,' Liz says. 'So it's never come to that.'

'I think I could donate an egg to my sisters, but not for a stranger,' I say.

'I couldn't do it,' Fiona says.

'Poor thing, missing out on motherhood …' Tam commiserates.

'Imagine never being able to breastfeed …' Helen says.

'Yeah …' Ereka sighs. 'Though in my case, I'm done with it. It's enough now,' Ereka says. 'I have had enough.'

'Yeah, you should stop,' Liz says. 'Kylie's nearly starting school, isn't she?' My eyes grow to saucers. None of us has ever spoken out loud a critical word against Ereka. Liz must be drunk.

'Really?' Ereka asks. 'I know it's gone on a bit longer than I intended, but I didn't realise you had an opinion about it,' she twitches.

'Yeah, well, you don't have to give it up because of me,' Liz says.

'I won't,' Ereka says, her injury surfacing.

'We'd all have to give up eating if you were the measure, Liz,' I say, scuttling to Ereka's support.

'I didn't mean to be judgmental,' Liz says, backtracking. For all her intelligence, sensitivity jostles to get a word in. The virtue of always being right rings hollow when compared with the halted considerations of compassionate silence.

'I admire you for doing it for so long,' Fiona says to Ereka. 'I didn't do it at all.'

'Really?' Helen asks, incredulous. 'Why not?'

Fiona hums a bit, then says, 'I had no milk. Just dried up.'

'That's a myth, you know,' Tam chirps. 'Apparently it's all about hormones and emotions—you have to get enough rest and liquids. Every mother produces enough milk to feed her baby.'

'Well, I must have been an exception, then,' Fiona says, smiling frigidly. And with that, she excuses herself to go to the bathroom. She pads out of the room. Silence follows her.

'Did I say something wrong?' Tam asks in a whisper.

'No, not at all,' Helen says. 'Don't be so oversensitive. She needs to do a wee, that's all. These daiquiris catch up with you eventually.'

Tam darts a look my way to gauge my reaction. I don't know what she has said that has somehow shifted the energy in the room, but I feel it too. There is an edge, where there was none before.

'I didn't mean to be one of those "breast is best" kind of mothers,' Tam says.

'But breast *is* best,' Ereka says. 'We all know that. It's no big deal, some women just struggle, and some don't.'

'I struggled,' Dooly says. 'I mean, I persevered, but I struggled.'

'Yeah, but some of us don't actually like the idea of breast-feeding,' Liz says, 'and it's a pain in the arse to have breastfeeding mothers raise their eyebrows at you when you take out the formula and start shaking a bottle. Some of us can't,' she says, eyeing the door through which Fiona has just exited, 'and some of us don't want to. I had no desire whatsoever to do it, didn't appeal to me at all.'

'You didn't even try?' I ask her.

'No,' she says and shrugs. 'The idea of it was repulsive to me. In fact, I went on business to New York a few weeks after Chloe was born, and my breasts were so engorged, I was standing in a public toilet room expressing, and a huge black woman came up to me and said, "Mam, are you pumpin' and dumpin'?" And I said, "Yes I am." She was so outraged and said, "Do you know there's a breastmilk bank on the corner of 51st and 77th?" And I told her, "I don't have time for that, I'm on business." She practically spat on me!'

'There's a lot of ill-feeling to mothers who don't when they can,' Ereka says.

'As if it matters in the end,' Liz says tiredly, as if we really ought to catch up with where she's coming from. 'Who are we to judge the choices other mothers make? None of us knows what goes on behind closed doors,' she says. 'I didn't breastfeed and my kids are perfectly healthy and happy,' she continues. 'My breasts are part of my sexual identity, and that's how I want them to remain. They're mine, so I should be allowed to have a say in the matter. All this pro-breastfeeding propaganda is just another way in which women get guilted into losing control over their bodies. It's like the abortion debate.'

'Having an abortion and not breastfeeding your babies—how are they the same?' Tam asks, ruffled by Fiona's exit for which she feels responsible, and the spiral of conversation which seems to have slipped from our control.

'It's other people telling me what to do with my body,' Liz says. 'First it was men telling us what to do, and now it's other mothers. Haven't we won these debates? Why do we choose to regress when we live in a first-world country, and we have the right to make up our own minds about what is right for each of us?'

'You've got a point,' Dooly says meekly. She has inadvertently cupped her breasts in her hands and is holding them protectively.

'I'll say,' Liz says.

'Because it's better for the baby,' Tam says. 'It's as simple as that.'

'A baby is only part of the equation,' I intervene, taking over from Liz. If I'm honest, I did perhaps end breastfeeding a little earlier than Jamie would have liked after Frank got a mouthful of breastmilk in a moment of unchecked ardour. 'There's also the mother. What about what's better for her?'

'Well, most mothers,' and I can feel Tam measuring out her words and testing how this will sound to Liz and I, 'feel that what is best for their baby is best for them . . .'

Both Liz and I shake our heads.

'What a load of rubbish,' Liz says. 'Children are separate beings from their mothers.'

'I found breastfeeding much easier than bottles,' CJ says, chipping in with a safe tangent. 'It was a pleasure. I didn't have to go out laden with bags and things, just a nappy and some wipes, and the tits came along for the ride. It didn't even strike me that it was better for the baby—it was just more convenient for me.'

Fiona pads back into a room taut with the righteous tug-of-war among us. She catches Liz's glance and gives her a small smile. She wanders over to the food table, and picks up an artichoke. She pulls off a leaf, and puts it in her mouth. She screws up her face and quickly spits it out. 'Yuuuck,' she says.

'Fi, you have to put some dressing on it,' I say.

'I can't be bothered,' she says. Liz gets up and goes over to her. Together they stand surveying the food. Liz puts her hand on

Fiona's shoulder. There is a quiet understanding between them from which the rest of us are excluded.

I desperately don't want the evening to take a nose dive. With all the similarities we take for granted among ourselves as mothers, it is our differences that most stridently and divisively speak our individuality. We forget what a fraught arena motherhood is, and how the harsh pollutants of our judgments (of one another as well as of ourselves) damage the fragile ecosystems of our friendships. In this world it is not only, as CJ has determined, a battle between mothers and non-mothers. The more bitter acrimonies chafe at the inner thigh of motherhood—between the natural-birth mothers versus the Caesarean-birth mothers; the breastfeeding mothers versus the bottle-feeding mothers; the stay-home mothers versus the career mothers, each of us clawing for justifications and consolations for the choices we have made.

But, even as I feel the edge as I sit among my friends, I have no regrets about having kids. I was lucky to fall pregnant easily and birth mine. But adoption would have been my Plan B. In fact, I haven't given up the idea of adopting in the future. When I articulate this, Frank actually looks up from the television. 'Do me one favour,' he says, 'Just wait for me to die first.' Frank unashamedly admits that the coffers of love and nurturing have been plundered by his own flesh and blood and are bare when it comes to the needs of waifs and orphans.

At least he's honest. But I may still be able to weasel an adoption out of him. I mean, what else is worth doing in this lifetime but loving little people? What could be more significant than teaching a child to tie his own shoelace? What stirs the heart more completely than watching a six year old leave her tooth under her pillow for the first time? What superior human purpose is there than comforting a child when he wakes up from a nightmare? When

I consider all the astonishing accomplishments on earth, the cures for diseases, the scientific breakthroughs, the overreaching technologies that have been invented, I wonder whether it is they that finally matter. Or whether it is the heaven in a toothless grin, saying, 'I love you to the stars and back', that makes the world go around.

'What would you be if you didn't have kids?' I ask the girls, aiming for lightheartedness.

'Thin,' Ereka says.

'Divorced,' Dooly shrugs.

'Fucking a different man every night of the week,' CJ says.

'Exactly what I am now,' Liz smiles, her hand still firmly on Fiona's shoulder.

'A good remedial teacher,' Tam says modestly.

'Travelling overseas every six months,' Helen laughs.

'And you, Fi?' I ask.

Fiona ponders. 'A clueless childless person who rolls her eyes when people with kids sit next to her on the aeroplane. Breastfeeding.'

We all laugh. Liz releases Fiona from her grasp.

'No, seriously, maybe I'd be in some third-world country, doing some meaningful work there, teaching maybe.'

'What about you?' Helen asks me. 'What would you be without your kids?'

I barely think. My answer slips off my tongue before my brain gives the go-ahead.

'Miserable,' I say. 'Utterly miserable.'

mothers don't get sick

Suddenly Helen is holding her tummy. 'Ooooh,' she moans.

'Too much food?' Liz asks.

'It's pregnancy nausea,' she groans

'Do you want to lie down?' Fiona asks.

She shakes her head. 'I'll be fine, it passes quite quickly.'

I come from behind her and put my hands on her forehead, giving it a gentle squeeze.

'Could you not do that, Jo?' she asks kindly.

'Sorry,' I say, 'I thought it might help.'

'I just need to be left alone for five minutes, and I'll be fine,' she says, lowering her head into her hands. I hate seeing her unwell. I rely on her robustness, her invincibility. Helen doesn't get sick. Without her, there is no party.

'Can I get you some water?' I ask. She nods.

In the kitchen, I fill a glass with tap water, and remember I've got some butterscotch schnapps in the freezer for the rest of us. I put the frosted bottle on a tray with eight small shot glasses—maybe Hel will revive in time.

Back in the lounge room, Helen is still in the same position in which I left her, head in her hands. Dooly, Tam and Fiona are looking on, concerned. Liz is sipping a glass of red. Ereka is doubled over, painting her toenails a burnt orange colour, and CJ is on the floor, doing a yoga cat stretch. I pass the glass of water to Helen.

'You sure it's not that tummy bug that's doing the rounds?' Tam asks Helen. 'I was off work all of last week with cramps, vomiting and diarrhoea. And so was most of the staff. My boss was frothing at the mouth—and then he got it.'

'Nah, it's pregnancy nausea,' Hel says. 'I never catch what's going around.' She holds the glass of water, but doesn't take a sip.

'I catch everything that's doing the rounds,' Dooly says. 'My immune system is so shoddy, since . . . you know, last year.'

I smile at her. Someone's got to acknowledge her pain, so masked in the nonchalance of a phrase as prosaic as 'last year'.

'How about some schnapps? It'll put fuel in your tank,' I say.

'What the hell . . .' she says, taking a glass.

'Who else?' I ask, touting for takers.

Helen lifts her head up and gives a weak smile. 'Just give me a moment—and I'll be ready. It will either settle my stomach, or make me hurl.'

She is such a rock, is Hell's bells. Revived from the brink of demise. She's got the constitution of an elephant, like Mrs Large, the mother of Laura, Lester and baby elephant who tries—without success—to have a bath with a tray of tea and some scones away from her children. *Five Minutes' Peace* by Jill Murphy is the bedtime book I always select to read to my kids when it is my turn to choose. The story ends with all three of her kids joining her in the bathtub. Mrs Large gets out of the bath and goes down to the kitchen, 'where she had three minutes and forty-five seconds of peace before they all came to join her'.

I get to read bedtime stories to my kids by six p.m. in winter. The premature darkness gives me a conspiratorial wink. Between early nightfall and my kids' time illiteracy, I can have them asleep by seven o'clock, believing they are having a late night. It is so effortless to abuse their trust. But exploit it I will, if it means I can get them to sleep more quickly, because that is when I love them the most. Even when I am unravelled with exhaustion, devotion for these maddening, beloved creatures seeps into my bones, when they are silent and needy-less. Only then can I exhale, and confess my own unforgivable frailties: I am tired. I have a headache. I don't feel so good.

As mothers, our right to get sick belongs in the same category of rights as joining a travelling circus of knife-throwing, fire-eating gypsies. It is overly ambitious—not to mention downright foolish—to contract a raging temperature, a mind-splitting migraine or anything as lingering as a slipped disc. In the event of such ill-fated circumstances, the best advice is: pretend. Feign health. 'I'm just fine, thank you.' Dose yourself way over the 'should-not-operate-heavy-machinery' threshold, and carry on regardless. Because if children sense weakness, you are done for. They will tear you to shreds.

In much the same way Aboriginal people have no concept of Western 'ownership' of land, children have no language for maternal illness. Children are designed without the synapse that connects the words mother and sick, and are as blind to a mother's sickness as they are unmoved by our suffering. *Mothers don't get sick.*

'So have you had to take lots of time off work?' Tam asks Dooly.

Dooly nods. 'But I've run out of sick leave and compassionate leave, I think I'm in leave-debit at the moment ... I just drag myself to work no matter how I'm feeling because I just can't face telling my boss "I won't be in today".'

'I hate having to call in when the kids aren't well. You can just hear the resentment, as if I'm taking a day off to go see a movie or go to the beach,' Tam says, declining the schnapps.

'You should hear the tone when you have to call to say "My husband isn't well". If it's not a heart attack or cancer, there's no sympathy. Especially if it's because of depression . . . there's not a lot of understanding about mental illness,' Dooly says as she smells the schnapps before having a sip. 'Mmmmm, yummy . . .' she says approvingly.

'When Gabriel's sick I have to cancel all my appointments for the day. Some of my clients who are mothers understand, but my male clients just don't get it,' Fiona says. She holds her glass, but doesn't rush to taste it. 'I'm always scared I'll lose a client if I say no, so sometimes I get a babysitter in and end up paying her what I've just made in my hour of work,' she grumbles. 'But I shouldn't complain, at least I'm my own boss.'

'Workplaces are not mother-friendly,' Liz says. 'They're not designed to be. If they were, they'd be running at a loss. I won't have,' she says, gesturing with her hand.

'Oh come on,' I say. 'Just try it,' I plead.

'What part of no don't you understand?' she asks me, lightly but enough to sting. That's the catchphrase we use in anti-rape advocacy. This is just a shot of butterscotch schnapps, for fuck's sake.

'That's a bit harsh,' Ereka says to Liz. 'As a mother yourself, how can you justify that workplaces don't help mothers out? It's why every working mother I know is torn between work and home.'

I find myself nodding vigorously in concurrence. Dooly and Tam join me.

Liz laughs. 'Look, for those of you who believed the feminist propaganda that women can and should be able to have it all—family, career, sex life—just look at the reality. How many of you are happy with the mothering you are doing and feel fulfilled at work?'

Fiona tentatively puts up her hand.

'Yeah, well you run your own business,' Liz says.

'I still feel torn . . .' Fiona says.

'So what is your point?' I ask Liz. 'Do you think it's perfectly okay that workplaces don't give a shit about mothers?'

'As a boss, I understand the financial realities that you just can't have an unreliable workforce that depends on whether little Jonny has a snotty nose, or little Suzie's twisted her ankle, or little Patsy's mother wants to go on a school excursion. You just cannot run a business like that.'

'You are the anti-feminist,' I tell her. 'Why don't you stand for government? John Howard would just love to have you sprouting all that family values crap.'

'I just tell it like it is,' she says.

'But it's not fair,' Dooly says.

'You sound like one of my kids when I tell them it's time for bed. Yes, it's not fair, but that's how it is.'

The body language in the room has subtly shifted. Liz's legs are crossed, as are her arms. Some of us have turned our bodies away from Liz's conservative philosophising.

'How can you defend such injustice?' CJ pipes up.

'Because I am first and foremost an employer, and this is a man's world. If you want to succeed in a man's world, you can't let pregnancy and motherhood interfere with that. Get yourself a Lily,' Liz says to us. 'I've never had to stay home or cancel an appointment because of a sick kid.'

Fiona laughs uncomfortably. 'She's always been conservative—as long as I've known her,' she says of Liz. 'At school she tried to convince our PE teacher that there shouldn't be separate girls and boys races at the sports carnival and that we should all race against one another.'

'I still think we could've beaten the crap out of those pansies,' Liz says. Despite the distraction of Fiona's reminiscing, it sits unspoken among us—the canyon between the financially secure and the financially insecure, despite our shared 'middle-class' label. The telltale signs of economic security: 'get a Lily'. The smug comfort of those who never worry about having enough money at the end of the month when rent has to be paid three times, instead of two due to a quirk in the calendar. I look at Dooly. She smiles back at me. Unified in our quiet disdain. I've weathered similar clueless derision from men before. It's much uglier in women, though.

'But I want to be with my kids when they're sick,' CJ says. 'I have to get a babysitter in if I'm due in court or there's something I just can't change. But I feel so guilty about leaving a sick kid with a stranger.'

Helen sits up now, unruffled by the tensions in the room. 'You're all trying to cut yourself up into too many pieces,' she says. 'What's wrong with just being a mother? You're all so stressed out trying to do everything.'

'Maybe some of us want more out of life than changing nappies and ferrying kids to and from their after-school activities,' Fiona says, shrugging. I find myself thinking that if Liz were my old school friend, I'd take her aside and tell her to tone it down a bit. I think Liz's boldness sometimes stuns Fiona into a fugitive silence—she so seldom ventures a strident opinion.

'Well, it was good enough for my mother, and it's good enough for me,' Helen says.

'Times have changed, Hel,' Ereka says. 'Isn't there so much baking and burping you can take? I think we're lucky we've got opportunities our mothers never had, but in some ways it's harder to have the choice and not be able to fully exercise it. Sometimes I wish I hadn't been born with such a yearning to paint—I'm always so disgruntled feeling like I never get to do what I was put on this earth to do. And anyhow, what are you gonna do when your kids grow up and leave home, Hel?'

Helen cocks her head to the side, smiles and says, 'I'll go to Italy for three months. I'll bake cookies for my grandchildren. I'll go to matinee movies, and I'll drink lots of wine.'

I am trying to gather my thoughts but Dooly, who has been sitting nestled in silence, suddenly talks in a tone that is surprisingly assured. 'Liz, the injustice of how the world works is not a small thing, like bedtime for your kids. I'll bet women in every country feel the unfairness of it. It's a gender battle, and when I hear a woman defend the way things are, it just makes it more difficult for women like the rest of us who really enjoy being mothers, and also enjoy our work, to have a fair go at doing both.'

I give Dooly a huge grin. She may not be able to say boo to a goose but she can tell Liz where to get off. And without an ounce of offensiveness. But she's not finished.

'Some of us can't afford to or don't want to delegate mothering to hired help, and some of our households depend on our incomes. It's a catch-22. And for most of us, it boils down to a choice between working and feeling guilty for missing out on school concerts, and doing homework, or staying at home, being a full-time mum and missing out on promotions and advancements, and being bored witless sometimes. If that's what we choose, our sacrifices are often invisible to our husbands and children. Staying home all day with kids looks like "doing nothing" in male-speak. Which is a laugh, really, but is reinforced by women in the workforce who apparently think the same way. It's a gender problem, Liz. Like it or not. Because there are two things I am pretty confident no man I know has grappled with: how to insert a tampon and how to juggle work and family.'

Dooly gets to the end of her diatribe and is glowing with indignation. I have never been more proud of her. Beneath all that dowdiness, Dooly is a fired up feminist, sharp as a whip. How motherhood has encrusted her with scaly domesticity.

CJ starts clapping. I join in. Ereka and Tam follow. Even Fiona, tentatively.

Liz shakes her head. She's used to disgruntled employees.

'Can we just agree to disagree,' she says, blithely.

But I seize my chance. I want a concession from her. I bring out the big guns. 'What would you do if one of your children was diagnosed with a terminal illness?'

She exhales and gives me a strained look. The shadow of her mother's early death hovers close, and I want to pull it closer. 'What do you want me to say? That I'd give up work and stay home, and be a perfect mother . . . I don't think about my children dying and I don't think about myself dying.'

'Well, you should, because it could happen,' I say.

'What do you tell your kids when they ask about death?' Helen asks, motioning for me to pass her a glass of schnapps, which I do.

'I tell them I'm not going to die for a long time, and that they're not going to die for a long time, and that when it happens, they will be ready for it.'

'And they're happy with that?' Helen asks. Liz nods.

'They've inherited your resilience,' Helen says. 'Nathan got so upset when I told him that I'm gonna die someday. He thinks I'm invincible because I can fix plastic swords with sticky tape and remove splinters and know where babies come from.' She dips the tip of her tongue into the glass.

How bittersweet is that thought. Our children don't believe we can get sick or die, because in their worlds we are omnipotent, omniscient. We're endowed with the comforting touch to heal all manner of heart sores, including best-friend meanness; not-being-invited-to-a-party rejection; being-called-horrible-names sadness; and being-branded-uncool cruelty. In the cradle of our arms, in the soothing tones of our lullabies, the world is a safe place of butterfly kisses. A never-never land of unbreakable hearts and happily ever afters.

But someday our cover gets blown. A goldfish floats to the top of the bowl. A grandparent passes away. CNN broadcasts live from the Middle East and we don't get to the remote control in time. And our children turn to look at us with tears in their eyes, and say, 'I don't want *you* to die, Mummy.'

So we hold them and rock them and ease their minds with our words. We tell them we are young and well. And that life is long and precious. And that all things die. Someday. But that day is far far away. We utter these inanities even as we anxiously await biopsy results, and cross our fingers that the 374 en route from Bondi Junction won't knock us down tomorrow. We tie ourselves up in bogus assurances. For their sake as well as our own.

We are terrified of frailty, that blood in the stool, that migraine aura, that darkening mole, anything that might rob us of our ability to care for our children. When a baby cries, there is a cellular override in our bodies that can dull the pain of a fresh Caesarean incision or momentarily shift a blinding headache to the backseat

so that we can respond. Not that we are indispensable—Liz has shown we are not—but our children make us feel that way. The crushing weight of that apprehension is enough to induce psychosis. Lovers who tell one another, 'I cannot live without you', are borrowing from the authentic emotional narrative of the love between a child and her parents. I am convinced it is the insight of this symbiotic neediness that largely accounts for the ubiquity of postnatal depression. Once we grasp, with penetrating lucidity, the sacred implications of parental responsibility, a concession of defeat before even trying is probably the only truly rational response.

'Imagine having a terminal illness,' I muse, 'and having little kids to look after . . .'

'Like my friend Marion,' Fiona says.

'What's wrong with her?' CJ asks.

'Ovarian cancer,' Fiona says darkly.

'Is she going to be okay?'

'No,' Fiona says. 'They got it too late. She's having chemo, but they're saying she's only got a couple of months.'

'God, that is terrible,' I say. 'How old are her kids?'

'Eight and six, two little girls, Emily and Janet.'

'I cannot bear to think of it,' I say.

'How old is she?' CJ asks.

'Forty-two,' Fiona says, sighing. 'She's young.'

'How would anyone handle that?' Tam says. 'It's not part of the bargain, is it, when we decide to have kids.'

'But you know what I found really interesting,' Fiona says, her voice soft with pain, 'as soon as she found out about the cancer, she just started withdrawing from her girls. She hardly has anything to do with them any more, she leaves their care up to her husband, her mother and the nanny.'

I'm struck by Fiona's choice of word, 'interesting'. It is heartbreaking is what it is. 'Interesting' is for anthropologists and scientists, not mothers like us.

'Wow,' Helen says. 'That's heavy.' We all stop what we're doing. Thinking of Marion.

'I think if I knew I had two months left to live, all I would want to do is spend as much time with my kids as possible, you know. Just fill up . . .' Ereka says.

'We can't judge her,' Liz says. 'We don't know how we would react in her situation. She must be broken inside.'

'Maybe it's just too hard to say goodbye,' Tam suggests. 'Maybe she's in denial.'

'What about closure?' I ask Fiona.

'She's written letters to both her kids for when they're older, and bought them presents for their eighteenth birthdays, beautiful diamond necklaces and matching earrings, which she asked me to buy and wrap for her,' Fiona says. 'It's very sad.'

I feel hot tears prick my eyes. 'Dear Lord, what a distressing task.'

'Yeah, I didn't enjoy it, but I feel very moved to be part of it,' Fiona says. 'And someday I will tell those girls all the stories I can remember about Marion. In fact, I've starting writing some down so I don't forget.'

I think to myself that I really should go for tests to check out those stomach pains I get. And maybe get a mammogram. A colonoscopy. And an ultrasound for my ovaries. Since Jamie's birth, my preoccupation with my health has escalated. Frank calls it my freakish obsession. I am consumed with thoughts about Fiona's friend Marion. I wonder whether she spent most of her mothering years as a stay-home mum or as a working mother, thinking that she had all the time in the world to be a mother to her girls as they flowered into adulthood, only to have it snatched away from her.

I feel a churning sickly feeling in my belly, that good old friend fear, that swept into my life on the day Jamie was born and attached itself to my skin like a leech. On the day that Marion dies, the sun will continue to shine and the traffic will go on flowing. People will tell jokes over coffees as they always do and the newspaper will still get delivered. Only two little girls will be struck by how odd it is that for everyone else it's a day like any other—sunny with some showers in the east, expected traffic delays along the Hume Highway, regular decaf lattes and daily newspapers which do not (how could they not?) blaze the headline that has changed the world forever: MUMMY DIED.

I wonder why I didn't think all this through before I decided it would be a good idea to have children. Or why, when I fell pregnant, no one took me aside and said, 'What'll your baby do if you die?' instead of congratulating me. I do have a faint memory of lying in the bath sometime during my second pregnancy and weeping for no reason, as if a tide of sadness was washing through me. Hormones, the doctor called it. Maybe it was an inkling of how unprepared I was to promise a child my immortality.

My faith feels so rickety in the oncoming unpredictable storms that life will bring. My confidence in my own health is so flimsy when I consider how much longer I need to be around to remind Aaron to wash his hands before dinner, to turn the car around because a news item for 'Show-'n'-Tell' has been left behind, to run onto the field at half-time with a bottle of Gatorade, fit Jamie with her first bra, a perfect dress for her formal, buy Aaron his first razor and remind them both about safe sex.

Liz is the only one among us who has had the foresight to put structures in place so that the world will continue even if she dies.

Perhaps she is like Moses when God appointed him to lead the Jewish people out of Egypt, who said, 'Why me? I'm just a humble shepherd with a stutter. Find someone else.' And so Liz found Lily.

The rest of us, foolhardy pilgrims blinded by groundless conviction that 'all will be well', blithely soldier on, never pondering who will take up the slack if we are struck down in mid-stride. Maybe we could all learn something from Liz, who does not revere motherhood as if it were written in stone, decreed by heavenly dictate, unexchangeable like a soul mate, but rather treats it like a favourite outfit you can choose to wear or lend out. And that would certainly be useful on days when we feel sick.

All those who'll drink it have a glass of schnapps. 'Here's to good health,' I say.

We all clink our glasses and down the schnapps. Like a glorious shot of caramelised morphine, it burns all the way down.

Five minutes later I am holding Helen's head over the toilet bowl as she brings up my butternut-ricotta pancakes, Thai curry—without the coriander—the sushi, the salad and even those beautiful artichokes which don't look as good coming out as they did going in.

Contrary to popular conviction, mothers do get sick. Especially on a cocktail of strawberry daiquiris and butterscotch schnapps.

what'll the neighbours say?

I return from the bathroom, a bit ashen myself. Vomit and I are not easy companions, despite my abundant encounters with its viscous, intermittently lumpy, desiccated mass. But somehow my own children's vomit is infinitely more tolerable than that of anyone else's. Even my dearest Helen. I feel pretty nauseous myself now.

'How is she?' Ereka asks me.

'She'll be fine, but she had a big one,' I say, shuddering.

'There are consequences to that much eating,' Liz says haughtily.

'Oh go jump off a cliff,' I say.

'Like Thelma and Louise,' CJ chimes in.

Ah yes. *Thelma and Louise*, depending on how you look at it, is either a great feminist statement, or a pitiful reminder that women would rather drive off a precipice than be shackled to male control. I personally felt vindicated when Thelma and Louise emphasised that there are consequences to men's bad behaviour, like refusing to apologise for sexist gestures and touching a woman without her consent. Admittedly, emptying the barrel of a gun in someone's chest or blowing up his truck could, if you wanted to split hairs, be construed as somewhat of an overreaction. But on the other hand, maybe not.

A friend of mine once reversed into a man's car deliberately because he had touched her on the bottom as she walked past him. 'It was sheer bliss,' she said dreamily when I asked her how it had felt. 'Insurance covered it, so it cost me nothing, but the look on his face when my battered-up old car slammed into his new BMW—well, that was priceless.' I am certain that at a particular point in my life—pre-children—I could have equalled such indignation had a stranger, without invitation, placed his hands on any part of my body. Especially my belly. So when my pregnant tummy began to show and people approached me, hands first, to pat it, I had to remind myself that a correctional facility (while your mother serves out her sentence for grievous bodily harm) was a less than ideal place for my unborn child to start life.

Though there are established social taboos, workplace policies and even laws that regulate how, when and where it is acceptable to stroke other people's bodies, these injunctions seemingly don't apply to pregnant women. That baby bulge, apparently, is there for the fondling. Hand in hand with this norm is the expectation that pregnant women are to graciously acquiesce to the fondles of all those who are fondling-inclined.

Pregnancy strips us of our right to bodily autonomy in the same way that the state prosecutes an assailant on behalf of an injured party, who is only there as a state witness. Similarly, in pregnancy, we become our baby's ride, nothing more than a living incubator. So when a pregnancy (in *our* bellies, causing *our* bulges under that ridiculous pinafore-type shirt we wear, resulting in *our* babies, for which *we* will be financially and emotionally responsible) is untimely or undesirable for whatever excruciatingly personal reason, we must plead and beg to obtain state 'permission' to terminate, which may or may not be granted under certain compelling conditions and within particular time-frames. Like it or not, once that sperm fuses with our ovum, that clump of mitosis becomes state property and can be used against us in a court of law.

With the same unrestricted entitlement they feel towards taking the weight off their feet on a park bench, older women approach us with the brand of alarming familiarity usually only manifest in co-dependent family members and mothers-in-law, declaring noisily, implacably, 'It's a boy—look how it's sitting.' Or 'I know a girl when I see it—I've had six. With girls, the mother is ugly, with boys, she glows.' We are expected as civil members of society to suffer this onslaught of agonising scrutiny and babbling opinion with good-natured grace, without ever battering a geriatric with her own walking stick or offering to give her a ride to the nearest RSL to do something useful like play the pokies.

Unhappily, once the baby's out, the focus moves from our bellies to the contents of our strollers. Strangers will stop us in the street to kiss—yes, put their god-knows-where-they've-been lips to our babies . . . uugggghhh. Matronly bystanders will proffer unsolicited counsel—'It needs a burp', 'Have you changed its nappy?', 'Maybe it's tired'. The accepted mores of pregnancy and new-baby etiquette dictate that appreciative smiles and courteous acquiescence are called for. Wherever we go, henceforth, the eyes and ears of strangers are now attuned to us like high-frequency radars. There is no privacy in motherhood. Nappies and all, it is the ultimate public and political arena.

Unfortunately for Frank, a series of unfortunate circumstances conspired against him one memorable summer's day when he bore the brunt of a stranger's interference. It was one of those unbearably hot January afternoons where the family outing is doomed to

failure; but staying in all day is a threat to the cat's life, the very walls of the house and whatever intermittent stalactites of fragile sanity still cling on. We drove past a beach at which Jamie, five at the time, declared she wanted to swim. The parking lots, however, were jammed with cars and long queues. So on we drove. But Jamie, with the determination of a Rottweiler, insisted that she wanted to go to *that* beach. We explained. Nowhere to park. If we could, we would. Sorry, but there'll be another beach. We'll have ice creams and a wonderful time will be had by all. End of story.

But Jamie wanted *that* beach. *That* beach. By now, even the airconditioning had turned on us, blowing hot sticky air, gluing us to our car seats with perspiration. Parking within walking distance of a beach was an option rapidly diminishing, when finally, blessedly, someone was reversing out of a spot just as we drove up. It was not at the beach Jamie wanted. We piled out of the car. Jamie refused to get out. She whined and growled. We cajoled and implored. She screeched and thrashed. We promised and threatened. She got out of the car. All the way from the car park to the beach, she publicly drew attention to her dissatisfaction with piercing screams, while I waddled ahead with Aaron in my arms.

Eventually Frank exploded. 'You go to the beach with Aaron,' he told me, 'I'm taking Jamie back to the car. She doesn't deserve to go to the beach.' And with that, he picked her up yelling and kicking and stormed back to the parking lot.

In that unappealing condition, perspiring inconsolably, fuming with irritation, and clutching a squirming squealing five year old who was screaming, 'I want my mummy,' Frank attempted to open the car door. A stranger, a middle-aged woman in an ill-fitting bikini, approached.

'Who is this man, little girl?' she inquired of Jamie.

I believe Frank gave her a perishing look.

'I'm her father,' Frank told her.

'Is he your father?' the woman asked Jamie.

'No!' Jamie screamed. 'I want my mummy.'

Perhaps we all nurture the humble fantasy of someday rescuing a child from drowning, an old man from choking, or in this woman's case, a child from the grasp of an indisputably obvious pedophile. This was her chance.

'Lady, I understand you are motivated by the best intentions, but right now you are interfering, my daughter is having a tantrum and I am trying to teach her a lesson,' Frank told her. She left reluctantly. Disappointed.

When he relays the story now, Frank does so with enormous admiration for this meddlesome stranger, who took her life in her hands in approaching him on that day. Frank still claims he feels 'dirty' at the obvious implications of her intrusion. Perhaps if more strangers were willing to pose uncomfortable questions, fewer children would be abused and neglected. But the reality is that, on the whole, mothers are not abusing nor neglecting their screaming, bawling, hysterical little darlings. Generally speaking, most mothers are just trying to get through the day, without losing their minds and without attracting the prying eyes, accusing questions and interrogating glances of strangers who wouldn't swap places with them—not for a winning Lotto ticket. As mothers, we know we are a condemned breed. Damned by our children, castigated by others and, mostly, by ourselves.

Here, though, in the lap of our friendship, we can confess our terrible sins. Each week one of us has a story to share about some hideous maternal atrocity we have committed. Once shared, we can live with the guilt. Sometimes, the stories even seem funny, and our laughter sets us free. In the ubiquity of our imperfection we take heart.

Helen returns to the lounge room, triumphant.

'Are you okay?' Tam asks.

'Perfect,' she says. 'And ready to start again, anyone going to join me?'

We all groan. For now, we are all full. Helen returns to the table with renewed enthusiasm to start all over again. The rest of us are rubbing our bellies and yawning. We have no children to put to sleep, no sexual advances to dodge. Tonight, we are unencumbered.

And just at this point, Tam's mobile phone rings to the tune of Beethoven's fifth symphony.

'I thought you switched that thing off?' CJ says to her.

Tam actually blushes. 'I had to keep it on . . .' her voice trails as she ferrets in her bag for her phone. 'Excuse me,' she says, embarrassed, and opens the door onto the balcony before answering the call.

'Fucking Kevin can't even put those kids to sleep without her,' Helen says, returning to the lounge room with a full plate.

'But why does she keep the phone on?' CJ says. 'If the phone was off, he'd just have to cope, wouldn't he?'

We all silently agree. Tam, we all know, is a 'perfect mother', but nestling within our chocolate-covered praise is the sourball of our censure. Sometimes you can be too perfect I muse, watching her through the window, standing on the balcony with her back to us. Is her brand of motherhood an innate outpouring of devotion, or the inflations of over-compensation . . . for what, though? Her own mother's conditional affection? A deflection of emotional energy from Kevin's infidelities? What peculiar brand of distress is responsible for this unwavering dedication? It is just as well Tam is indifferent to our opinions of her. Not even within our inner circle is safety assured. Even among our nearest and dearest, there is still the heart-stopping fear: 'What will they think of me?'

'She's always on duty,' Liz says as if reading my thoughts.

'That's how she wants it,' CJ remarks.

The conflagration of our disloyalty is as sudden as it is delectable. I shift uneasily on the sofa. But I comfort myself in the knowledge that Tam talks about me behind closed doors. Helen has let slip a few comments that Tam has made about how I mother Aaron. There is a silent understanding among us that as soon as our backs are turned, we are all fair game. Helen and I have gossiped about Tam's neurosis and how she sublimates all her energy into her kids because it's just too hard to face what Kevin is doing. Liz and I have commented that 'all Ereka needs to do is say no to Kylie breastfeeding once and for all'. Fiona and I have wondered how CJ's sexual frustration will affect her kids later on in life. When Liz's been unavailable, we've all clustered around the feeding pot of our denunciation of her hands-off approach to her kids like a gaggle of hungry chickens.

'Do you think she ever doubts that what she's doing is wrong?' I ask. 'I mean, I so often feel like I've made a mistake ... but I get the feeling she never does.'

'She never does,' Helen says.

'She doesn't seem to ...' Dooly says.

'If she does, she'd never admit it to us ...' Ereka says.

'Maybe we could torture her with gluten and extract a confession from her ...' Liz says wickedly.

We chuckle. As mothers, we are always playing to an ever-present jury—the neighbours, the strangers we stand next to in supermarket queues, our children's teachers and, of course, one another. Keeping up appearances, withholding that admission we are so eager to wrest from Tam, is therefore vital. Mothers must, like illusion artists, exude the chimera of being in control, making the pitch from one awkward boo-boo to the next appear seamless, and as if this screeching, shrieking attachment to our leg is normal: 'Gaylord's just had a bad day'; 'Seymor's just very tired'; 'Angelina's disappointed we have to go'. We pretend that the constancy of the effort is not unstitching us down the midline. That we don't crave to switch it off, leave it on the side of the road or sell it on eBay. That the smear of jam or mucus on our shirt has no impact on our self esteem. That we actually intended to go out with a sticker on our bum saying, 'Big Fat Liar', or 'Beware: Sudden Farting'.

'At least she doesn't have to worry about DOCS,' CJ says. 'Which I do all the time.'

The Department of Community Services (DOCS) is always on the lookout for those of us who, despite Nature's nod of approval that we are indeed fit to be mothers, are totally unfit. Conduct such as torture, cruelty, neglect and abuse are all tell-tale signs that we're not managing the stress of motherhood as well as we could and DOCS ought to find other mothers for our children. I am terrified of DOCS. I am terrified because from the screams and yells that emanate from our house, any reasonable neighbour would be entitled to conclude that my children are the victims of a pair of warped vindictive psychopaths masquerading as parents. In fact, ask Aaron and he will probably agree that I *do* torture and abuse him: I insist he eats at least half of his peanut butter toast before he is allowed his juice. I remain steadfast in my command of 'tidy your room before you watch television'. I am also pretty confident that years of watching Barney the purple dinosaur will someday be regarded as a form of psychological torture.

CJ laments that of all the privations TFB inflicted on her, having to move from a freestanding house to a semi is easily the cruelest. Every 'Go to sleep, you brat!', 'If you hit your sister again, you can sleep outside tonight', and 'Shut up and don't answer back you little shit' is gossip-fodder for the neighbours. 'I'm living

in a glass bowl,' she complained to me one night on the phone. 'I can't even shout at my children in peace, without Mrs fucking Hernandes giving me dirty looks in the morning.' Life in a flat or semi or an apartment is torment for a mother. There are too many common walls, curious ears and witnessable transgressions. All mothers must be able to stop the show every now and then and retreat to the dressing room of her imperfection. Or in Tam's case, the balcony of her perfection.

'Yeah, let's just hope Tam doesn't dob us in to DOCS,' Liz says.

'Now we're being nasty,' Dooly says. I wonder if social workers are genetically incapable or just rigorously trained to resist the delicious illicit gratifications of gratuitous backbiting.

Frank, however, is no social worker. I still smart at one of the cruelest jibes he has ever hurled my way. I was leaving to check out the park at which we were having Jamie's fifth birthday party the following day, so I would know where to hide the clues for the treasure hunt. I had only spent the past month organising the party. The invitations had each been fastened with a ribbon attached to a balloon that said, 'Special Delivery by the Party Fairies'. I had lain awake at night devising seven brilliant interlocking clues that would eventually lead to a large stash of treasure—a gift, individually wrapped and labelled for each of the thirty invited children. This was going to be the most spectacular, unforgettable, exciting birthday party on the planet.

'Get a life,' he said to me.

Frank just didn't get it. It is an intricate business organising a children's party. Success hinged on the checking and double-checking of every fine detail. The execution of this spectacular treasure hunt depended only on good weather and cooperative children. I had seen to the rest.

Of course, neither the weather nor the children obliged. It was windy—my clues blew away, the children got bored, fought over the puzzle pieces, and one of the more zealous competitors spotted the treasure long before the final clue led to its detection. By the end of the morning, I had a migraine headache. On the way home in the car, Jamie had snarled that I was a 'horrible mother' when I suggested she wait until we got home to open her presents. It was a disaster no matter which way you looked at it.

Back home, I collapsed on my bed. As I lay listening to Jamie ripping wrapping paper and ploughing through new gifts, each of which held her attention for all of thirty seconds, a tidal depression engulfed me. I swore blind I'd *never* do another kid's party again. That was it. It was over. Frank came to sit on the bed beside me. 'You care too much,' he said. 'It was only a kid's party.' But then he said more kindly, 'To them, it doesn't matter how much effort you put in. More is never enough. Really, when it comes to kids, less is better.'

The simplicity of his remark hit me like a slap to the temples. A cringing insight dawned. What had all this fuss been about? Jamie? No—she'd have been just as happy with a five dollar sponge cake with five candles and a movie, as long as I'd called it her 'birthday party'. Was it for me? I can make chocolate leaves in my sleep and stuff a mushroom like it's nobody's business—I have nothing to prove to myself. No, as pathetic as it sounds, this was my declaration to the world: 'Look at the kind of mother I am. Look to what lengths I go to make my child's birthday special. See all the time and effort I have put in? Aren't I a good mother?'

But the truth is that no one even noticed or cared about the extravagance of my efforts, and the ones that did notice called me crazy. Helen, who heats up two pizzas and hires a DVD for her kids' parties, was especially ridiculing. 'You're a real sucker for punishment,' she had sniggered. When it comes to my own misfortune I suppose I am, as much as I hate to admit it, the undisputed author.

'Is anyone in the mood for dessert?' Helen asks now, having just completed a second helping of everything. Her empty plate sits on her lap, traces of coconut milk and a stray leaf of rocket marking the site of her second innings.

'I am!' Ereka says.

'All right. We'll just wait for Mary Poppins to come back in and melt her chocolate,' Helen says. She takes the rocket leaf and wipes up the coconut milk before eating it up.

From the comfort of the galleys, we all snigger at Tam in the dock of our judgment, enjoying the fact that for now it is she, not us, who is subject to peer verdict. It's just a matter of time before we will take her place. At some point, we will all fail and be found wanting. Even by our dearest friends.

If I consider it, there has only been one person who has spared me his judgment. And of course, I fell head over heels in love with him. Ask any new mother, and she will tell you she is besotted with her children's pediatrician. Helen jokes that she scours for any excuse to take her kids to see Dr Strickland. Her lust for him (and he is middle-aged, paunchy and combs a ribbon of hair over his bald patch) is driven by the fact that 'he's just so . . . so . . . nice to me. He asks me how I am and he actually waits for the answer. He cares that I've had disturbed nights, and he comforts me that they will soon pass.' And, she says dreamy-eyed, 'he puts his hand on my shoulder when I leave, and tells me to "take care of myself".' It's a veritable seduction if you ask me.

In those early days after our babies are born, our children's pediatricians are just about the only adult male company we get. Other than our depressed sex-starved husbands. I saw Aaron's

pediatrician's eyes above his facemask in theatre moments after I had given birth. He handled my newborn baby with a tenderness and respect that aroused my desire, despite the spinal block numbing me from the waist down and the gaping entrails of my abdomen awaiting suture. In the weeks that followed Aaron co-operated—he became colicky. Then he obliged me with chest colds and ear infections. Lactose intolerance. Then he needed grommets. Unfortunately, after the grommets were put in, he got well. Those waits between vaccinations dragged on and on. But eventually I could rely on an unexplained temperature, a runny poo or a few mosquito bites to warrant another visit. I would eagerly join the other new mums in the waiting room, made up with exaggerated effort to hide those black rings under my eyes, wearing clean clothes for the first time in five weeks. And there we'd all wait, each of us believing that somehow we were special. Eventually my turn would come, and batting my eyelashes at the doctor and flashing my most flirtatious smile, I forged ahead, undeterred by the challenge to remain alluring with fresh posit all over my shoulder.

But unfortunately the world is not made up of our children's pediatricians. It is made up of ordinary, stressed people in a hurry, whom we only hope will turn a blind eye to the mayhem of our mothering instead of condemning us or dobbing us in to DOCS. Show me a mother who hasn't said a prayer of thanks for the blessing of a closed door behind which she collapses into a scream, a good cry, or hysterical laughter.

Tam comes back in. 'Sorry,' she says apologetically. 'Just needed to say goodnight to my boys—they couldn't sleep without hearing my voice.'

We all smile. And secretly stoke the embers of our silent censure.

CHAPTER 14

dignity, above all, dignity

Tam scampers off to the kitchen to start melting the chocolate. Our all too hasty smiles on her return from the balcony and our keen inclusions of her into idle musings about how the specials at Kmart compare with prices at Target were a dead give-away that we were bitching about her. But she scurried past us, pretending not to care. Once Tam's dessert is made, her duties accomplished, she will be able to leave, which is what she's been angling for since the pancakes. I have stretched out on my belly on the couch in the lounge room, and can hear her clattering about in the kitchen.

Helen says she's going to see if Tam needs any help and makes for the kitchen. But really, she's going on a peacemaking expedition—how much help does anyone need to melt chocolate and pour it over frozen berries?

I confess that I am not a huge fan of frozen berries, they're altogether tasteless and unless you know what you're eating, they might just as well be frozen peas for all your tastebuds can tell. Frozen foods do not move me. I mean, I am grateful and all that I live in the twenty-first century to benefit from such mother-loving inventions as freezers, tumble driers and dishwashers. But the idea of eating frozen berries—much like threesomes and beach picnics—is considerably more alluring than the experience itself. Flavour lives in such close proximity to the life force that once the malevolence of polystyrene, plastic wrapping and microwaves have had their way with food, it is somewhat battered and exhausted, with only a faint allusion to former glory—much like our bodies, all these maternally occupied years down the line. It's a pity we can't freeze our pre-pregnant bodies and hire another one to use for our childbearing years.

'How's the sexiest bum*b* in the park?' Helen says, giving my bottom a pinch as she goes past to help Tam out in the kitchen.

'Every inch still there,' I say, laughing.

'Helen's got a thing for your bum?' CJ asks.

'Naah, not her. Some old fella,' I chime. 'Last week I'd just done a lap of Centennial Park and was getting back into my car when an old man knocked on my window and motioned for me to open it. I was in a huge rush to get to school to pick up the kids and was irritated that he might ask for money or, even worse, a ride somewhere. I rolled down the window and said, "Yes? Can I help you?" and in a thick European accent, and between several yellowed and missing teeth, he told me, "You've got the sexiest bum*b* in the park",' I say, trying to give my best rendition of his accent.

'How disgusting,' Liz declares. 'Weren't you offended?'

'That's harassment,' CJ says.

'Are you kidding?' I say. 'I won't have a bad word said against him. He is the first person to have flirted with me in years. It made my week.'

'I see dignity is not high on your list of personal attributes at the moment,' Ereka says teasingly.

'Welcome to my world,' I say. 'When it comes to male appreciation of my body, I will unashamedly accept all offers.'

'Yeah, I'll also take what I can get,' CJ quips in.

'Dignity, girls, above all dignity,' Liz drawls at us.

Let's face it—the fresh meaty bodies we once possessed, these days are no more than the corpuscular equivalent of defrosted mincemeat. But I console myself that it is still possible to whip up a fine bolognaise sauce with thawed mince, and get away with it if you truss it up with a dash of red wine and a few well-placed bay leaves. At some point, you've just got to work with what you've got.

And right now, despite my banter about elderly strangers, what I've got, if I can bear the truth of it, is phone call envy. Tam's goodnight call has exposed an emotional stowaway on board the vessel of my ridicule: that my children have gone to sleep already without my having told them 'I love you' perhaps for the first time in their lives. Did I tell them 'I love you' before I sped off this afternoon? I can't remember now. We are big, my kids and I, on proclamations of love, the more outrageous and ridiculous the better. 'I love you up to the highest mountain,' Jamie says. 'And I love you down to the mermaids,' Aaron responds. 'I love you to the galaxies, the most distant stars, the furthest point in space,' Jamie says. 'But I love her more,' Aaron competes. 'No, you don't,' Jamie quips back, instigating a conflagration of hostilities, so that no one is left loving anyone at all.

I can't shake the superstition of this thought that maybe in my haste to escape from my children I've just broken a chain of 'I love yous' so cherishingly assembled. I need a distraction and so I pull out Little Nutbrown Hare, one of Aaron's favourite toys, from my handbag and start to sew on his left foot with the needle and thread I keep in my Mother's Survival Kit alongside my pendulum.

200 secret mothers' business

Little Nutbrown Hare is a wobbly bit of material full of beans whose foot has frayed, and who has been leaking a slow trail of innards all over the house. I have been carrying him around in my bag for weeks, wrapped in plastic, waiting for a moment to fix him. He is the soft toy that goes with Sam McBratney's book, *Guess How Much I Love You*, a lovely story in which Little Nutbrown Hare tells Big Nutbrown Hare that he loves him up to the moon. To which Big Nutbrown Hare responds, 'I love you to the moon—and back.'

The book and Little Nutbrown Hare were one of my first purchases as a 'mother-to-be', when I was just a few weeks pregnant with Jamie. All teary-eyed and dribbling with announcements of 'I'm pregnant' to the gum-chewing, nose-ringed teenager behind the counter in the bookshop, who just shrugged and said 'Cash or credit?', I wanted the world to know I was going to love my babies. And how I do love them. Frank often suggests that I drop the 's', because 'you're supposed to mother them, not smother them', he reminds me. I can't help it. They bring out an intensity of emotion I did not know existed until they got here and wrenched it out of me.

'Motherhood and dignity don't hang out together,' CJ says. 'In fact, I'd go so far as to say they're on totally different sides. You pick a team, and you're at war with the other one . . .'

The girls all chuckle.

'Wouldn't it just be more convenient all round—not to mention much kinder—if they told us at that first gynaecological check-up to abdicate and check in our sex appeal, sex drive and anything "taut", "pert" or "unblemished", at the counter, upfront, sign on the dotted line,' Dooly asks.

'You all just give up too easily,' Liz says. 'You can always get warring factions to negotiate. That's why Lilys were invented.'

'Even you must have had some low moments in pregnancy,' I say. 'Surely you didn't outsource the gestation did you, Liz? Or is there something you're not telling us?'

'Ha!' she chortles. 'If I'd thought it through properly, I might have ... And yeah, I didn't much enjoy leaking breasts while chairing a meeting.'

'My favourite was discharge that looks like soft-boiled egg whites,' CJ says.

'Piles,' Fiona chirps.

'Losing my hair in great clumps. Actually my episiotomy was pretty rough,' Dooly says.

'Do you think we'd have gone through with it if we'd known the full extent of the toll on our bodies?' I ask.

'It *is* magical and miraculous as well,' Ereka offers.

'At times,' Dooly adds.

'Well, nobody's going to tell you the truth, are they?' CJ says. 'Our mothers all just want grandchildren so they sure as hell aren't gonna say, "don't do it", the medical profession would go bankrupt if we all stopped procreating, and the government needs us to churn out future generations. It's a grand conspiracy of silence. A trap, and we're the bait.'

As CJ speaks, I recall during my newly pregnant joy trying desperately not to mind as my body slowly turned into a bloated blue-veined vessel for the life that was taking root inside me. I consciously reminded myself (every time I looked in the mirror) to resist the socialising forces of an anorexic society, which dictate that women should have lean and slender bodies. I reread Andrea Dworkin. But there was no escaping it—I was fat, and it made me miserable. For the first time in my life, men looked at me kindly, patted my head and offered me their seats. I started to crave one look of lust, one chauvinist remark, like 'hey sexy'.

As the weeks became months, my body began to feel like a portaloo I was lugging around with me. Frank watched in fearful fascination as I stacked pillows around myself in a desperate attempt to find comfort at night, alarmed that he was responsible for the gargantuan cushion-monster I had become. I taught Frank to chant the mantra for when I was begging for drugs in childbirth, 'Accept the pain, accept the pain,' which he did, with a look that only marginally concealed his concern for my mental health. 'Thank God I'm not a woman,' he said more than once. At least it was honest feedback on just how horrible a distortion I had become.

'I think getting mastitis, a week after Jamie was born, was probably one of my low points,' I say.

'I also had mastitis,' Tam says, returning from the kitchen with a tray of frozen berries and a pot of melted chocolate, Helen by her side. 'It was horrible.' She puts the tray down on the coffee table.

'What the hell is that?' Helen asks.

'Only someone who has never experienced inflammation of the breast ducts because your baby is not latching properly would be so ignorant as to ask,' I say. 'And just for good measure, it comes with a raging temperature, in my case, the crippling tenderness of a Caesarean scar, breasts rock hard to the touch, pain as if your breasts have been doused with petrol and set alight, and a screeching underfed newborn, oblivious to the anguish of its food source.'

'It sounds like a walk in the park,' Helen says.

Ignoring Helen, I ask Tam, 'Did you put cold cabbage leaves on your boobs?' I feel endeared knowing we have something in common for a change.

'I did,' she says.

'What for?' CJ asks.

'It's supposed to help,' I say. 'But then again, I was desperate. I would have rubbed Mongolian goat turds on my breasts if anyone had suggested it would help.'

'And did it?' Dooly asks.

'Who the fuck knows? It was either the cabbage or the antibiotics. But I smelled funny for weeks. Frank would turn to me, sniffing in the middle of the night and say, "What *is* that smell?" and I'd just clench my teeth and say, "Me, okay?" And he'd smile weakly and murmur, "Oh", before turning his back and pretending to fall asleep again knowing that he'd just sabotaged any chance of sex in the next year. Sadly though, neither of us have had the same relationship to cabbages since then.'

'That's no great loss,' Helen says.

'You're just not thinking right about cabbages,' I say to her. 'What about sweet and sour red cabbage with honey and aniseed. Or stuffed cabbage with rice and dill . . .'

'I can live without cabbage,' Helen says.

'I went to see a lactation consultant,' Tam says, clearly unmoved by the loss of cabbages from my culinary repertoire. 'It really helped.'

'What for?' Ereka asks.

'To show me how to breastfeed properly,' Tam says.

'Isn't breastfeeding supposed to come naturally, like breathing or urinating?' Helen asks.

'Often A-type personalities, you know, perfectionists, control freaks, find breastfeeding a challenge,' Tam says.

'How hard can it be?' I ask. 'Africa has survived on the bosom of breastfeeding mothers. Without the aid of lactation consultants and breast pumps.'

'It's not a left-brain activity,' Tam says, as if that explains it. I don't have a clue what she means.

'So what did you do there?' Helen asks.

'I sat on a couch in a lounge room with seven other new mothers, while Barbara "but please call me 'Barbie'", tweaked and twisted our nipples into our babies' mouths at fifty dollars an hour per head.' Tam smiles, sheepish now. 'It was like this coven of delirious, bloated and bewildered young mothers, wincing when the suction felt like clothes' pegs on our breasts, or silently crying while babies bawled and buckled in frustration. But every now and then we would all get it right, and there would be a silver thread of silence for a few precious seconds.'

'I didn't even realise some women couldn't breastfeed,' Ereka says.

'Yeah, it was much harder than I thought it would be ... But I got it right in the end. I was glad to have got it right.' Tam says.

'Breastfeeding is what saved me,' CJ suddenly says.

'Really? How do you mean?' Dooly asks, eyeing the pot of melted chocolate and sliding the tray towards herself. It seems like she's forgotten all about the orange scarf, which still hangs over the dining room chair where CJ left it. I'll bet Luke is tossing and turning in his bed. Not.

CJ inhales deeply. 'I just got to love my body again, because it knew what to do. Despite the fact that Tom had found me repulsive during my pregnancies, and had been screwing around, my body was still something beautiful.'

There is a large pause as each of us absorbs this information. We all knew CJ booted Tom out, but none of us knew why.

'I hate men who don't find pregnant bodies beautiful,' Helen says.

'It's quite common,' Tam says wryly. 'So much of Kevin's work is done on women post-birth, to get it all back in place for husbands who are not interested in their wives' bodies any more.'

'Fucking men,' CJ mutters.

'How did you know he was screwing around?' Liz asks, leaning forward, a gesture of intimacy.

'That is a story in itself,' CJ says. 'But if I don't get a cigarette, I can't tell it.'

'I've got one for you,' Fiona says, making for her bag.

'Fiona?' Tam says in disbelief. We're all incredulous.

'Oh so fucking what?' she says, the word 'fucking' sounding outlandish and prim coming from her. 'I only have one every now and then,' and with that she hands over a packet of Dunhill Lights to CJ.

'There's no smoking in here,' Helen says. 'My parents would have a fit.'

'Don't have one,' Tam says. 'You've been off them for months now.'

'And look at what a wreck I am,' CJ says, hitting the underside of the pack and holding up a slim white cigarette.

'You'll be sorry,' I say, but CJ ignores me.

'Are you coming?' she says to Fiona. Fiona inhales deeply and follows. She and CJ go outside to the balcony.

With that there is a hushed silence in the room.

'Can you believe Fiona smokes?' Dooly says softly.

'Can you believe Tom was fucking around while CJ was pregnant?' I say.

'It's really common,' Tam says, 'for men to freak out when their wives get pregnant.' I look at Tam. I get the feeling she's telling us something, but she doesn't say anything more.

We all sit quietly contemplating our men's reactions to the changes pregnancy wrought on our once-were-luscious bodies. Dooly succumbs, and dips her finger into the pot of melted chocolate. Liz leans back and squeezes her temples with her manicured hands. Ereka collects her hair and twists it into a braid.

Tam takes a frozen berry in her fingers and puts it in her mouth. Helen looks at me, I look at Helen. As we sit, waiting for CJ's return from the balcony, her lungs balmed with corroding nicotine, I consider how seven years of motherhood have stripped me of all the tantalisations of my former self. Whatever vanity I once possessed, mostly accrued by the privilege of youth, has fled my clutches.

Glenda Kierans. Why I suddenly remember her is no mystery. She was the wife of that man I had a crush on when I was twenty years old. We'd all been sitting on the beach and Glenda, who must have been in her forties, took my arm with affable firmness and walked me along the shore. 'It's obscene to grow old,' she said to me. And then she gave me a look I can picture perfectly in this moment. It was a look that took it all in—the way I noticed with barely concealed disgust her pubic hairs sticking out untidily from the crotch of her bathing costume; my vain comparisons of our limbs—hers dimpled with cellulite and speckled with varicose veins, mine smooth and browned by the summer's sun; my proud pitying of her, unfairly advantaged as I was, she so past it all, and I so utterly gorgeous.

She should have said, 'Leave my husband alone, little girl', but she had more dignity than that. She charitably permitted me to wallow in the unjustified limelight of my youth, only alluding to the inevitable justice of it all that someday I, too, would be the forty-year-old mother with a husband hankering for a glimpse of an unwrinkled cleavage. And that is all I was back then—an unwrinkled cleavage. I understand that now.

In those days, I would agonise with hair-wrenching gloom over the size and imperfect pertness of my breasts. I minded terribly about clothes size as if the difference between a 12, a 14 or 16 were matters of life and death. But now, like Glenda Kierans, I am happy

if I can fold my breasts into a sensible bra and find a pair of trousers in my cupboard without some inexplicable stain on them. The odd grey hairs on my head that made their first appearance sometime during my second pregnancy have meandered south for the winter. Of late, the wrinkles between my breasts have extended their lease into full-blown ownership. I cover up in those large and ridiculous SPF50 ultraviolet protection t-shirts on the beach now, and douse myself in sunblock. Bolting the door after the horse has fled the stables, I admit, but what's a girl supposed to do? Surrender? Call on Kevin for a nip and tuck? Not I. At least, not yet.

Most of us will chirrup that having our beautiful children is worth all the distortions, mutilations, wounds and physical indignities that follow—the stretching and tearing of perfectly delectable body parts, the slicing open of unmarked bellies, the diffusion of tight hazelnut nipples to the size of small dinner plates and the foreverness of those stretch marks.

'It's amazing really that any of our husbands still want to fuck us,' Helen says, as if reading my thoughts.

'Oh come on, Hel, that's crazy. We're still beautiful—in a different kind of way,' I say.

'In a sumo-wrestler kind of way?' Dooly offers.

'I'm proud of my body,' Ereka says. 'I know it's not much to look at these days, but it's loaned so much of itself without expectation of reward, it's done some hard yards, earned its medals and has been a kind and generous vessel for bringing life into this world.'

'Well said,' Tam says to Ereka.

'And I think that Jake appreciates that . . .' she says wistfully.

'I'd like to get my body back,' I say. 'I want a self of my own to return to, for someday when all my work as a mother is done. So I can go kayaking around Australia. Or hiking in Spain. Or on a walking tour of Tuscany with other middle-aged women and widows when my children have flown the coop and Frank is sailing around the world on his yacht. I still have plans, even if they don't include sex appeal.'

The girls laugh softly.

We all share the same fate—though motherhood has sapped us of our dignity, our taut and unscarred bellies and our haughty breasts, fate has not been entirely unforthcoming. It has bartered our youth for something else: acceptance. I know that's not very romantic, but it takes the edge off the grief. So we don't have flat bellies any more, but our strong arms can do the seamless transfer—from the car seat to the cot—without waking the baby. The breasts we once barely covered with itsy bitsy teeny weeny bikini tops are no longer male eye-magnets, but they've stopped a baby's crying. Handsome men don't scare us any more. We are mothers, for godsake. We can wipe a bottom squeaky clean with the very last wipe, remove all traces of vomit from cashmere, and tell whether a child has a temperature just by feeling its forehead with the back of our hands. Don't fuck with us.

Here, together, the unspeakable secrets of motherhood are laid bare. That our bodies are riddled with incrementally worsening imperfections, like the hairs on our big toes the beauticians always wax off at no extra cost to the full leg wax, the smell of our menstrual pads, the patches of hair we are losing, the menopause that is beckoning, the distinctive odour of our husband's day-old semen oozing out of us as we bustle between drop-offs and pick-ups. It is an unloveliness in which we all share and pretend is not there, and that we laugh about until we cry.

Three years ago, when Tam had her operation to fix the vaginal-birth induced incontinence—she couldn't sneeze, laugh or cough without wetting her undies—we all pitched in for the most colossal bunch of pink roses, with a card that read: 'If you can't be a good example, then you'll just have to be a horrible warning'. And when we get together and we're drunk enough, we do a show and tell and compare: whose got the biggest tummy flap? Whose breasts are the saggiest? Whose varicose veins the ugliest? Whose stretch marks the most hideous? Invariably someone's got worse breasts than you, but your flap is bigger, or someone's got horrible stretch marks but your varicose veins are worse. There is comfort in displaying all our horrors to one another and in the shared reality that none of us will be spared the fate of decrepitude. And as soon as anyone gets too depressed, we bring out more wine or another plate of something fabulous to eat.

We've done a spring-clean on our heroes. Gone are the days of coveting a body like Bo Derek or buns of steel like Jane Fonda. We now know that women do not age naturally like Cher. Our new champions are Jamie Curtis, who recently posed for a series of real middle-aged photos and Maya Angelou, who jokes that her breasts are having a competition to see which one can reach her knees first.

In this bevy of middle-aged bodies, riddled with premenstrual, menstrual or post-menstrual hormones, there are twenty-one pregnancies (including four miscarriages), seven Caesarean sections, ten vaginal births, and godknows how many days of mothering on the clock. Hundreds of punishments, time-outs, treats and rewards. Thousands of kisses and cuddles and of telling little people, 'I love you to the moon and back'. It's an impressive tally.

Little Nutbrown Hare's left leg is now fully re-attached. I sigh and return him to my bag with a great sense of accomplishment, for I am A Fixer of Wobbly Bits—as long as they aren't attached to my body.

Helen stands up. 'It is time for us to eat again,' she says. 'Are you men or mice? Squeak up.'

I look down at my belly, which has become a horrible warning of the obscenities of growing old, and mentally tell myself that I will not have any dessert.

Saying 'no' is sometimes the only way we can show that we love ourselves—to the fridge and back.

CHAPTER 15

a hunchback in a bikini

Aside from Dooly's stray finger, and the single berry Tam ate, Tam's dessert remains untouched. The melted chocolate, like a brittle spinster, has hardened in the waiting. I imagine Tam will take it personally. I should make a point of telling her that if you want people to trust your food, you have to trust it yourself. Our fears overshadow even our best intentions. There's no substitute for honesty. Tam's so scared of her own dessert that she's inadvertently put us off it too. The frozen berries, now thawing, are bleeding on the plate. They're only good for a smoothie now.

Suddenly that kids' song pops into my head, the one about the 'big brave mouse' who marches through the house and declares that he's scared of nothing . . . except for a cat . . . a dog . . . a mousetrap . . . and so the list grows. Like that mouse I, too, am 'not afraid of anything'. And since motherhood my list of exceptions has expanded exponentially.

I confess that courage has never been my middle name. I have always been nervous by disposition—scared of big waves, flying, boys in fast cars, cancer, roller-coasters, anaesthetics, and the list goes on. I am also (forgive me Ereka) terrified of being fat. Though I am probably fat by certain adolescent standards, I refuse to meekly submit to that label. I was once thinner. Before I had kids. But, contrary to all reasonable expectations of losing my pregnancy kilos, fuelled by myths of breastfeeding as an assured weight-loss regime, that weight did not just slither off me like a sloughed pelt of blubber after birth. It has hung on with gritty determination. From the grimace on my midwife's face as she ripped my stomach muscles apart, I knew with unsullied clarity that the days of my flat ironing board of a stomach were over. In its place, I now have a flap. A flap is something, I must admit, I could have done without.

Which is why when Helen says, 'Who's ready for zabaglione?' I get a clenched feeling in my belly—somewhere in the vicinity of my flap. CJ and Fiona have returned from the balcony, the leeching odour of smoke sneaking in with them. Smoking. It's a tricky one to hide; its smouldering betrayals, like those that cling after a huddle around the barbie, call for a vigilant suppression. It explains Fiona's cleanliness fetish. Does she sneak down to the end of the garden or lock herself in the downstairs loo for a smoke on the sly? I am quite thrilled at the thought that she has a secret life, even if it revolves around a pathetic carton of fags emblazoned with the warning, 'Smoking Can Kill You'. It's more than I've got. Some of us eye Fiona cautiously—trying to sniff out what other little devilish activities she's covertly engaged in. The smoking. The kickboxing. It's like she's living two lives. Others of us are restless with agitated curiosity to hear CJ's story. But first, there must be dessert.

When it comes to sweet food, I cannot and would never vie with Helen. She is the queen of the cherry-on-the-top, the final taste left in the mouth, the undulating tones of vanilla pod, crème fraîche, cocoa and strawberries. If I am, among my friends, the

Iron Chef of the savoury, she is the mistress of the mousse. Willy Wonka would have keeled over for her.

But I distrust desserts. In much the same way that I am wary of sweet-talking men. Desserts are the Don Juan's of the dinner table, seductive but calorie concealing, allowing one a faint rush of pleasure which deserts one later in the misery of the bathroom scale. A spoonful of sugar may help the medicine go down, but it also makes your flap hang low. And right now, mine needs no more help. Liz, of course, sees a good time on a plate and condescendingly declines to be pleasured. She just smiles and says, 'No thanks.'

Helen's dessert tonight is zabaglione, the classic Italian dessert made of egg yolks, caster sugar and Marsala wine stirred over simmering water to a thick cream. Its perfection—which has been known to cause people to roll their eyes in ecstasy upon tasting— requires a dedicated serenity I simply do not possess.

I stand up and head for the kitchen to boil the kettle—the only way I am going to make it through the quicksand of the zabaglione is with a stiff cup of black coffee. I admit it, I am scared witless of Helen's desserts.

When I return, a steaming mug in my hands, the girls are all clustered around the dining room table, slurping up Helen's sugared masterpiece and CJ is saying, ' . . . I thought I was going mad . . .'

'Back up, CJ,' I say. 'How could you start without me? Start again, please,' I implore. I squeeze my bottom onto Helen's chair, although our two behinds are really more than one unfortunate chair can reasonably accommodate. She shifts up and I brace myself against the table.

CJ sighs. 'I was just saying how my first two pregnancies were not great. Tom didn't want to have sex with me at all. I thought that was just normal . . .'

We all nod, familiar with a concerned husband declining sex during pregnancy, afraid of 'hurting the baby'.

'So I thought, okay, this is just a passing thing,' CJ continues, in between mouthfuls of zabaglione. 'It was quite hurtful at times. He didn't ever touch me, or my tummy, throughout the pregnancies. And he didn't want to be present at the births either. He said it would affect how he saw my "cunt", as he put it, which I suppose should have alerted me to his state of mind.'

'What's wrong with calling it a "cunt"?' Helen asks. 'I like that word.'

'Do you?' Fiona flinches. 'I find it . . . crude.'

'Oh, it's okay,' I say. 'It's when and where . . .'

'Yeah, in the right context,' Helen says. 'It works a treat for talking dirty during sex . . .'

'That would just turn me off,' Fiona continues.

'So when you want Ben to touch you there, what do you say, "please touch my vagina? My female genitalia"?' Helen asks.

Fiona grimaces. 'I don't really have to use words,' she says, clearly reddening. 'You can do a lot with body language . . .'

'I find you don't really ever have to ask a man to touch your fanny,' Liz says. 'It's more like asking him to stop, that's a problem.'

'Even if you want him to stop, you still have to call it something,' Helen says.

'Just saying stop usually suffices,' Liz says.

'The point is that CJ was *pregnant* at the time,' Fiona says, labouring the word.

'Yeah, you can't call a vagina a cunt when you're pregnant,' Ereka agrees. 'That's just fucking disrespectful.' The others, excluding Helen and I, nod.

I wish we could pursue this conversation so I can gain some understanding of how our genitals get promoted to the desexualised

sanctity of 'vagina-dom' in pregnancy, and then go back to common cunthood sometime post-birth. But we have interrupted CJ's story, and given how long we've all waited to hear 'what really happened' it takes precedence. 'Please go on,' I say, looking at CJ.

CJ hungrily returns to telling her story.

'Tom wanted sex really soon after Liam and Jorja's births, long before my body was ready but I complied because I knew he needed it. But then when I fell pregnant with Scarlett, it was like he couldn't bear my physical presence. I'm sure I repulsed him. And you know how you just sometimes know things . . .'

'Intuition,' Fiona says.

'Female right-brain activity,' Tam adds.

'I knew from early on that something was very wrong. He was working late all the time, and even more unavailable than he usually was. We were booked in for an ultrasound, and he was meant to come and join me. And he just didn't show up. I called him on his mobile, but it was on voicemail. When I finally got him, he made up some bullshit excuse about a meeting. And so that night I confronted him. I just asked him straight out, "Are you having an affair?" The outrage that ensued was, I suppose in retrospect, very telling. He called me a jealous cow. Mad. Insane. Paranoid. Hormonal. You name it, I've been called it.'

I am aware of a burning sensation in my chest, partly because I know what's coming. The loneliness CJ is describing, the distrust of one's own sanity, has a resonance that feels ancient—women have been branded insane and hysterical since the beginning of time.

'You know he was so convincing that I actually believed that I was going mad. I just could not shake the feeling that he was with someone else, but every time I raised it, he laughed at me. And I started to get scared that maybe I *was* losing my mind, because

I used to trust my feelings and I could no longer tell what was real and what was not.'

'Jesus!' Ereka exhales. She has paused, her spoon midway between bowl and mouth.

'How did you find out?' Liz asks. 'Were there other tell-tale signs?' She shifts in her chair. Crosses her legs.

'You won't believe this. It was actually very simple. One night, he was in the shower and had left his mobile phone on the bed. Without even thinking, I picked it up and pressed redial. I had no idea who I was calling, whether it would be a business colleague or what, but I just dialled.'

'And what happened?' Helen asks, captivated.

'A woman answered the phone. And I said to her, "I apologise if I have got the wrong person and if I sound like a mad woman. This is Courtney-Jane Cranson, Tom Cranson's wife. Are you having an affair with my husband?"' CJ says, grimacing.

'What did she say?' Dooly asks.

'There was a stunned silence for a minute, and then this woman said, "I am so, so sorry. I didn't know he was married".'

Not a word is spoken as we all take this in.

'Fuuuuuuuck . . .' Helen says.

'And I said, "Yes, he is. He is the father of my two children, Liam and Jorja, and we are expecting our third child in eight weeks' time".'

'Phew,' I say.

'And then—get this—*she* started crying,' CJ says. 'It was the weirdest thing. Here *my* life was falling apart, and *she* was crying. And you know what, I felt sorry for her. And I told her I was finished with him and she was welcome to have him. And I gave her our address and I told her to please come and pick him up because otherwise he would have nowhere to sleep that night.'

'This is like a movie script,' Dooly says.

'That was brave,' Fiona says softly.

'And when Tom came out of the shower, he found a suitcase on the bed, and I said to him, "Please pack your stuff and get out of my life and our children's lives. Both they and I deserve better. Your girlfriend will be here to pick you up in a while".'

'Did he deny it?' Liz asks.

'No, he didn't.'

'Did he say sorry?' Ereka asks.

'No, he didn't. He left that night, and came back once more to get some of his stuff. I let him know when Scarlett was born, that she was a girl named Scarlett—it was a name he absolutely hated when we'd discussed names, and I told him I would be changing all the children's surnames to my maiden name. And that was that,' CJ says, exhaling. She has not touched her plate of seconds yet, and now looks at it anew. 'I've actually lost my appetite in telling that story,' she says, pushing the bowl away.

'What a thing to have gone through,' Tam says, placing her hand on top of CJ's. Fiona puts hers on top of Tam's. I put my hand on CJ's shoulder, and Helen puts her hand on CJ's other shoulder.

'You know, it was my worst fear,' CJ says. 'I always feared that someday my husband would fall out of love with me and leave me. And he did.'

'You poor thing,' Tam says quietly. Moments pass, as we all mentally traverse the emotional heights of deceit, abandonment and rejection our friend has scaled. Alone. We close ranks in our enfolding esteem for her courage. She is a hero. We love her. No one will ever judge her again.

'And maybe I somehow co-created the situation,' CJ sniffs.

'Oh bullshit!' Liz says. 'It wasn't your fault. Why do women always do that to themselves?'

'I don't know,' CJ says miserably.

'Some things we have no control over,' Liz continues. 'Infidelity is a personal choice.'

'Maybe,' CJ says. 'But I am so afraid that if something happens to me, my kids will be all on their own. Tom's not a father to them. He's remarried with two other kids now.'

'I'll take your kids in,' I say to her. 'If you're struck down . . .'

'Yeah, we'll all look after them if anything happens to you . . .' Helen says.

'Which it won't . . .' Liz intervenes. 'You are not going to get cancer and die young . . . you're not.'

'Can I have that in writing?' CJ asks.

'Lawyers,' Liz says, shaking her head.

'Fear-driven mothering is very normal,' Tam says. 'All mothers are afraid of dying and leaving their children.'

I nod vigorously.

' . . . but at least you know your kids will all have fathers to take care of them if you die,' CJ says, and the tears stream down her face, unrestrained.

'You're *not* going to die,' Ereka says to her.

'You're going to be around to get drunk with us for a long time to come,' Helen says.

'Only the good die young,' Liz says jokingly.

CJ sniffles, and forces a smile. 'Yeah . . .'

I have a huge lump in my throat. Like CJ, my overriding intuitive emotion dominating my mothering experience is fear. I eye the zabaglione. I *must* resist.

'You know what frightens me?' Fiona says, softly. 'When I am alone with Gabriel, and Ben is away on business and Kirsty's with her mum, I get scared that I'll have an aneurysm or a heart attack or something and die on the spot, and Gabriel will find me and won't know what to do.'

'Doesn't he know how to dial 000?' Tam asks.

'He does, theoretically, in an emergency. But what if the shock of finding me lying on the floor in a heap made him forget? What if no one found him for days?'

'We had a case study at university of a single mother who died of asthma,' Dooly says, 'and they only discovered her body and her eleven month old baby days later. The baby was soiled and starving and dehydrated.'

'Jesus, that's a horrible story,' Fiona says. 'That's my worst fear.'

'But Gabriel is old enough—he'd know to open the fridge and get food and use the toilet,' Liz says.

'Yes, but what about the trauma of finding me?' Fiona asks.

'You can't protect them from everything,' Liz says.

And of course she's right, but we all want our children to live fearlessly, unrestrained by the countless 'what ifs?' that abound. So, for their sake, we muster courage. We try to be brave. And when we can't, we lie. We tell them we are not afraid of big waves ('I'm just cold, so not swimming'); flying ('these little pills are for Mum's headache, sweetie, flying is *such* fun!'); cancer ('Mum's going in to hospital so the doctor can check out that she is okay, there's *nothing* to worry about!'); roller-coasters ('someone has to wait with the bags and hold the ice creams'); anaesthetics ('it's like being in the most lovely peaceful sleep'). But our children read through the lacy transparency of our trying, to the stark semantics of honesty beneath. You can just as much hide your fears from a child as you can a hunchback in a bikini.

'Tyler asked me the other day what I was scared of, and I told him I couldn't think of anything,' Dooly tells us. 'And Luke said,

"I know what you are afraid of". "And what is that?" I asked. And he said, "You're afraid of me and Tyler dying".'

'God, he's got you pegged, hasn't he,' Liz says.

'When I asked him why he said that, he answered, "Because we are your treasures. Your most precious things . . . and because you can't have any more babies".'

'He's too smart, that one,' Helen says, licking her spoon.

'I cannot think about my children dying. I don't even want those two words in the same sentence,' I say. There's a Jewish superstition that when you talk about death, you have to spit three times. It's to scare off the evil eye. I spit three times now—in the opposite direction of the zabaglione.

'That's disgusting,' Helen says to me.

'It's to ward off the evil eye,' I say.

'You know what's weird? I used to wear a piece of rose quartz around my neck,' Ereka says, 'for good luck and healing energy. I started wearing it when I began spotting in my pregnancy with Olivia,' she continues. 'I was about eight weeks pregnant when I started bleeding. And I remember crying, pleading with God. Let me keep this baby. I'll never walk past a beggar again without emptying my wallet. I'll never say fuck again. I'll go to church on Sundays. I'll sponsor a third-world orphan and sell my paintings to dig wells in Africa . . . and I'd rub my rose quartz like it was a lucky charm.'

We're all quietly pondering the same unspeakable possibility— that maybe the spotting was a 'sign'—but we all keep reverentially silent. We must be careful what we wish for.

'It felt so unjust to be in the throes of imagining "my baby's" sex, its features, trying out names, only to fear it being snatched away,' she continues. 'I remember the moment when I accepted that I couldn't change what was going to happen. I was driving my car, and suddenly this bird landed on my bonnet. Just landed, like it had fallen out of the sky. I stopped my car, and wrapped it up in my scarf, it seemed like it was dead. When I got home, as I was walking to the front door, it stirred, and suddenly flew out of my hands. And in that instant, I just surrendered. I realised I couldn't force the pregnancy to hold. It was not my decision.'

'What an amazing story,' Fiona says.

'It's funny, I would never have interpreted a bird landing on my bonnet like that,' Helen says.

'I took it as a sign,' Ereka says.

Helen shrugs. 'Your brain is wired differently from mine. I would have flicked it off my bonnet and carried on driving.'

'I think that's an amazing story,' I say to Ereka.

'Yeah, I think so too. The bleeding continued for a few weeks, but when I heard the ga-thump ga-thump of her heartbeat for the first time on the scan, I swear I cried as if my heart had just been broken.' Ereka smiles in the remembering.

'It is so special when you first hear that heartbeat . . .' Dooly says wistfully.

It is. We all agree.

'What did you do with the rose quartz?' I ask Ereka.

'I threw it into the sea after Olivia was born,' she says. 'It wasn't lucky at all, was it?'

'It was just a piece of stone,' Helen says.

'Yeah.' Ereka smiles sadly.

'You should have kept it,' I say to her.

'I couldn't . . . I wanted to get rid of it,' she replies.

I nod. Some of the girls carry on eating. Within the silence, spoons clink against plates.

Then Dooly says softly, 'I was terrified of childbirth. I was so scared of the pain. Those antenatal classes where they show you natural childbirth actually made it worse for me—I wished I hadn't seen it.'

'It actually had the opposite effect on me,' I say. 'It helped me to make up my mind that I wanted a natural birth, with midwives.'

'Are you mad? Without any drugs?' Liz asks.

'Well, I wanted to try the natural route, but things didn't go as planned.'

'A Caesar?' Fiona asks.

I nod. 'Oh yeah. After thirty-four hours of labour . . .'

'You were crazy to go on for so long,' Helen says. 'What were you thinking?'

'That I wanted a natural childbirth,' I say.

'And what went wrong?' Fiona asks.

'Jamie's head was not properly positioned, I barely dilated, and even an epidural didn't help.'

Was it hubris? Arrogance? Maybe, but I like to think it was something more temperate, like faith, that impelled me away from the terror-driven allopathic route, to preparations for a natural, vaginal, midwife-assisted birth. But that look of weary compassion in my midwife's eyes when she quietly consoled me, 'The only way this baby is coming out is if we cut her out,' shook me rigid. Like an object from the clutches of rigor mortis, the fantasy of the birth I wanted to give my child had to be pried from my grasp. To prove my mother wrong. To take away her words, 'women die in childbirth. It is irresponsible of you to put your life and your child's life at risk by wanting a homebirth'.

Now, with Ereka as one of my dearest friends, I know better. My artless longing, stoked by a couple of natural childbirth books, to experience a different way of giving birth from the fraught recollections of my mother's, could have escorted me to a sorrowful ending. To the ending of which my mother warned me: 'Things

go wrong'. It was the one philosophy about life I wanted more than anything to prove unfounded. A courier no more trustworthy than luck's indifference delivered my healthy baby into my arms.

In the weeks that followed Jamie's birth, that realisation induced in me a series of panic attacks, which developed into a fear of flying, and persistent thoughts about dying. Before Jamie was born I feared not having a normal healthy baby. I imagined that post-birth, I'd be off the hook. Ha! The relief of birthing a normal baby was almost instantly flooded with a tsunami of fears: fear of cot death. Fear of fever. Fear of dehydration. Fear of choking. Fear of suffocation. Fear of her rolling off the bed. Fear of allergies. Fear of her falling. Fear of accidents. Fear of her drowning. My joy at being a mother was a tiny flicker on the radar compared to the extended family of anxieties that arrived uninvited.

'I booked my Caesareans at my first obstetric appointment,' Liz says. 'Both my kids' births were quick and easy, there was no hoping for this or that. Why do you torment yourselves with all this stuff? It's hard enough without adding all this anxiety on top of it.'

'There is a lot to be said for natural childbirth,' Tam jumps in.

'Like what? A stretched vagina? An episiotomy? Hours of excruciating pain?' Liz laughs.

'A drug-free birth, for one thing,' Tam says. 'And a sense of achievement, of having done it the way nature intended, without all that intervention.'

'If it wasn't for intervention, Jo and Jamie would probably have died in childbirth,' Liz says. 'So much for a sense of achievement.'

'Yeah, just making it through alive and well is a sense of achievement,' I say. 'But having children has made me more vulnerable than I ever imagined it was possible to feel.'

There are nods of agreement all around me.

'Maybe that's what having kids is about,' Fiona says. 'To make us confront our mortality.'

'To confront mortality period,' Ereka says. 'I mean, just having a child is like putting your worst fear—that something terrible will happen to them—out there.'

Fiona begins to plait her long hair into a braid. We all watch her, mesmerised by the rhythm of her hand movements.

'Losing a child must be the worst thing that could happen,' Helen says.

'What could be harder?' Dooly asks.

'Spit three times,' I tell the girls. Fiona, Dooly and Ereka all oblige. Liz shakes her head. Helen just snorts.

'I used to work with a young woman, called Tharshni,' I say. 'She was beautiful and clever, the kind of daughter any mother would be madly proud of. She was coming home from law school one day, and was knocked down by a car outside her house. Her mother rushed out, and cradled her while they waited for an ambulance,' I tell the girls. I pause. 'She died in her mother's arms.'

There is silence now among my friends. 'Can you think of anything sadder in the world?' I ask.

Everyone has stopped eating her dessert. My friends look at me and shake their heads.

Liz breaks the silence. 'If your child was to die, in whose arms would you want her to die? Yours or a strangers?'

I look at her with big eyes. There is something startlingly comforting about what she has just said.

'You're right, Liz,' I say. 'I've never thought about it like that.'

'Stop being so morbid and have some pudding,' Helen says to me.

'Yeah,' my friends all agree.

I pick up a bowl and a spoon. I am petrified of how vulnerable and exposed I feel as a mother. But apart from my children dying ... and me dying ... and big waves, flying, boys in fast cars, cancer, roller-coasters and anaesthetics ... I'm not afraid of anything.

Except maybe Helen's desserts. And judging by the chorus of mmm's and aaah's around me, it's a pretty lethal one. I approach the dish with caution, my dessert spoon poised in defence.

CHAPTER 16

the vagina dialogues

I try not to think about those jeans I have been trying to fit into over the past year as I dish up a second helping of zabaglione onto my plate.

Given the timid neuroses to which I am intermittently prone I prefer, on most occasions, to play it safe. But on a plate I am rather more adventurous, easily persuaded to abandon apprehension and embrace the serendipity of, say, a cold melon soup. Or a meat dish, that once upon a time squeaked or neighed rather than moo-ed or baa-ed. There are those people who are content to stick with Vegemite on toast or spaghetti with meatballs, never wondering what coriander-studded goat's cheese and porcini or black pepper mud crab with green papaya salsa might taste like. I, however, would avoid sex with these people.

Cooking programmes generally rouse a comparable response in me as hard-core porn shows do in others. The way Jamie Oliver handles a trout, the passion that Ainsley Harriott displays towards fresh herbs, the ecstasy Nigella Lawson oozes over a pot of simmering mussels, I admit it, turns me on. Nigella Lawson? The woman practically orgasms over a taste of eggplant with cumin. And it's that time of night, so I don't care who knows—Helen's probably already blabbed it out—I had a fling or two with women during my sexually adventurous years.

Ever since Helen wrestled this juicy tidbit of my history out of me last year, she has pestered me for details. Lesbian sex is one of her favourite topics of conversation and she brings it up at least once a fortnight. Hearing the stories of my affairs is just titillation for her. I've told her that she should really get it out of her system and have a quick girl-to-girl roll in the hay, but now that she's pregnant again, she'll have to reserve that for her next life. Helen will die regretting that she never had sex with a woman, but she really ought to have done that all before she had kids. When motherhood dawns, you might as well hang up to dry—with all the nappies—any of your sexual fantasies that range beyond heterosexual monogamy. Unless of course you do what my cousin Deidree did, and have the kids, dump the husband and move in with a woman just as you slide into your forties.

Now, between mouthfuls of zabaglione, Helen steers the ship of our friendships into the shallows of joyous inanities to give us a break from the depths of despair we have just crossed. She prods, as she always does, like a child wanting to hear the same story for the hundredth time. 'So Jo, tell us what it's like to have sex with a woman.'

Before I even get a chance to consider whether I want to play along, spin a fanciful story or tell her to put a cork in it, Ereka pipes up, 'It's highly recommended.'

We all turn to look at her. I smile, I might have guessed. She's a bloody hippie after all.

'No way!' Helen gasps. 'You, Ereka?' And she falls about in her chair, laughing.

Liz is wide-eyed, but Fiona and CJ are laughing too with prurient pleasure. What voracious curiosity we have in other's carnal antics.

'Don't all women want to have sex with other women?' Ereka asks.

'Not me,' says Liz (see, I told you she's sensually challenged).

'What's the oral sex like?' Helen asks, scavenging for detail.

'It's very wet,' Ereka says.

Dooly and Helen are giggling like silly teenagers.

'Of course it's wet,' CJ says. 'What else could it be? There's not a dry patch for miles.'

'No, but it's wetter than you expect,' Ereka says quite earnestly.

'Who was it with?' (that's CJ).

'Was it a one-night stand or a relationship?' (that's Tam).

'Why did you ever go back to men?' (Dooly's question).

Ereka fields all these queries with equanimity, and does not descend into the quagmire of loutish inquisitiveness, holding herself with as much dignity as it is possible to muster when your girlfriends are giving you a hard time about your penchant for clitoris.

'Did you use a strap-on dildo?' Helen asks.

'Actually, lesbian sex is not about penetration,' Ereka says, managing to grace that question with a serious response.

'Aw c'mon,' Helen says.

'Pornography is made for male audiences, which is why you always see women humping each other with strap-on dildos—they're just replacement penises because that's what men think women want. But it's not,' Fiona pipes up.

We look at her.

'What?' she asks, shrugging.

'How would you know what women want?' Helen asks her.

She smiles. 'I don't really . . .' then blushes. 'Okay, well, if kissing and all that counts . . .'

Helen shrieks, 'Oh surely not! You too? What's going on here? How come I got left out in the cold?'

'It's not too late,' CJ says.

'I don't think David would take too kindly if I told him I wanted to have sex with a woman. Not unless he could join in . . .'

'And really, what would be the point of that?' Ereka asks.

Around the table I make a head count. 'I am one, Ereka is two, Fiona is three—do I hear a four somewhere? Anywhere?'

'It wasn't really sex,' Fiona says.

'You and Bill Clinton. It's close enough,' Helen says. 'Anyone else?'

'Helen's practically in, because she's so keen,' Fiona adds, uncertain about whether she can bear to be lumped in this motley crew of mothers with a dykey past.

'But who could I do it with?' Helen asks.

'What about that tall brunette at preschool—what's her name? Jacqui?' Ereka says.

'Jacqui Senderwood?' Helen asks.

'Yeah, little Samantha's mum,' Ereka says.

Jacqui Senderwood is one of those mums who arrives for drop-off in her running shoes and black tight-fitting gym outfit. In summer, her bare tummy reveals a series of muscles that are almost irresistibly inviting to the touch. She is buff and beautiful and sexy despite being the mother of two kids. She is also aloofly unfriendly. Very fuckable.

'Naah, she's not my type,' Helen says. 'She's too much like a man. I think I'd like a more girly kind of woman.'

'You'd love a snog with her,' CJ jibes. 'Just think how you could melt all that bitchiness by going down on her . . .'

Helen pauses to think about this scenario. She's not completely disinterested.

'Listen to us,' Tam says, tensely.

We all stop and look at her.

'We're mothers for godsake! I really am uncomfortable about the way we're talking. Imagine if our kids could hear us.'

'Tam, your kids are not here, and you can stop being a mother for one minute. You need a good lesbian fuck,' CJ says to her. We all guffaw in laughter. Tam blushes visibly.

'It has never appealed to me,' she says.

'Liar, liar, pants on fire,' CJ sing-songs.

'I am not lying, why should I? I actually find it quite a repulsive thought,' she retorts. 'And if it's so great, why don't you have an affair with a woman if men are so crap?' Tam asks CJ, deftly deflecting the focus from her.

'Yeah, why?' Helen asks, jumping on the bandwagon.

'Why?' we all chime in.

'I haven't met the right girl,' CJ says.

'And besides, let's face it, there's nothing like a good hard cock,' Helen says.

'Like this?' CJ says, leaning for her bag and removing Harvey. She puts him on the table, right next to the almost empty dish of zabaglione. We all met Harvey on our last girl's night out. We were at a restaurant and Tam had excused herself to go for a wee, and when she returned an enormous large-veined bright pink plastic dildo was standing upright in her plate of stir-fried vegetables. I don't know who was more embarrassed, Tam or the poor waitress on her way back to the kitchen carrying a tower of dirty plates. CJ calls him Harvey because ever since she saw the movie *The Piano*, she claims no man can ever live up to Harvey Keitel's seduction of Holly Hunter, a standard 'which clearly does exist, even if it is only in some filmmaker's head'. I did point out to her that the movie was directed by a woman, but she pooh-poohed the unassailable point. 'If you want romance, kiss a woman,' I always tell her.

There in that Thai restaurant, with Tam smouldering in discomfort, refusing to eat any more, CJ told us that 'Harvey is my most reliable and, frankly, most satisfying fuck to date. He never comes before I do, he gives it to me hard, and he is easy to clean—can even go in the dishwasher' (to our shrieks of disgust). But we all wanted a turn to hold him, so passed him round the table making lewd remarks and comparisons with the 'real thing'; though Tam said it was 'unhygienic' and made us look like a bunch of lesbians. She didn't shut up about the fact that we'd never be allowed back in that restaurant again. Most of us just wanted to brush up against that sense of being single again—in the market for a good large dildo, instead of the tired, sex-weary monogamous once-were-kittens, now worn-out pussycats we are.

Now Tam says to CJ, 'Please put that thing away.'

'Harvey is very hurt that you don't like him,' CJ says.

'Kiss and make up,' Helen says, taking hold of the dildo and passing it to Tam.

'Gross!' Tam says. 'That thing's been in . . . in CJ's . . .'

'What?' CJ says.

'Your vagina,' Tam says.

'And what have you got against CJ's vagina?' Helen asks. 'Huh?' she adds in, for emphasis.

'I happen to have a very nice vagina—a little underutilised and a little stretched after three births, but a perfectly good one otherwise,' CJ declares.

It seems pernicious, a little cruel even, that the expectations of our poor vaginas are biologically conflated to include both a firm glove-like grip during sex as well as stretching to the size of a baby hippopotamus's yawn at birth. At a glance, the circumference of the average penis fails to suggest that the self-same aperture in which it fits best will also, at a push, squeeze out a large leg of lamb. Once having done so, however, the latex of our genitalia tends to slacken. And just at that point when our husbands are desperate for as much affirmation as we can rally in our exhaustion, their libidinal efforts engender as much arousing friction as the stirring of paint with a rather scrawny twig.

'Do you know that after I had Cameron, David had the gall to ask my gynaecologist if he could "tighten" me up a little?' Helen says.

'Show me a single man who doesn't think that, even if he doesn't say it?' CJ says. 'They're never satisfied, even if you spend the rest of your life doing those stupid pelvic floor exercises.'

'What did your gynae say to that?' Tam asks Helen.

'He told him to get a penis enlargement if it was a problem,' Helen says, snickering.

'Good on him!' Fiona says.

'But is it a problem? For your sex life?' Tam asks. 'Kevin sometimes does vaginal reconstructions after birth.'

I'll bet he does, I think.

'Things could be tighter,' Helen says, 'but we make do. I would never suggest to David that he gets his gear enlarged. I love him just as he is, and so we sometimes have anal sex.'

'I beg your pardon!' I say, looking at Helen. 'You do *what*?!'

'Anal sex,' she says, shrugging. 'It's not so bad.'

'Gross,' Tam says.

I am forced to agree with Tam. 'What could be worse than anal sex?' I say. 'It's all those porno movies David watches, next he'll have you geared up in black leather with a mask, and he'll be

standing over you with a whip. You've got to get him to throw out that collection of pornos,' I say. 'And you've never told me that before,' I quip. 'Why have you never told me that?'

'You've never asked me,' she says. 'And I like those porno movies, too.'

'What's so terrible about anal sex?' CJ asks. 'I'd take it any which way.'

'I don't think I could do anal sex,' Ereka says. 'Isn't it . . . messy?'

'No messier than ordinary sex,' Helen says. 'Men find it a huge turn-on.'

'I just don't get how that can be a turn-on for you,' I say to Helen.

'Have you ever tried it?' she asks.

'No, because I find the thought of it repulsive.'

'Well, how can you reject it if you've never tried it?' she asks.

'Yeah, that's not like you,' Liz says. 'You've tried everything else, from what I can make out . . . what's the big deal?'

'I've tried it,' CJ says. 'Tom used to love it—you've got to be in the mood. I just don't understand why you, Jo, who are such a sensual, open-minded person when it comes to sex, would get freaked out by it . . .'

The girls are all looking at me. I feel silly, and I can't locate the explanations for why the notion of being face down with Frank climbing over me like a canine in mating season is actually . . . quite funny. I want to be able to keep CJ's descriptions of myself as 'sensual and open-minded', and either I've got to concede that anal sex is perfectly okay and preserve these generous appellations, or risk having them snatched away like freshly baked biscuits I'm not allowed to eat.

'I don't need to have sex with a dog to know I don't want to have sex with a dog,' I say, feebly.

'It's not the same,' Helen says. 'And it's a turn-on for David, and that is a turn-on for me,' she says, standing. 'And there are fresh figs, four different cheeses and glazed ginger for those who are sensual and open-minded,' she declares, heading for the kitchen.

'Get your fanny tightened if that's the problem,' I implore after her. And then, raising my voice so she can hear me from the kitchen, 'My gynae told me that if I had vaginal births, I'd never have a tight pussy again. You should have had Caesars,' I say.

'He actually said that?' CJ asks.

'*She*,' I say. 'I only go to female gynaes. And yes, she actually used those words,' I declare. 'Only another woman would be candid enough to tell you the truth.'

'God bless her,' CJ says.

'She probably charges more for Caesareans than natural births,' Liz says, ever the businesswoman. 'I'll bet she encourages all her patients to have Caesars.'

'You are such a fucking cynic,' I say to her.

'A realist, thanks,' she retorts.

'I couldn't go to a female gynaecologist,' Tam says, positively squirming, clutching her glass of water.

'Why not?' I ask.

'I'd feel very odd to have a woman poking around there.'

'But they own the equipment, so they understand it better,' Ereka says.

Tam shrugs.

'You've got vagina-phobia,' I say. The others laugh, Tam doesn't. Helen returns to the dining room table with a platter of cheeses, fresh figs and a dollop of glazed ginger pieces that smell heavenly.

'Yeah, you won't even touch Harvey because he's been in my vagina,' CJ says.

'CJ, I drink a toast to your perfectly good vagina,' I say, lifting the butterscotch schnapps and refilling my glass. All at once three other glasses are proffered for refilling. I refill them and we all clink.

'To CJ's perfectly good vagina,' we chant, and we drink a huge slug of our schnapps.

'What about my perfectly good vagina?' Ereka says.

'Let's drink a toast to your perfectly good vagina, too,' I say, and we clink glasses again and drink a toast to Ereka's.

'And what about yours?' Helen says to me. 'Yours is the one that's been under the weather.'

'Yes, how is your vagina?' Liz asks.

They are all alluding to the cone biopsy I had a few months ago, after a regular pap smear revealed I had stage CIN III pre-cancerous cells on my cervix. I still get a shiver when I consider how easily that reminder from the lab 'You are due for your next pap smear' might have sat scrunched up in my bag for months before a spare hour presented itself for me to see to it. As it turns out, I had to get an immunisation certificate for Aaron's preschool records from my doctor, and remembered about the pap smear just as I was walking out the door. The assiduousness with which I used to guard my own health has been dissipated by my dependants—it is no surprise that the category of women most at risk for cervical cancer is that of young mothers, distracted by small children. In taking care of others, mothers like us habitually forget to take care of ourselves.

'It's beautiful. Back to its old self after six weeks of discharge I would hate to describe. And by the way, have you all been for your pap smears?' I ask, looking around the table.

I see three heads nodding—Fiona, CJ and Tam.

'What about the rest of you?'

'I'm booked in next month,' Liz says.

'And a mammogram?' I ask her.

'I'll go next year,' she says.

'I'll have a pap smear after the baby is born,' Helen says.

'I'll go, I'll go, all right?' Dooly says to me. 'It's not my most favourite reason for going to the doctor,' she says. 'I find it humiliating and uncomfortable and the name is horrible—who is Pap? What gets smeared?'

'Actually, it's named after a Greek doctor, Papanicolau,' Tam pipes up. 'Pap is just short for Papanicolau.'

We are all pretty impressed. All those lectures and seminars have paid off. Tam cascades information that would be most useful on TV quiz shows, like *Who Wants to Be a Know-It-All?* and *The Most Annoying Link*.

'He convinced his wife to let him experiment on her every day with a speculum for twenty years,' she continues.

'Kinky bastard,' Helen quips.

'That's an interesting variation on foreplay,' Liz chimes in.

'Thanks to him, I am here to live another day,' I say. 'Let's drink a toast to Doctor Papanicolau,' I say.

'And to our perfectly good vaginas?' Dooly asks.

'Let's not forget our perfectly good vaginas,' I say.

With that, we clink our glasses and drink toasts to all our perfectly good vaginas, a little ragged and tired, but still in fabulous working condition. And to Doctor Papanicolau and his speculum and his very obliging wife.

the complementary penis

Harvey has pride of place in the centre of the table amongst the blue-veined Roquefort, the vintage cheddar, the oozing Brie and the fruity Gruyere. A fine sliver of any one of these, pressed against the body of a pink half-fig, irresistibly comparable to a beautiful vulva, with a wedge of glazed ginger is the stuff of which sheer sensual ecstasy is made. Tam has left the dining room (she 'cannot bear looking at that thing') and is in the kitchen, tinkering with the kettle and a teabag for a cup of chamomile tea and after that, she 'really must be going'. Harvey's hardly more offensive than a zucchini or a banana—does she shudder at the greengrocers too? What an unsettling place the world must be to one in whom phallic objects evoke tremulous agitation. Perhaps she should increase her dose of Prozac.

'So, do you ever feel the need to masturbate?' CJ asks, fired up after our perfectly good vagina toasts. Those who don't do it, talk about it. Incessantly, it appears. Hers is a gratuitously general question, left on the table for anyone in the mood to engage.

'How do you mean?' Fiona asks, breaking a fig with tenderness.

'With your husbands around for sex whenever you feel like it, do you ever masturbate?' CJ's cut a chunk of each cheese for herself, but is more interested in the conversation than the creamy textures on her plate.

'Like being in a hotel and feeling like you have to use the facilities?' Dooly asks. CJ nods. She reaches for a chunk of glazed ginger.

I giggle. 'Frank reminds me often, "this relationship comes with a complementary penis—feel free to use it at any time".' I lick a dribble of soft Brie from my finger. 'But mostly I am too tired for sex. I just want to get into bed and not have anyone bother me until morning.'

The others bob their heads in concurrence.

'As soon as I start taking off my makeup, Jake considers that foreplay,' Ereka says.

'All I've got to do is bend over to pick up kids' socks,' Helen says, talking with a mouthful of Gruyere, with its hint of fruit and nuts. 'They're like dogs that are just waiting to jump into your lap. You have to avoid eye contact.'

'You're all bloody spoilt,' CJ whines. 'Do you have any crackers for this?' she asks Helen.

'We've got figs and ginger, darling, crackers are for kids,' Helen responds.

CJ pokes her tongue at Helen. 'Cocky slut,' she says.

Dooly has taken a wedge of cheddar and is gnawing at it. 'Every now and then I'd welcome it if Max wanted to have sex,' Dooly says. 'His medication has really destroyed his libido.'

'So do you masturbate?' CJ asks.

'Naah,' Dooly says. 'It's boring.'

'Have an affair,' Liz suggests. She has taken three figs, skipped the cheeses. I want to wail for the deprivations she willingly inflicts on herself.

'No, I couldn't,' Dooly says, nibbling, nibbling.

'Why not? He's not satisfying you, why don't you find someone who does?' Liz continues. It's often a guess with Liz, whether she's playing at devil's advocate or is just pathologically tactless.

'I have a thing about infidelity,' Dooly says. 'I'm a bit old fashioned that way ... and I'm surviving without sex. I'm doing okay.'

'No one should have to survive without sex,' I say. 'Can't you tempt him?'

'With what?' Dooly asks. 'Drooping breasts and a roll of fat? Yeah, that'll really get him fired up.'

'With your perfectly good vagina,' I say to her.

'I think he'd rather watch CNN,' Dooly says. Tam returns from the kitchen, a steaming mug in her hands.

'Why don't you go into a sex chat room on the internet?' Helen asks, passing me a fig belly she's stuffed with a tiny chunk of each cheese. 'My sister says they're fun, she's in there all the time.'

'Just be careful, there are some weirdos out there,' CJ says.

Several of us give her the 'oh really?' eye. 'Yeah, okay, I've done it every so often ... what's the big deal? I'm single, lonely and sex-starved, so don't judge me.' CJ says.

'Naah, that would feel like cheating too,' Dooly says. 'I'm fine. Sex is not that important to me any more. Sleep is what I need these days.'

'Talking to someone over the internet about sex would feel like cheating on Max?' Liz asks. She's had a bite of one of the figs, but it looks like it's failed to enthuse any of her tastebuds.

'Absolutely,' Dooly says, reaching over for the bottle of red wine, and filling her butterscotch schnapps glass.

Liz shakes her head. 'It's just words, no touching, no exchanging of bodily fluids. I don't get it.'

'How would you feel, Liz, if Carl spent hours in a chat room talking to someone about having sex?' Tam asks as she sips on her cup of warm urine-coloured tea.

'Honestly? I'd be fine about it.'

'I'd feel Kevin had cheated on me,' Tam says.

'I'd rather David did the chat room thing than go out and have actual sex with someone else,' Helen says. 'I mean, I could probably live with it, if that's what he was up to, but not if he fucked someone else. If he did have an affair, I'd leave him and take the kids with me.'

'How's that a punishment to him?' CJ says. 'Don't you mean you'd leave him with all the kids to look after.'

'Yeah, that's it,' Helen says, giggling. 'Can you imagine, he'd have a nervous breakdown after a week.'

'I've got a friend whose husband was chatting to guys on the internet. He was really into all this gay male porn,' Fiona says.

'I wouldn't cope with that,' Tam says. 'I mean, that would feel like serious rejection.'

'But he wasn't acting on it,' Fiona says.

'Could she prove that? I've had plenty of clients whose husbands do lots of things behind their wives' backs, without letting a single clue slip. And he was probably fantasising about guys while he was fucking her,' CJ says.

'The thing I really wouldn't cope with, is if Frank was a cross-dresser. I think I could handle and forgive everything else, but if he got off by dressing up in women's clothing, I think I would have to call it a day.'

'Can you see Frank in high heels and fishnet stockings?' Helen says to me, laughing. The two of us start giggling. Dooly lets out a small laugh.

'So there'd be no room for forgiveness for an affair?' Liz asks, breaking through our laughter.

'Absolutely no way,' Helen says.

I sneak a peek at CJ. She stood her ground, followed through on the 'you deceive, you leave' principle. In the aftermath of infidelity, once the glow of moral righteousness wore away into the torpid pastels of the daily grind, does a shameful regret surface, an intermittent wondering about whether she and her kids would have been better off had she swallowed her indignation and fought for reconciliation?

'What about your history together, your common values, your friendship?' Liz says. She's abandoned the figs now altogether.

'Once there's a breach of trust, it would be hard to find your way back,' Fiona suggests.

'What about an emotional connection with someone else?' Liz proposes. She is leaning back in her seat, arms crossed.

'Even worse,' Helen says. 'Sex is one thing, but if David was carrying on an emotional relationship with another woman . . . God help him. And her.' She lifts the cheese knife and holds it up to her throat.

'Hang on,' I chime in. 'I still have feelings for some of the men I have loved in the past. I didn't stop loving them when I met Frank. I just promised that I wouldn't carry on sleeping with them . . . Can you make me another one of those?' I ask Helen. She obliges immediately.

'So how does Frank know you're not fantasising about other men when you're having sex with him?' Liz asks.

'He doesn't,' I say.

'Do you fantasise about other men?' CJ asks. 'And women, in your case.'

I don't answer directly. 'I don't consider that infidelity,' I say. 'Everyone has the right to his or her own sexual fantasies.'

'And if Frank was fantasising about another woman while having sex with you?' Liz asks.

I consider this unlikely scenario. 'As long as he didn't shout, "Oh Lucy!" while he was coming, I'd be none the wiser . . .'

'Or "Oh Patrick!"' Helen throws in.

'Yeah, that would come as a bit of a shock,' I concede. 'As long as there are no fishnet stockings.'

'So what you don't know, can't hurt?' Liz asks.

'Yeah, I guess so . . .' I say.

'I really *must* be going,' Tam says, her tea now finished. No one bites. She doesn't move.

'So what do you fantasise about when you masturbate?' I ask CJ. Tam's eyes follow the lead of my question to rest on CJ. She's not going anywhere.

'Anyone, and anything . . .' she says. 'James Spader. Guy Sebastian. Eddie McGuire . . .'

'You're sick,' Liz says.

'I don't know where you get the energy to think about sex,' Dooly says to her. 'I hardly ever think about it any more.'

'I think about sex all the time,' CJ says. 'When I'm cross-examining a witness, when I'm standing in line for my coffee, when I'm shopping for groceries . . . and Harvey's okay for the basics,' she says. 'But he can't give me a back rub. And I miss the conversation.'

'Yeah, I'd take a back rub and conversation over sex any day,' Helen says.

'At least you don't have to get into arguments about birth control,' I say to CJ.

'Why don't you just use condoms?' Fiona asks me.

'I hate the smell of rubber when sex should smell like sex. Smell is one of the best parts of sex,' I say. 'Of life, in fact. Just smell these cheeses, this ginger,' and with that I practically inhale the little fig-half Helen has prepared for me.

'I'm still using the pill,' Fiona says.

'Me too,' Ereka says.

'I hate having to remember to take it every day,' Tam says.

'Just get a loop in,' Liz says. 'Then it's over, no one has to remember anything at the last minute.'

'But then it's still up to us,' I say.

'When it comes to the prospect of you falling pregnant, who would you rather leave matters up to, an unreliable man or yourself?' she asks matter-of-factly. 'Look at where it's got Helen . . .' She nods in Helen's direction.

'I thought I was too old to fall pregnant, and honestly, we have sex so rarely these days,' Helen says.

'How often?' CJ asks.

'Once a month, maybe,' Helen says. 'In a good month.'

'What a waste of a complementary penis,' CJ says. 'What about you, Liz?'

Liz inhales. 'Whenever Carl wants,' she says.

'Which is how often?' CJ pushes.

'Most nights,' she says.

We all stop eating cheese. We turn to face Liz. Helen breaks the silence first.

'Are you mad?' Helen says.

'Do you feel like it?' Dooly asks, wide-eyed.

'After a long day at work? You must be joking. I just want a long hot bath, some time to read the newspaper and a mug of peppermint tea ...'

'So why do you do it?' I ask.

Liz pauses before she answers. 'Some people need to take pills to keep their cholesterol in check, and I have to have sex with Carl to keep him in check. It's just easier for me that way.'

We all look sceptical. I'm a bit horrified, to be honest.

'I know how to manage people,' she says, 'and giving in to sex is like short-circuiting a protracted negotiation process in the office. It is infinitely more efficient. And it's usually over really quickly.' She looks at each of us in turn. 'You should all try it sometime ...'

'You mean you don't come?' Helen asks.

'Sometimes, it depends on my mood. But I'll teach you all a little trick, it's called KY jelly, and it's over before you know it, and you can get back to your book, or just go to sleep.'

We must all be looking like we've just witnessed a car accident. '*What?*' she says.

'I don't know ...' Fiona says. 'It just doesn't sound like it should be ...'

'My husband is sexually satisfied, we seldom fight, and that's a recipe for a happy marriage,' Liz says. 'What about you, Ereka?' Liz asks, in search of an ally. 'Don't you and Jake also have sex every day?'

Ereka smiles. She and Jake were childhood sweethearts. He collapsed into an abiding love for her when she was no more than a girl, with ripening sensuality that he alone watered, nurtured, brought to life. In public, Jake still touches Ereka's hair and holds her hand. For all those who don't believe in soul mates, Jake and Ereka are indisputable evidence. Of course he supported her desire for a home birth. And he continues to defend Ereka to his family,

who blame her, his mother in particular. For putting the baby at risk. For tempting the gods (as if the gods need tempting). Neither of them is stuck in self pity, despite a only human covetousness for the lives the rest of us, with 'normal kids', have been granted. The easy road.

Once, in a moment of intimacy, when I confessed to Frank my guilt at how having one Ereka in our midst is the statistic that grants the rest of us safe passage, he had smiled and said, 'Someone has to draw the short straw.' Ereka once also uttered to me the bizarre sense of relief she feels in having Olivia. 'When your worst fear manifests,' she said, 'it's over. The waiting for something bad to happen dissipates, and you can get on with your life.'

'We often have sex,' Ereka says. 'Not as much as we had when we first met, but quite a lot. We sometimes just lie and hold each other. We kiss a lot.'

'Kiss?' Dooly asks. 'I can't remember the last time I kissed Max. I don't mean a peck hello, but a real deep-tongued kiss.'

'We never kiss any more,' Helen says.

'I don't really want to,' Fiona says.

'I don't need to,' Liz rejoins.

We all sigh. How did we all turn up here, smooch-deprived in our late thirties and early forties, zealous believers in the power and glory of The Kiss? Only the other day, driving past two young lovers totally engrossed in a deep kiss, I hooted, waved and yelled from my window. They looked up, bewildered at the passing traffic, mistaking my reaction for a conservative objection to their public exhibition of passion. But I was celebrating. I was rejoicing. I was insane with jealousy. At his Knebworth concert Robbie Williams pulled a young woman from the audience and started to kiss her. I know this, because I bought the DVD, which Frank has caught me replaying several times. 'It's a sad day,' I've heard him mutter, as he returns from the fridge with a beer, 'when your wife's having an affair with a DVD clip.' I don't mean to be a voyeur. But I used to be that passionate. That kissable. That desirable. And I miss it.

I tell the girls now about that Robbie Williams kiss.

'You are a fucking adolescent, Jo,' Liz says.

'I miss that part of adolescence,' I say.

'Why don't you try kissing Frank like that?' CJ suggests.

'He would think I was having an affair,' I say. But I secretly promise myself that I *will* catch him off-guard one of these nights, when I am not too tired, and when the kids are asleep, and the laundry is folded, and the dishes are washed: I will kiss him. I will kiss him like Robbie Williams kisses that girl.

'It's just that there's usually not the time to prolong all that foreplay,' I say, sadly. 'I miss those long languid lovemaking sessions we used to have when we were young … before kids came along.'

The girls all nod in agreement. The sexual buffet of yesteryear is gone, replaced with mini bite-sized chunks. And how we all miss that holding out, holding back, and leaving the bed only to do an urgent wee or raid the fridge for refreshments so you could start all over again. These days, sex is a conflated furtive and conspiratorial act, behind closed doors, in the dark. Scheduled. After they're asleep, before *CSI*. Between six-thirty in the morning and the padding of little feet across the corridor. Pencilled in along with swimming lessons, mufti day and vaccinations. But an appointment for sex is for men who use prostitutes and, frankly, I've never understood it. When foreplay is 'You've got twenty minutes', my libido sort of loses interest, preferring the allusions of mystery and the anticipation of the unknown. Post-kids, sex is just another chore awaiting a tick.

'You're just all dogs in the manger,' CJ pouts. 'You've got the complementary penis and you don't even use it. Even for a quickie. A quickie is better than nothing.'

'We get to have more than a quickie,' Ereka says. 'But that once got us into trouble. Kylie walked in on us once while we were having sex. She was three at the time, and was just standing at the door watching us—godknows for how long. By the time we registered she was there, I had had an orgasm, but Jake was still going at it. I just gripped his shoulders, and said in my Mummy voice, "Darling, what's the matter, have you had a nightmare?" and of course Jake just stopped in mid-thrust and lay there, turned his head and smiled at her.'

'So what did you do?' Helen asks, sucking on a knob of honeyed ginger.

'I slipped out from under Jake and went to her, and took her back to bed. What else could I do?'

'I wonder if she'll bring it up in therapy one day,' Liz says.

'I've no doubt she will,' Ereka says. 'Hopefully she won't be too scarred by it.'

'I would die if my kids caught us having sex,' Dooly says. 'I don't know how I would explain it to them. You know how you feel grossed out at the thought of your parents having sex? Well, I feel grossed out at the thought of my boys knowing I have sex.'

'Someday, the penny will drop,' CJ says. 'When they realise where they came from.'

'Luke's asked me about the birds and the bees, and I've told him the basics, but I don't think he's put it all together in his head—you know, that me and his dad have actually done it. I don't want my boys to think of me sexually. I'm their mother,' Dooly says.

'Boys have a sexual attachment to their mothers,' Tam offers.

'I know about all that Freudian stuff, and it makes me squirm,' Dooly says.

'Cameron likes to squeeze my tits and play with his willy at the same time,' Helen says.

'Good God, I wish you hadn't said that,' Dooly says.

'That is way too much information,' Liz adds.

'It's normal,' Ereka says. 'Kids have a sexuality too, and it's totally innocent.'

'So what do you do when your boys get erections?' Helen asks Dooly and Liz. 'Smack their hands and tell them to say ten Hail Marys?'

'Don't be silly. I just pay no attention to them, and hope they'll go away,' Dooly says.

'That's exactly what I do with David's erections,' Helen laughs.

'Your poor husband,' Fiona quips, giggling though.

'Kieran's got an enormous penis,' Tam says. Gifted and well hung? He's gonna be something that boy, someday. And then, as if she's just heard herself replayed, 'God, is it okay to say that?'

'No, you're going to burn in hell for being the first mother who ever looked at her son's penis and thought, you are going to make some woman really happy one day,' Helen says. 'All mothers do that, you silly tart,' she says, teasingly. Tam seems overly relieved. She takes a piece of Gruyere and eats it as if she's really enjoying it.

'We had Gabriel circumcised, because we thought it would be more hygienic, and now I am really sorry we did it. He's got a really small penis,' Fiona says. 'I think they took too much off in the circumcision. And I worry about it—you know, I would hate him to have a small-penis complex when he grows up.'

'He's only little,' I reassure her. 'You can't tell how big it will be when he is older by the size it is now.'

'How little?' Helen asks.

'Tiny, this big,' she says, showing us a centimetre between her thumb and forefinger.

'Oh, it will grow,' Ereka says reassuringly.

'Don't worry about it,' Dooly says. 'It's not your problem.'

'The length doesn't matter,' Liz says. 'It's the width—volumetric displacement.'

True, we all nod.

'Besides, there's nothing you can do about it,' I say. 'It's out of your hands.'

'We still worry about things we can't change,' Fiona says innocently.

As if by some choreographed gesture of sympathy, we all look at Ereka. She smiles weakly. A silence laps around us.

And then Ereka says, 'I worry that Olivia will never know the joy of sex. It has been such a source of pleasure for me in my life, and who knows if there will ever be someone who will love her and take sexual care of her . . .'

We are all stunted by this statement. Our flippancy spent. Penis size an indulgence. Ereka's concerns for Olivia extend into the vast unknowable future. Whether she will be able to go to school, have friends, fall in love, whisper secrets . . . The rest of us take all these things for granted.

One night, while I was putting Jamie to sleep, we had a precious conversation I have stored away, a treasure from her childhood, about her first kiss that still awaits her. I stroked her hair as together we wondered excitedly who the lucky boy might be. She sighed happily and closed her eyes as her imagination conjured up Peter Pan and other boyish heroes. These moments are not Ereka's to enjoy.

As much as the destiny of motherhood desexualises us, so does disability. In a world in which the contortions of anorexic, botoxed blondes are revered as beauty, the unassuming sexuality of disabled people is rendered imperceptible, hidden beneath a shroud of pitying responses.

We all feel humbled by Ereka's comment. Helen puts her hand on Ereka's arm. I love her for not uttering some stupid platitude like, 'Don't worry, there will be someone out there for her . . .' She just keeps her hand on Ereka's arm. No one rushes to rescue Ereka from the heartbreak of this inevitability. We all lower our eyes into the sadness, and hold it together, for a time.

CHAPTER 18

a survivor in our midst

Tam still hasn't left.

Even after we broke up and Fiona joined Ereka on the balcony for a joint in solidarity against the immensity of all that has been said. They both return from the balcony, arms linked.

'Okay, who's for a foot massage?' Fiona says, reaching for a bottle of massage oil from her bag. 'I concocted this one myself—geranium, rosemary and citrus.'

'I'd love one,' Ereka says. I offer to give it to her.

She lies back in the big easychair, and I sit on a little poof at her feet with a towel on my lap. Her feet, like the rest of her, are hefty and her heels are cracked and dry. The feet of a mother, literally worked off her feet, who never has time to go for a pedicure or apply that peppermint foot lotion she gets each year on Mother's Day. In those feet, the labour of mothering is mercilessly evident.

'How're you doing, Ereka?' I ask her, rubbing her left foot with a handful of oil. 'I mean, how are you *really* doing?'

'Okay, I guess,' she says, sighing deeply. She closes her eyes and takes a deep breath.

'And how is Olivia?' I ask, gingerly.

'She has good days and bad days,' Ereka says, not opening her eyes. I do not say any more for now, and concentrate on massaging her big toe, and then the indents between her toes. Her foot grows heavier in my lap. I do not rush to fill the stillness.

Then she says, 'Sometimes when she is asleep, I go and look at her and imagine what she would be like as a normal child, you know. When she's asleep, she looks just like any normal kid.'

I take this in. As difficult as it is for me to listen, I want to be generous enough to allow her the space to talk the way she good-naturedly puts up with our incessant nattering about our kids. But when Ereka speaks of Olivia, I feel uncontained, in the way I do when I'm unable to tidy the disarray of a room where nothing has its right place. I stumble, reaching for the appropriate questions—intimating interest, not prurience, support, not invasion.

'It must hurt you so deeply,' I say, wondering if that just sounds lame, a token.

She smiles, her eyes still closed. 'It hurt for so long to accept that she was not going to just get better, or just one day wake up and be okay. Sometimes I think I don't know what not hurting feels like.'

My fingers falter. I gather her entire foot between my hands, and I cup it with tenderness.

'Do you love her?' I ask, bravely.

'Oh yes,' she says. 'It's impossible not to love your own child. But do I wish that she had never been born? Or that maybe she had even died in childbirth? I would be lying if I said no. Sometimes, when I'm out in the park or on the beach and I see all these happy families, these ordinary children running about and growing as they should, I get this feeling I used to get when I was a little girl, and was the only one not invited to the party. And I want to stamp

my feet like a kid and say, "It's not fair, I also want two normal children. Like everyone else!" I must have some huge karmic debt to repay,' she says wryly.

'My life is not a choice I made,' she says. 'Despite what people think. I never imagined for one minute that I would be caring for a handicapped child when I fought so hard for a home birth. I honestly thought I was doing something wonderful, bringing my child into the world without fear, without drugs, in our own home. It was supposed to be such a good start for all of us. I didn't go into it with ignorance, you know. And maybe in the end, I'm paying the price for my own pig-headedness.' She sighs and the clinking of her bracelets tinkles into the silence around us.

Suddenly the room has grown quiet. I am aware that everyone has been listening to our conversation.

'You could never have known how it was going to turn out,' I say. 'You did the right thing in the face of the unknown—imagining it would turn out well. You can't live always preparing for disaster,' I say.

'I know this will sound strange, but having Olivia has prepared me for disaster,' Ereka says. 'If she died, for example, I know I would survive it. Ironically, she's given me strength to endure whatever life brings my way ...'

'Having her has made you stronger?' I ask.

This question is too much for Liz, and she ventures, 'No one is ennobled by suffering, Jo. All that New Age theory about our wounds and how we have to work through them is just masochistic nonsense. We would be just fine without them.'

There are murmurs of agreement—from Helen, Dooly.

But Ereka does not rush to agree. 'Maybe,' she says. 'I mean, some days what I would give not to have to watch her struggle just to do the basics. I watch her trying, trying—to walk, to talk, to exist fully—and always falling down, failing, not making it. And I know that for the rest of her life, that is the pattern she is destined to repeat, over and over again. Some days I just accept that she *is* existing fully, as *Olivia*, which is different from a Kylie, or a Jamie, or even an Ereka. And sometimes, I just wish she could be like everyone else. But she won't. She'll always be who she is. At least with Aaron, Jo, even with all his behavioural challenges, you know he will grow out of them.'

'Or not, as the case may be. I just pray he doesn't become a bigger and more terrifying version of who he is now. A teenage thug. In gangs. A drug dealer or, Christ, my biggest fear in having a boy, a rapist . . .'

There is a hushed silence now over the group.

'Mothers of rapists and murderers always stand by their children, in the news, you know, you always hear that,' Ereka says. She has opened her eyes and is looking at me.

'What would you do, Jo?' CJ asks me from the other side of the lounge room where she is holding a magazine, but hasn't paged through it in minutes.

'If Aaron ended up as a drug addict, rapist or murderer?' I shudder as I say these words.

'Yeah,' CJ says.

'I don't know.'

'Would you leave him to rot in jail?'

'I might,' I say. 'At a certain point, I think we are entitled to walk away from our children.'

I think now of my friend Matty, a survivor of domestic violence and a women's rights activist who, with patient fortitude, has raised three children on her own. She devotes her life to healing other women. She opened a domestic violence counselling unit in a hospital in one of Johannesburg's townships to which women flock each day to nurse their physical and emotional wounds. Recently, after months of her teenage son's rampage of drinking, staying out late and (she suspected) drug-taking, Matty left all his possessions out on the street and changed the locks on her doors. And she told him, 'My son, you know I would give you the clothes off my back and the food from my mouth; but I will not lay down my life and die for you. I have worked too hard to be alive. And I will not let anyone—not even you—take my life away. I love you. But I love myself more.'

'I couldn't,' Tam says. 'They're my babies.'

'If they contravene everything sacred I have taught them, they lose their right to claim me as their mother,' I say.

'You're a very principled person,' Fiona says.

I bristle, exposed. 'Yes, maybe I am . . .'

'You just have a very strong ethical sense of what is right and wrong,' Ereka says, softening the blow. I know she is alluding to my poorly concealed disdain for people who take drugs; though surely she knows that in her case, I make an exception. People with handicapped kids should be allowed whatever vices they need.

'What if one of us did something that in your eyes was despicable?' Liz asks. At some point in the evening she must have taken off her linen suit because she is now wrapped up in her maroon nightgown on the sofa.

'Like what?' I ask.

'Like . . . like take cocaine, for example,' Helen says.

They all wait and look at me.

'You're right, I wouldn't be impressed.'

'Would you still be friends with us?'

'Yes, if it was a one-off. If it became a habit, maybe not.'

'What if we had an affair?' Liz asks.

'I would encourage it,' I say jokingly, trying to lighten the mood.

'What if we did something truly terrible, like kill someone?'
CJ asks.

'It depends how it happened—was it a car accident or was
it murder?'

'Murder,' Tam says.

'Like who?'

'Carl,' Liz says.

'It would also depend.' I am thinking now of Tam feeding
Kevin some black-eyed peas, like Mary-Anne and Wanda in the
Dixie Chicks' song 'Goodbye Earl'. I am sure Kevin would end up
being a missing person that nobody missed at all, other than his
obscenely wealthy sagging clientele.

'Or one of our children,' Fiona says.

'On purpose?'

'Yes,' Fiona says.

I am silent. There is great discomfort in this room.

'Like that woman, what was her name? Folbigg?' CJ says.

I take my time to answer. I don't want to be misunderstood and
the territory is ripe for misunderstanding. 'I hate what she did, but
somewhere I feel like . . . um . . . I feel sorry for her.'

'You should feel sorry for the innocent children she killed,' Tam
bites back.

Wasn't she leaving after dessert?

'I said, I hate what she did,' I continue. 'But none of us knows
what she went through . . .'

'She just didn't want kids any more,' Dooly says. I sense Dooly
wants to help me out, but she's battling.

I am starting to feel embattled. 'Folbigg's a bad example, but
remember that American woman . . . um . . . Yates. Andrea Yates?'

'I remember,' Liz says.

'Who was she?' Helen asks.

'She had five kids. She was diagnosed with postnatal depression after about the third, and her husband insisted they have more kids, and she home-schooled them. One day she just drowned them in the bath.'

'Christ!' CJ exhales.

'She must have been insane,' Helen says.

'What are you saying about her?' Liz pushes.

'I'm saying that nobody gave a fuck about her. Nobody cared enough about how maternally overburdened she was. She was diagnosed with postnatal depression, but society just discarded her. Why are we surprised that she ended up killing her kids?' I say. I am feeling hot and angry now.

'She killed her kids, Joanne,' Tam says, speaking like I am retarded. 'Killed them.'

'I know, and it's horrible and terrible and my heart goes out to those little souls,' I say. Doesn't one woman here get what I'm saying?

'But you feel sorry for her,' Ereka continues. I have long stopped rubbing her feet. They feel like leaden weights on my knees.

'She was left to sink or swim by herself . . .'

'So she drowned her kids?' Dooly says in a tone that doesn't feel supportive. I guess I'm sounding lame.

'It was them or her,' I say.

There is a chilly tension in the room. They are all receding from me, I am on an island somewhere distant and unreachable and their voices are becoming more and more indistinct. I want to shout, 'Don't leave me here, please stay and understand . . .' Suddenly this group of my closest friends is a crowd of strangers, and I am lost and cannot find a familiar face.

The silence lasts. I am almost desperate for reprieve. Not even Helen throws me a life jacket. I will die here alone.

'I suffered from postnatal depression,' someone says.

My eyes gratefully turn to the source of this blessed revelation. Fiona? Calm, collected, gentle Fiona?

'Really?' CJ asks. Fiona nods. Something reluctant in the intonation of Fiona's disclosure warns, tread gently.

'What was it like?' Helen asks, trundling in.

Fiona inhales deeply. Slowly exhaling, she starts to speak, 'It's the most afraid I have ever been. I wanted to die, I remember that. I lay in bed all day long while Gabriel cried and cried in his cot. When I thought I was going to lose my mind, I'd sometimes put him at the far end of the house so I couldn't hear him. I didn't get out of my pyjamas for weeks and weeks, and I stayed under my covers, watching TV.'

'How did you keep it together?' Dooly asks, genuinely moved.

'Well Kirsty, who was eleven at the time, was amazing. She would go to Gabe when he cried and change his nappy, and take him out for walks when I couldn't get out of bed. She was my saving grace. Truly, I don't know how I would have coped without her.' Fiona smiles at us. 'And my mum also helped a lot—she moved in with us for a while.'

This is a staggering confession. I am not abandoned. The tide is turning, and they are edging back to me. Wanting to hear more, nobody speaks.

'I would look at Gabriel, and feel nothing. I thought I must be evil, or defective, or have something horribly wrong with me. As if I was made without a womb or a heart. I wanted so much to feel that maternal love everybody says you'll feel, but every time I reached inside myself, I drew a blank. I hated Gabe's crying, it was such an accusation of my inadequacy. All I ever wanted to do was to get out of the house, and come home and have him asleep.'

There is shock on some of our faces. Tam has actually cupped her hand over her mouth. Spurred on by our horror, Fiona continues.

'Sometimes I would take him for walks around the park and people would stop me and ask me if I was all right, and I'd say, "yes, why?" and they'd say, "because you're crying". And I hadn't even felt that the tears were just running down my face ...'

'You poor thing,' Ereka says. 'How did Ben cope?'

'He was just bewildered by it all. I mean, he was supportive—but he was distracted with his business and was often away. He always made sure my mum was staying with me, and that Kirsty was around. But I think there were times when he just wanted to run away from the whole nightmare of his second wife and this child he'd agreed to have for my sake but which it turned out I couldn't cope with.'

'What do you expect from a man?' CJ says.

'Actually, he did okay. I think the fact that he was already a father really helped. He took me to a psychiatrist who specialises in postnatal depression, and I went for counselling. It eventually came right. But by then, Gabe was almost two. I'm okay now though ...'

'Of course you are,' Tam says, demeaning all that has been shared with a blunt inanity.

'Is that why you haven't had any more kids?' Helen asks, probing.

Fiona nods. 'I just cannot go through that again. I cannot do it to Gabriel. Or to Ben. But especially to myself.'

'You could take medication,' Helen suggests.

'I don't want to,' Fiona says. 'I figure that I got through this with a few scars, and things are good now, but I don't want to go there again.'

My relief and gratitude are irrepressible. A survivor of postnatal depression. A real-life survivor. In our midst. Such a nestled egg of a secret among us, cracked open, exposed in all its raw clarity. I look at Fiona with affection. She is the kind of mother I always wish I could be, but I don't envy the guilt she must carry inside her for those two precious lost years. I still cling to the memories of my children's infancy with passionate nostalgia for the boundaryless closeness and pure human intimacy as mother and child touch, hold and love, free of the cynical restraints of *enough*.

Fiona's little secret, wrapped in the secret of her smoking, swathed in the smells of her aromatherapy oils. It's quite a brew, but we all must find ways to survive in the end. I feel mostly the sadness of knowing too much as I look at Fiona. Does she really know what she lost? Yeah, of course she does. She kicks the shit out of a punching bag twice a week.

'But you would never have contemplated hurting Gabriel?' Tam asks.

'Not him, but me. I did feel suicidal some of the time . . .'

'There's a big difference between committing suicide and killing your children. We have the right to do what we like with our own lives, but we don't have the right to hurt our children,' Tam sputters.

'Do mothers see themselves separately from their children?' Dooly asks her tentatively. 'Maybe for mothers, the line between their sense of self and their children's is blurred . . .'

'But we *are* separate people, and what we do to ourselves we have no right to do to them,' Tam continues.

'Like what, for example?' Helen asks.

'Like take drugs. I get so angry with pregnant women who shoot cocaine or heroine, and drink themselves into liver failure and basically cripple their unborn babies.'

'So, if you had been suffering from depression while you were pregnant, you would not have taken drugs, because it could affect the baby. Now that your kids are out of your belly, it is okay to take drugs, because you are not affecting them?' Liz asks. Tam must be ruing that Prozac now.

'Exactly,' Tam says, as if Liz has just nutshelled her entire philosophy on life.

'And what if you had been so depressed when you were pregnant that you had committed suicide?' I ask. 'Should you wait until your baby is born before killing yourself?'

'You are being totally ridiculous,' Tam says.

'I'm just trying to understand your logic,' I push.

'Mothers have NO RIGHT to hurt their children,' Tam says, her voice rising in pitch. 'It's an inviolable principle. No matter what they are going through.'

'So children are more important than their mothers?' I ask.

'Yes, they are. They are helpless and innocent and they have a right to our protection,' Tam says.

I wouldn't disagree with her gratuitously, but there is something very challenging about her approach to motherhood. It is that exigent conviction, despite all the banter about 'self care', that a good mother is a selfless one. We'd all rather self-abnegate to our detriment than risk the damning adjective 'selfish'. To Tam, children surpass their mothers in the hierarchy of existence. But to locate mothers against children on a hierarchy is disingenuous. In symbiotic relationships, if the host dies so does the parasite. As an advocate for battered women many years ago, I was forced to concede that the only guarantee for children of safety from violence and abuse was safe, protected mothers. Otherwise children are always at risk of abuse—not only by raging fathers, but by their distraught and broken mothers.

We mothers are fenced in a pen of expectations that we will cope, even if we cannot; that we will refuse ourselves to provide for our children, even if we cannot breathe from the pain inside us. Airline policy for oxygen masks released in the event of a loss of cabin pressure dictates: put yours on first, then attend to the children. Otherwise everyone is at risk of dying. We could do with a new theory of motherhood based on this prudent principle. Sometimes survival demands the sacrifice of altruism. Not always *you first*, sometimes *me first*. I want to articulate all these thoughts to my friends, but I don't know where to start. Tam is intentionally misunderstanding me or not wanting to hear what I am saying. I try again.

'What would have happened to Gabriel if Kirsty and Fiona's mother had not stepped into the gap?'

Tam shrugs. Fiona says, 'He would have to have been cared for by Ben, or a nanny.'

'What if Fiona had no Ben? What if he did a Tom on her and abandoned her when she was pregnant? What would have happened to Gabriel then?'

'Foster care,' Fiona says.

'Mothers like us are in the minority—most women in the world do not have the material benefits we have. I, for one, have no network of support that I could draw on—other than all of you—if I slumped into a depression. What I'm saying is that what drives a woman to kill herself or her children is desperation. And no woman should ever be that desperate.'

A few heads are nodding in agreement. I feel very hot and bothered after this encounter. I need some air.

'I need some fresh air,' I say.

I stand up and open the door onto the balcony, closing it behind me, and I breathe in the cool night breeze, gripping the steel

railings with my hands. They have imbibed the chill of the night.
We all think, ensconced in our first-world trappings, that motherhood is like real estate—you have to own it exclusively for it to
mean anything. Indigenous people understand land better. It is for
the use of all of us, a communal space we all share. With mutual
responsibility and support.

The door to the balcony opens behind me. It is Dooly.

She stands quietly by my side for a whole minute before asking,
'So have you ever fantasised about it?'

'About what?' I say.

'About . . . you know, getting rid of your kids?'

I laugh. 'Are you mad? I can honestly say I have never fantasised
about that. I've fantasised about being away from them for a
week, about having someone to help me feed and bath them at
night, but that is as far as it goes.'

She smiles weakly. 'Really? Have you never, when they are just
in that insane irrational state, just imagined what it would be like
to be . . . free?'

I look at her now. She is telling me something. I don't want to
judge her. I choose my words carefully.

'No . . . not really . . . I long for some time away from them, but
I don't long to be rid of them. Do you?'

'I sometimes wonder whether it would just be easier if we were
all wiped out in a car accident, or an aeroplane disaster. You know,
it sometimes feels all too hard . . .'

'It's hard to be a person,' I say. 'Hard to be a mother . . .'

She doesn't answer. She just gives me a look full of terrible
whispers.

I put my hand on her shoulder. 'Don't go there,' I say. 'It's
normal to feel cornered. It really is.'

She nods.

'Don't say another word,' I say softly. 'You will be misunderstood. Even here.'

'I haven't said anything,' she says.

I squeeze her shoulder, and together we stand there looking into the empty night, its views shrouded in darkness, stripped of something we both barely understand.

CHAPTER 19

the terminator

When Dooly and I return to the warmth of the indoors, the lounge room is almost deserted. Helen has taken Fiona and CJ upstairs to the huge spa bath (with eight jets) to run a bath. Liz has gone to the loo, though why she needs it is anyone's guess—she's hardly imbibed enough to necessitate the use of her excretory functions. Dooly says she's going to 'check out the bed situation' and disappears down the corridor. Exhaustion is driving each of us to our primal comforts. I wonder if any of us will make it through the DVDs I have brought. I am now longing for my bed at home.

Ereka smiles (she's just got *one more*) and jingles her way out onto the balcony she's been befriending all night with her cannabis ash. A trail of smoke ribbons out behind her like a gossamer scarf. There's a lot of tidying up to do around us, but I am hoping the others will offer to do it the way Frank always jumps up to load the dishwasher when I've spent the day cooking him up a kingly meal. It's a fair trade, you've got to admit. And I fucking hate cleaning up.

I wander over to the kitchen to spy on the leftovers which may need to be Tupperwared or covered in plastic. Tam is standing over the sink rinsing out the dish in which she brought her (untouched) berries. 'I've left them for you in a Tupperware in the fridge,' she says curtly. She *does* take it personally. I regret not even tasting her efforts, the way you wish you'd not bullied someone when you see the distress it has caused.

Tam is quiet. There is a frail delicacy to her face for which I feel marginally responsible. She always seems so self assured, as if Kevin's infidelities—even if they have never shifted gear from the verbal to the physical—have taken their toll. Prozac is for depression, not self-delusion. And Tam is no fool.

'I'm going to go now,' she says softly. She seems remote and marooned. I hate being misunderstood. I approach her gingerly.

'Tam,' I say, 'I'm sorry if what I said earlier was offensive, I really didn't mean it to be ...'

'It's okay, Jo, I know that,' she says.

'I didn't mean that it's okay for mothers ...'

She interrupts me. 'I know what you meant.'

I want to finish my sentence. I'm not convinced she understood what I meant, but I get the feeling she's made up her mind about what she's heard. ('Guess what? Joanne thinks it's perfectly okay for mothers to kill their children, poor Aaron, what that child must go through with a mother like that.') I can almost hear the gossip behind my back. I don't want to lodge a bigger wedge between us or make matters worse. When someone's got a knife in her back, sometimes trying to pull it out is only going to cause more bleeding. But I can't resist.

I try to reach out again. 'I abhor it when mothers hurt their children,' I say. 'I loathe myself when I shout at mine, when I smack them or lose patience with them. I just understand that sometimes women snap, and then they are lost . . .'

Now Tam turns and faces me, clutching her dish to her chest, her hands folded across it in what I am sure in body language is a gesture of 'get out of my face'. Something in her demeanour is anguished; a muscle is twitching on the side of her left eye. Is she about to cry? I suddenly feel afraid.

'I know what you all think of me,' she says.

'What do you mean?' I ask.

'I know you all think I'm neurotic, overprotective and obsessed with my boys . . .'

I shift uneasily from one foot to the other, finding it difficult to hold her gaze. 'No, not really, Tam. You know, each of us does it the way we think best . . .'

'Don't bullshit me,' she says. 'I know what you all think, and I don't care. My boys *are* precious. My boys *are* everything to me. If you want to judge me for that, go ahead.'

'No one judges you,' I say feebly.

Tam laughs a bitter laugh. 'What's wrong with just admitting it?'

'We all have our idiosyncrasies,' I say.

'Yes, we do,' she says, nodding. 'All of us have things we have to live with and deal with. And each of us does what we can to stay in the game.'

I nod. I want us to be friends again.

'And I've been meaning to tell you that I will replace that butterfly net Kieran broke, okay?'

'What?' I say, silently cursing Helen for not keeping her fucking mouth shut!

'My boys tell me everything,' she says.

'It was just a stupid butterfly net,' I say, sounding pathetic.

'I'll replace it anyway.'

'Please just forget about it,' I say. How small and petty a rod and some mesh seem now, and how insidiously I have punished her for it. I don't know what else to do to make things better. I flounder in my basket of appropriate responses, grappling for a reconciliatory rejoinder.

Before I can come up with anything, she says: 'Kevin made me have an abortion eight years ago.'

Now I can look her straight in the eye. I don't move. I don't say a thing.

She continues. 'I fell pregnant when it was inconvenient for him. He was studying. He was not ready for children. He promised me that if I had an abortion, we could try again the following year.'

I still say nothing.

A shaft of shame unsheathes itself inside me. I am nervous and she can sense it. It was only twice. Erotic dreams are not consciously desired. In dream language, they probably mean the opposite. I didn't even tell Helen. I just shelved it. It doesn't count for anything. I still think Kevin's a bastard. I don't envy Tam being married to the guy your friends are fantasising about. Momentarily, I want to confess to her, but I don't. Something else inside me is unfolding, the clean laundry of fresh understanding, the unravelling of creases, the smoothing out of all I do not know in the small backyard of my judgments.

'And you know what's the worst part of that story?'

I shrug.

'I did it. I went ahead and had an abortion—an abortion of a perfectly normal pregnancy. Because it *inconvenienced* my husband. He was writing exams. It did not suit him.' Her voice is clipped and sour.

'Do you want to know what it means to hate yourself? Do you want to know how it feels to regret every single day of your life being such a wimp? Just look at me.'

I exhale and shake my head. 'Tam, I'm so sorry ...'

'I should have told him to go fuck himself and gone ahead and had my baby.' The venom in her voice hits me like a slap to the face, the word 'fuck' startling coming from her. Tam uses 'Drat!' and 'Fiddlesticks!' as expletives of anger, modelling, always modelling appropriate behaviour for her boys. But in this moment, I realise that even she knows that they are just poorly concealed Barneyisms for filthy invectives that have a power and a satisfaction no number of 'Gee golly whiskers!' can deliver.

'You did what you thought was right,' I offer weakly.

'It wasn't good enough. It was unforgivable.' Her voice is raised.

'I don't think you should judge yourself so harshly,' I say.

'I couldn't judge myself harshly enough. I deserve nothing but condemnation for what I did.'

'I disagree,' I say.

'And I'm still married to him ... do you believe that? I'm still married to the man that made me have an abortion because it was *inconvenient*.' That word has clearly become to her what 'hysterectomy' means to Dooly. A tag for everything that has been fatally expunged.

I approach Tam and wrap my arms around her. I wonder why it is that cruelty in men is such a turn-on for women. We're like eager little moths drawn to the suggestive brightness of a flame, never imagining that up close its warmth will burn the living daylights out of us. She does not hug me back.

'We've all done things we regret,' I say.

'Have you had an abortion?' she asks into my shoulder.

'No,' I say quietly.

'Then you can't know how it feels,' she says.

I do not answer this. She is right. I don't know. There is much I don't know . . .

'Forgive yourself,' I whisper in her ear.

She says nothing and does not move.

'I can't,' she says. 'That would be like letting me off the hook.'

Helen walks into the kitchen. 'What's going on here?' she asks loudly.

I raise my eyebrows at Helen, hope to God she has the sense to let this go. She catches my look and turns and leaves, saying, 'There's a hot spa bath ready for anyone who wants to hop in.'

'I have to go home now,' Tam says and untangles herself from me.

'Don't you want to stay over?' I ask.

She shakes her head. 'I really do have to get up early tomorrow morning.'

'Okay,' I say. 'I'm really glad you made it tonight.'

I walk Tam to the door and hold it open for her. I stand in the doorway and watch as she gets into her car. I hold her confession in me like a stone. I think of how Helen will react when I tell her, with vindicated hatred of Kevin. CJ will shake her head in disbelief at how Tam stays with Kevin after all that. Liz will say, 'It's no big deal—I had an abortion because it didn't suit me, get over it, honey.' Fiona will be sympathetic and find an oil to ease the guilt. Ereka will be quietly sad for Tam, as will Dooly. As for me, I am already planning a spectacular gluten-free cake for her that will take me all day to bake.

'Don't you want to take your berries and chocolate home with you?' I ask. 'I'll run back inside and get them for you.'

Tam shakes her head. 'No thanks, you all share it among yourselves tomorrow. Take it home for the kids.' There is no trace of moral superiority in her voice. Have I imagined it all along?

I nod. 'Take care, drive safely,' I tell her. She starts up her engine and gives me a small smile through the window. I stand and watch as she reverses out the driveway, indicating first, despite the deserted street.

Self-hatred is a terrifying place of withholding. Never forgetting is a mighty commitment. It keeps us locked away from a forgiveness only we have the power to grant ourselves. But some of us choose to throw away the key, as if eternal punishment is the only legitimate atonement.

Motherhood is not a trifle. It is not a zabaglione or a dessert of frozen berries with melted chocolate. Motherhood is the ultimate matrix—between life and death. When all the romance and glory is stripped away, it is a wasteland with no consolations for the errors, mishaps and sins we unwittingly commit in the juggle between 'doing-the-best-we-can' for those we have brought to life and staying alive ourselves.

The sound of Tam's car hovers in the night, long after she has driven away.

the morning after

The idea was to have scrambled eggs with shallots, sun-dried tomatoes, feta cheese and sourdough toast for breakfast. But even I don't have the stomach or the energy to brave the kitchen, littered with the detritus of last night's feast. There is a tub of cinnamon and honey yoghurt left out on the counter—I hate that and fret madly with my kids when they leave the milk or butter out overnight. But who am I going to pick a bone with here, among mothers who should all know better? I feebly put it into the fridge now, though if it's going to be off it's already too late.

I survey the breakfast terrain with groggy eyes. My 'get-up-and-cook' mood is dog tired, but give me half an hour . . . I switch the kettle on, flick open a few kitchen cupboards in search of a coffee plunger, and find it right next to a half-full bag of luxuriously expensive coffee. I'm sure Hel's folks won't begrudge me a single shot of caffeine. The kettle clicks to boiling point. My head is stodgy with lack of sleep and a daiquiri overindulgence. Liz patters yawning into the kitchen in her maroon satin nightgown and a pair of red leather slippers.

'How did you sleep?' I ask her.

'Okay,' she says. 'The bed was a bit hard, but I did get some sleep. You?'

'So-so,' I say, spooning a double helping of coffee into the plunger, then adding another two. We need it. 'The sofa was a bit soft, and I struggled to fall asleep, but I got there eventually. I feel like I've been up all night with a sick child.' I pour the hot water in and sniff the aroma which, were it my lover, I'd caress hungrily each morning upon waking. Whoever first espied a coffee bean and envisioned the tang of a smoky slow-roasted double espresso was a fucking genius. Coffee is one of the few pleasures of which motherhood has not deprived me.

'What an irony,' she smiles. 'Can I have one of those?'

I plunge, pour Liz a coffee and slide the milk and sugar over to her.

'No sugar thanks,' she says.

'Of course not,' I say. 'Are you hungry?'

'I'm still full from dinner,' she says.

'Even if it were true, Liz, some things you should just keep to yourself,' I chastise.

Together we take our coffees and walk out into the lounge room where the morning waits for us.

We sit together on the sofa overlooking the morning harbour. The view is stark compared to last night, stripped bare in the naked light. I'm enjoying the quiet, the peace of it all, but I am aware that this is probably the first morning in the past seven and a half years when I have not had a child in my lap, snuggling into the cosiness of my body's leftover sleep-warmth. I feel peculiarly bereft. I look at my watch—it is 8.25 on a Saturday morning—they will have been up for hours now, nagging Frank about putting on the TV (which he will agree to) and maybe asking him when I am coming home (but not if the TV is on). It is no more than two or three more hours until I see them. I am suddenly longing to hear their voices, but I don't want this time to be over so soon. I'm just starting to relax and enjoy myself.

Around us, the tealights are all burned down and there is an ashtray with no less than five marijuana cigarette stubs in it. Ereka has had a bumper night. The dishes were just left last night on the coffee table, a side table and the dining room table—we didn't even stack them in the dishwasher. If I were a parent and we were the kids, I'd be furious with us.

'Do you think Tam's all right?' Liz asks.

'Why do you ask?' I say, turning to look at her. Her face looks tired, though there is something very lovely about it, stripped of its severity without the perfectly applied makeup and that harsh maroon lipstick she always wears.

'I noticed she got very emotional in our conversation and she left without saying goodbye,' Liz says.

'I'm sure she'll be okay,' I say. 'I think she just has a lot to deal with . . . Kevin's an arsehole, you know.' I am about to say, 'He made her have an abortion eight years ago,' but my tongue holds back. Tam's secret rolls back into my throat and down into my belly where it settles in a new place of holding, far from the shallows of idle chit-chat.

'I know,' she says.

She and I sit and sip our coffees for a while. I tuck my feet up under my gown and stretch my back over the arm of the couch.

'I'd hate to be married to an arsehole,' I say, coming upright again.

'You're lucky you're not,' she says.

'I know. Frank's a good man . . .' I think fondly of my Frank now. I get a renewed thrill when others recognise what a great guy he is, an observational distance from the all too often taking-for-granted that goes on between couples. 'But Carl's not an arsehole,' I say.

'No, he's not. He can be very moody, though.'

'Mediterranean temperament?' I suggest.

'Maybe.' She runs her fingers over her eyebrows, smoothing them into shape.

I stretch my legs out and cover them with my absurd towelling robe with my name 'Joanne' embroidered on the pocket—a gift from my mother for my thirtieth birthday. In the morning light, Liz is mellow. I look at her affectionately. All that sharp authority seems almost fragile in slippers and gown. She must be reading my thoughts, because the next thing she says is:

'I had an affair.'

I almost spill my coffee on my towelling gown. But I don't move. 'Really?' I say. I wonder what she saw in my face that has prompted this confession. 'With who?'

'Oh, it's not important . . . someone from my past, from university days, who resurfaced in my life unexpectedly,' she says. Will she say any more? I don't want to twitter with too many questions, a dead giveaway of nosiness, though my curiosity is bristling like an expectant father waiting to hear whether it's a boy or a girl.

'Someone who adores me—you know, in that way we are adored by people who are in love with an idea of us, not really the reality.'

I nod.

'Are you still having an affair?' I ask.

'No, I ended it. About two weeks ago.'

'Is that good or bad?' I ask.

'Some days it's good, and some days it sucks like you cannot imagine.'

'What was it like?' I ask.

She takes a sip of her coffee and does not look at me, but out at the 3.5 million-dollar view of the harbour, its still, flat water and the horizon before us.

'It filled a need in me that has been crying out to be filled for years now.'

'I suppose ... that can't be all bad?' I suggest.

'It was good for me,' she says. 'It revived a part of me, anyway. I miss passion. A husband just can't make you feel the way an illicit lover can. It's a flaw in the marriage template.'

Something resembling relief—it's not just the caffeine—is coursing through me now. I have always feared the day when a lover from my past might cross my path and make a mockery of the vows I took with Frank. I have no desire to be unfaithful to him or to break his heart, but in the wrong circumstances I fear I might be capable of both. Maybe fidelity owes more to the accidental virtue of absent opportunity rather than the legitmate highground of moral integrity.

'Did Carl find out?' I ask.

'Nope,' she says. 'I only tell him things on a need-to-know basis. He didn't need to know.'

'Wow,' I say.

'Yeah, but he's picked up that there's something going on. He wants us to go for therapy ...'

I take a long sip of my coffee. 'That's okay?' I say, hedging, hesitant about reading Liz's feelings.

'Really?' she asks. 'Why?'

'Uumm ...' I scramble for a response to meet the strictures of Liz's uncompromising logic. She has no patience for empty platitudes. 'I think all relationships can benefit from counselling. It's a chance to understand each other better.'

She sniffs. If she's not satisfied with that, she doesn't let on.

'I'm just afraid that the truth will come out and that Carl will leave me. And take the kids with him,' she says.

I inhale. 'Liz, don't imagine the worst,' I say. 'The therapy can be very positive.'

'I don't know how positively Carl will take the fact that I've cheated on him.' She laughs bitterly, looking beyond me out to the view. She closes her eyes and exhales deeply.

'Maybe he'll understand,' I say. I pause. 'And if he left you and took the kids, would it be so terrible? I mean, you'd still have your work...'

She opens her eyes and looks at me like I'm the dumbest kid in the class. 'I may not be a hands-on mother like you and Helen and Tam, but I'm still a mother. They still hop into my lap and plant wet kisses on my cheeks. I'm working my butt off so one day they'll have financial security and can do whatever they like—whether it's climbing Mount Everest or making those things, those what-d'you-call-'em ... dream catchers, out of feathers and crystals. Without those kids ... I don't know ... I don't want to lose them.' For the first time ever, her vulnerability peeps at me. It's just like anyone else's.

'You won't,' I say. 'Just lie in therapy. Don't let him know ... deny it.'

Liz laughs. 'I'll try, but I can't promise. Sometimes the truth is stronger than we are ...' She looks at me with narrowed eyes. 'So I must lie, hey? Interesting coming from you. Is that what you tell your daughter?'

'Oh fuck off, Liz,' I say. And then, 'Maybe if she was married and had an affair . . . I don't know . . . It's not black and white . . . It's a muddle all the way.'

'Would you cheat on Frank?' she asks me, looking me straight in the eye.

I shrug. 'I hope not,' I say. 'But you never know . . .' and I give her a huge grin. 'It'd be really hard to turn Robbie Williams down.' Inside I know this to be true: that before kids, I may have been precariously balanced on the fence between fidelity and infidelity; a nudge would have knocked me right off balance. Now that I'm a mother, I am far more firmly on the 'does not stray' side. I'm too weary, too encumbered to even steal a look over to the green grass. But I do not share this thought with Liz. I simply reach out and squeeze her hand. She does not respond.

'You know, it's just that my whole self esteem and the way I think about myself has taken a huge knock since the gestational diabetes, and I went through years when I felt so undesirable.'

There is a long pause during which my brain fumbles to grasp the slingshot of her words.

'What?' I say, turning to look at her.

'I got gestational diabetes when I was pregnant with Brandon, and I was really quite ill with it. That's why I have to watch what I eat.'

The thump of comprehension wallops me like a blow to the belly and the entrails of my own foolishness spill gushingly before me.

'Why have you never told any of us?' I ask.

'I don't need to lay that on all of you—it's *my* problem. I don't want you preparing special meals for me or anything. I manage.'

'I'd be happy to make you something special to eat,' I say.

'You're very kind, but really, I'm fine. I just moved on from food. I used to have such a sweet tooth . . . I loved lemon meringue pie. Now, eating for me is like paying taxes—I just do it because I have to.'

I want to gurgle out some garbled confession, to beg her to forgive me for the years in which I have held her beneath culinary contempt, for the arrogance of presumption, my shot-gun assumptions . . . But behind us we hear Dooly and CJ's voices. My pale gangly apology doesn't know where to sit, and wanders through my head, lost . . . too late.

•

Dooly shuffles in wearing an absurd pink fluffy nightgown, the kind our parents made us wear when we were kids, and some ridiculously huge fluffy footwear with Mickey Mouse faces on them, the black noses and ears of which make walking a hazard. Somehow she manages. Dooly—always taking the hard route—what's wrong with an ordinary pair of Kmart slippers? But this morning she looks happy, girlish. CJ is pacing about in her men's checked flannelette pyjamas, which I'm sure she wears just to feel close to men again.

'Fuck, I'd love a cigarette now,' she says. 'But I'm officially giving up again this morning. How could you all let me smoke last night? Call yourselves friends!'

'There was no stopping you,' Liz says.

'Have some coffee instead,' I say.

'What a crap movie that *Amy's Orgasm* was,' CJ declares. 'Who chose the DVDs?' Way past midnight, after we'd all soaked in the hot tub, we had all clambered onto the couch and watched two movies one after the other. *Amy's Orgasm* was spectacularly disappointing, as enduring other people talking about their orgasms generally is.

'Guilty,' I say. 'I'm sorry, I should just be in charge of the food, next time I'll leave the movie choice up to someone else.' I am still rewinding the past years of my friendship with Liz in my head, trying to recover all those times in which spiteful remarks about her eating habits have glibly slipped from my ignorant tongue. Fucking gestational diabetes. I am quite nauseous with guilt.

'Did anyone get any sleep?' Dooly asks.

'Some,' I say. 'Not enough.'

'A bit,' Liz says.

'CJ snores like a chainsaw,' Dooly says.

'Do not,' CJ says defensively.

'How would you know? You're asleep,' Dooly asserts. She comes now to join us on the couch, squeezing in between Liz and me.

'I refuse to be classified as a snorer,' CJ says. 'It is too humiliating for words.'

'Christ, what's becoming of us?' Liz says.

'Horrible warnings all round,' I say.

'I bought Dead Sea Mud for us all to put on our faces last night and I forgot all about it,' CJ says.

'We can do it now,' Dooly says enthusiastically.

'Forget it,' Liz says. 'I am way too tired.'

'Oh come on,' CJ says. 'It'll be fun. And then we can go and wake the others with our faces covered in black mud.'

'Not me,' pipes up Fiona's voice. She wafts in covered in an aquamarine hand-woven woollen shawl knitted no doubt by some organic farmer's wife, the proceeds of which go to feed hungry orphans in Indonesia. 'Won't it make a horrible mess?' she asks.

'Oh mess, shmess!' Dooly goads. 'Come on, when last did we do something for ourselves?'

That is all the encouragement CJ needs and she disappears down the hall to get the mud from her bag.

•

It is a scene from some modern French movie. We are all gathered around the breakfast table with hardening black mud on our faces, our eyes globular and starkly white against this ebony backdrop. Unfortunately, Helen and Ereka woke up before we had a chance to startle them with our muddied faces. Even Liz has agreed to be masked up, though in her opinion the package blurb didn't help, claiming that 'heroines from the Bible must too have used the mud from the Dead Sea, situated in the heart of the Promised Land, for a divine complexion'.

'I'd fire whoever wrote this,' she spurned.

I deftly deflected a disagreement with CJ about the Promised Land's occupation of the West Bank by offering biscotti speckled with roasted almonds and apricots for us to snack on while we wait for our masks to set.

The doorbell rings.

'Who the hell could that be at this time?' Helen says.

'Maybe your parents decided to come back early?' Ereka suggests.

'They have a key. And besides, they're only due back in a fortnight,' Helen says, trundling towards the door, barefoot.

We all wait.

'Tam!' we hear Helen say.

'My God, what's on your face?' we hear her exclaim.

'Dead Sea Mud—and don't think you're going to get away without some on yours,' Helen says.

Tam comes in, followed by Helen. When she sees the seven of us in our pyjamas and all mud-faced she bursts out laughing. 'If you girls could just see yourselves!' she giggles.

'How come you got back here?' Fiona asks. 'What about the boys' cricket, or was it chess?'

'I told Kevin this morning that he had to take them,' she says. 'And I just left.'

'Well, we're very happy to see you,' Dooly says.

'Though you should have come in your pyjamas,' Helen says.

'Do you want some coffee?' Ereka asks.

'No thanks, I brought my own chamomile tea, and I'd love a cup of tea.'

She sidles off to the kitchen to pour herself some tea. I try to catch her eye but she avoids my gaze, a strange incomplete smile on her lips.

•

It is finally now time to take leave of one another. Apart from Liz, who left early to go into the office to check on something, the rest of us are all still here, trying to leave. We have reluctantly bathed, showered and dressed ourselves, stacked the dishwasher, cleaned the table and emptied the ashtray and dustbins. We have divided up the leftover food. We have left a note of thanks to Helen's parents. The girls said I could take the tulips home. I didn't argue and I've wrapped them with their stem ends in a plastic bag with a bit of water, and secured it with a rubber band.

We lug our bags outside, waiting for the first of us to make a move of departure. Dooly is wrapped up in Luke's scarf despite the warm morning. There is no reason to tell him his scarf spent the night on the floor under Ereka's chair—I discovered it while we were tidying up. But Dooly may just confess, and spend the afternoon repenting. Helen's in the same clothes she wore yesterday—I think she may have even slept in them, taking only her Ugg boots off. Ereka has picked two daisies from Helen's mum's front garden for her girls, and is wearing them tucked one behind each ear. I convinced Tam to take home her berries to make smoothies for her boys. Fiona's little basket is filled with leftovers wrapped in foil. CJ's got her bottle of wine—we never got to drink it.

We go through a silent ritual of hugging one then another, until each of us has hugged everyone else. The threads of intimacy that lace us together are delicate and frail in the morning sunlight. Nights like the one we have just spent together will probably not come around again in a hurry and I'm already nostalgic for its passing. I want to cup this feeling, bottle it in a jar of coloured glass, write it down somewhere, but I feel it slipping away. It has been an extraordinary, ecstatic, glorious, heartbreaking island of time of confessions and anecdotes, stories and secrets. I wave at my friends, standing in a constellation at the side of the road, the tall and the short of them, the fat and the thin of them, a handful of unsung heroes.

'When shall we eight meet again?' CJ asks.

'I'll figure something out,' Helen says. 'Maybe a weekend away next time?'

'Bloody fantastic!' Fiona says.

'I don't know about a whole weekend,' Tam says.

'Depends when and where,' Dooly says

'So how about Weight Watchers?' I say.

'I'm in,' Ereka says.

'Me too,' Dooly nods.

'Get a life,' Helen says.

'See you all soon,' I yell out the window as I drive past.

I have a twenty-minute journey home in a car strangely quiet without bickering from the back seats. I dial home on my mobile and Frank answers. 'Can I pick anything up on the way?' I ask him.

'Get some milk and green apples,' he says. 'And no need to rush—everything's under control here,' he says.

'Meaning they are catatonic in front of the TV,' I say wryly.

'Not quite, but almost . . .'

'You're impossible!' I say to him.

'Thank you, my darling,' he says. 'I see a night out with the girls has mellowed you beyond recognition. Can I get the recipe?'

'I'll see you in a while,' I say. 'I can't talk, I'm driving,' and I hang up. Sarcastic bastard.

At the service station counter I am standing paying for the milk and green apples when I notice my hands, unrecognisably my own, with those garish red nails. I must get some nail polish remover, I've got none at home. I hold them out and gaze at them. Aaron is bound to ask, alarmed, 'What happened to your hands?' Jamie will beg me to paint hers too and we'll have to sneak into my bedroom to do it—Frank cannot bear little girls made up. I suddenly remember that I didn't find out which celebrity has over four thousand pairs of shoes, damn. Now it will irk me. Maybe I can look it up on the internet. Maybe I can find a completely sugar-free recipe, too, for lemon meringue pie for Liz . . .

Joan Armatrading's voice drifts through the service station on the radio they play as background music, 'More . . . more than one kind of love . . . there is more . . . more than one kind of love.' As I stand at the counter waiting to pay, I think now of the kind of love it takes to withhold your pain, the way Liz has, lest we pity her ascetic existence; the way Ereka does, abidingly around her unceasing anxieties for Olivia; the way Dooly does, bereft of a longed-for daughter. I think of the kind of love of those who always try to clear a path ahead for those that will follow, like Tam does, never resting in parental indolence. Of the love it takes to walk tall, with courage, like CJ did in kicking Tom out, setting a precedent for unimpeachable integrity. I shake my head in quiet wonder at the kinds of love we as mothers all must draw on—daily,

hourly, minute-by-minute; love which is the overlooked but indispensable roots that hold the world in place for our children.

I'm about to hand over my twenty dollar note to Jamil behind the counter when suddenly I grab two Kit-Kats for the kids, a mood ring for Jamie and a dinosaur keyring for Aaron. It's nearly over. This time away is almost done. I am almost a mummy once more. I leave the store, forgetting the nail polish remover.

I pull up slowly outside our house. I adjust the rearview mirror so that I can see my face. I look ragged. A night away from my kids has not, as I had imagined, rested me. I take a deep breath, and open the car door. With my bag over my shoulder, the empty dishes in my arms and the tulips balanced on my *fayanza* I make my way to the front door.

I don't get a chance to knock or yell out, 'Let me in, no hands!' because the door swings open and two small bodies fling themselves at my thighs and clutch me around the waist. 'Mummy's back!' I say as I am swallowed into the yelps and bounds of everything that has brought me home.

postscript

Six weeks after our evening together, Fiona found a lump in her left breast. She has been diagnosed with breast cancer and had to have a radical mastectomy combined with radiation and chemotherapy. All her gorgeous hair fell out, but the prognosis is good. Kevin, Tam's husband, did Fiona's breast reconstruction and threw in some of the latest implants, free of charge, which means she's now got bigger (and firmer) breasts than all of us. It seems that Kevin got to examine someone's breasts for free after all.

Helen's baby is due any day now. The amniocentesis has confirmed that it is a healthy baby, though she didn't find out its sex. But she's made me do the pendulum six more times. It's still a 'no' to a girl.

At her firm's Christmas party, CJ had occasion to kiss a woman. While it was 'quite fun', she has not thrown Harvey away, nor has she given up on the hope of finally meeting an ordinary decent bloke ('God knows if they even exist out there'). At Tam's urging, CJ did not put Liam on Ritalin, but is giving him high doses of

omega oils. Though the jury is out on his behaviour, his skin and hair are very glossy.

Dooly's mother unexpectedly had a stroke and passed away a month ago. Max organised for a cleaner to come and surprised Dooly with a spotless house. Dooly, while still mourning, says she's never known Max to be such a rock. Dooly hasn't had time to come to Weight Watchers' meetings, but she's reading *French Women Don't Get Fat*—'there's got to be a diet out there where you can eat chocolate'.

Tam gave up her part-time job to be more full-time with her boys. She is still on Prozac, and has decided to do a part-time course as a teacher for gifted children. She's trying to talk Kevin into having another baby, and though she wouldn't mind another boy, 'it'd be really nice to have girl . . .'

When she got home from her last overseas trip, Liz discovered a bruise on Brandon's arm, and eventually got it out of him that Lily's been hitting him and bribing him with lollies to keep it quiet. Liz fired Lily on the spot. Liz is desperate to find a new live-in nanny after all the temps she's tried, but 'Christ, there's a lot of crap help out there'. After Fiona's diagnosis, she went for a mammogram and is all clear.

Ereka finally weaned Kylie. And she and Jake went away to Bali for a week—by themselves—to celebrate their ten-year anniversary, leaving the kids with Ereka's mother. They ate, made love and read all week. When they got home, Olivia was fine, it was Kylie who had been suffering from separation anxiety. Ereka's lost almost two kilos on Weight Watchers'.

And me? I went on to write a book about our evening together, which I'm hoping like hell will sell gazillions so I can finally take Frank for that honeymoon in Paris we never got to have. Of course, we'll probably have to take the kids with us but, hey, that's motherhood for you. In the meantime, the housework continues. Aaron's started eating bananas and I've gone off Robbie Williams after Jamie said he looks like a chicken when he dances. It's a day-to-day grind of school runs, lunchboxes, karate and swimming lessons, punctuated by whingeing and bickering, and made bearable by cuddles and kisses which are running out faster than I care to admit as those teenage years loom ever closer.

But it all changes so quickly—today's burdens will be tomorrow's emptiness. Right now, my guess is that this is happiness. Or as close as it gets.

Acknowledgments

I owe my deepest thanks to so many generous women:

to Jane Ogilvie for finding me, believing in me and growing the idea for this book in me, for the many gifts of her friendship and the largesse of her spirit;

to Jo Paul, for saying 'yes' and for all the joys of working with a brilliant, astute and kindred-spirited woman;

to Jeanmarie Morosin for the quiet tendering of my manuscript with care and dedication;

to Belinda Lee for her insightful editing;

and to all those at Allen & Unwin for their incredible support and enthusiasm for this book;

to my gorgeous friends—and you know who you are—who were with me on 'that' night and on other similar nights; to the 'boat girls' and other beloved friends, scattered far and wide, engaged in the sacred task of mothering, for sharing the wisdom and laughter of their stories with me and for sustaining me through hard times with glorious food and friendship. Especially to Katrina, whom I love mightily, for sharing the joys of eating and the challenges of motherhood with me;

to my soul sister Tracey Segel, for the gentleness she brings to the world and for the kindness of her camera lens;

to my beautiful children Jesse and Aidan, for being patient with me and loving me despite all the mistakes I've made;

and to Zed—I am humbled by the blessings of your loyalty and love.

Joanne Fedler